THE
PUBLICITY
HANDBOOK

THE
PUBLICITY
HANDBOOK

David R. Yale

Printed on recyclable paper

NTC Business Books
a division of *NTC Publishing Group* • Lincolnwood, Illinois USA

Library of Congress Cataloging-in-Publication Data

Yale, David R.
    The publicity handbook : how to maximize publicity for products,
    services, and organizations / David R. Yale
            p.   cm.
    Includes bibliographical references and index.
    ISBN 0-8442-3285-8.   —   ISBN 0-8442-3286-6 (pbk.)
    1. Public relations—Handbooks, manuals, etc.   I. Title.
HD59.Y33   1991
659—dc20   90-23364

1995 Printing

Published by NTC Business Books, a division of NTC Publishing Group
4255 West Touhy Avenue, Lincolnwood (Chicago), Illinois 60646-1975 U.S.A.
Manufactured in the United States of America.

    4 5 6 7 8 9 VP 9 8 7 6

Dedicated to the memory of
Bobinsky Kusano
and
Sophie Riedel

CONTENTS

Foreword

Publicity can have far greater integrity, impact, influence and attention value than advertising—but only when it's actually used by the media you have targeted.

Whether you're a novice or a professional, David Yale's *Publicity Handbook* tells you how to increase your chances of success, so that you don't have to rely on luck—or prayer—to get media coverage.

It's a book that's worth reading—and re-reading—particularly the checklists and questions at the ends of chapters.

I own several hundred public relations and journalism books, including eight that I have written.

The Publicity Handbook is a more comprehensive and useful manual than any other book. I wish that I had it when I started as a publicist. In fact, I wish that I had written it!

— *Richard Weiner, Public Relations Consultant, New York, NY*

Introduction

I designed *The Publicity Handbook* for two kinds of readers: the seasoned professional, who needs a reference book to answer occasional questions about the finer points of publicity and keep up with new developments (like video news releases and satellite media tours), and the beginner looking for a thorough guide to publicity.

Publicity is a fascinating subject, and I made sure that *The Publicity Handbook* is just as interesting. Throughout this book you will find examples of both excellent and awful publicity material. The examples are in a different typeface, but in many cases, the format has been modified to fit the book page. The correct format is specified, however, for each type of publicity material.

The good examples are almost all real ones, and they are attributed to the organizations and publicists who created them. A few, however, have been created especially for this book, to illustrate specific techniques or procedures. These are attributed to groups in a fictional place called Plains City.

The bad examples are based on reality. Although people do produce this sort of material, the examples here are fictitious. All bad examples are attributed to organizations in the town of Chelm, a fictional place in a story by the Jewish writer Sholem Aleichem. According to the story, when the angels distributed people on the earth, they had two bags each. One bag was full of dumb people; the other was stuffed with geniuses. It seems the angel flying over Chelm was too low, and one of his bags got caught on a tree branch. All the fools landed in Chelm, and it's been a pretty foolish place ever since!

Throughout the book I have used *he* sometimes and *she* other times, since both men and women are reporters, editors, public service directors, and news assignment editors. I want this book to reflect the real world.

In the chapters that follow, many journalists and publicists share their opinions about publicity—and their likes and dislikes. I introduce them to you by name and title when you first meet them, and after that I give you a more abbreviated identification, to keep things simpler.

Finally, I have provided thorough checklists that will help you review the material in *The Publicity Handbook*, and keep your publicity campaign on target. Look for them at the end of Chapters 1 through 10.

Acknowledgments

I would like to thank the many people who helped me (directly and indirectly) with this book. To Professor Rose Zimbardo, who taught me how to write (and think) clearly; to Dale O. Johnson, who showed me how the system works; to V. Hap Smith and Peggy Voulkos who drafted me for my first publicity job; and Burton Weber and Virginia Lawler who taught me to write clear and concise copy—special thanks!

Many thanks also to Bob Asher, Bob Kusano, Evan Press, Esther Savin, Lydia Canosa, and Jim Kousoulas. My agents, Michael Larsen and Elizabeth Pomada, and NTC's editor, Anne Knudsen, were always available with thorough and thoughtful feedback and advice.

Ravelle Brickman read the entire manuscript of the first edition and provided both helpful criticism and encouragement. Leslie O'Bergin's continued votes of confidence were also important during the long task of researching and writing the first edition.

Sheila and Marc Calef, S. Lynn Diamond, Phil Douglis, Sharon Haver, Ken McEldowney, Andrew McGowan, Dan Schlesinger, Judy Lukin, Richard Weiner, Andrew Yale and Jerry Pozniak all read portions of the manuscript and provided helpful comments and ideas.

Thanks to Tom Glazer for permission to use the lyrics from his song, *Precious Sight;* Phil Douglis and Cliff McGoon, Editor of *IABC News* (now *Communication World*), for permission to use Phil's material on publicity photography; Cora B. Everett, Executive Secretary of the National Conference of Editorial Writers for permission to quote material from *The Masthead;* Judy G. Meehan, publications manager of The National Association of Broadcasters, for permission to quote from their pamphlets; Joseph Whitfield of PRSA for permission to quote from *Public Relations Journal;* Denny Griswold, editor of *PR News,* for permission to use excerpts from a case study; Jack O'Dwyer for permission to quote from *O'Dwyer's PR Services Report* and *Jack O'Dwyer's Newsletter;* Lee Levitt for permission to quote from *The Publicist,* and Regina LaPierre for permission to use material from *pr reporter.*

And finally, the dozens of journalists and public relations pros who gave their time and ideas to this book have made an invaluable contribution. To each of them, a special note of appreciation!

CHAPTER ONE

Your Role As Publicist

You've planned a special event for your organization. It took a lot of work, and you hope there will be a large crowd to gawk at that fire-eating sword-swallower who volunteered to add a touch of the unusual. But you're worried. What if *nobody* comes? What will you do with 100 lbs of potato salad and 30 cases of hot dogs? Will the event really promote your product? Raise the money you need? Bring your organization the attention you want?

Or perhaps you wrote, re-wrote and edited a press release about your improved new widget. You spent a fortune on slick photographs to go with it. And you mailed it to every newspaper and broadcaster west of the Mississippi. It's tough trying to break into the widget market.

Your company has a limited advertising budget. There's a lot riding on the results of your press release. For the company. And for you. What if nobody uses it?

Both the rookie and the old pro find that publicity for products, corporations, nonprofit groups, community organizations, government agencies, trade associations, and small businesses is a major concern.

But even if you have no formal training in public relations, there *are* publicity techniques you can use to make sure your message will be heard. This book will help you learn them. And you'll have a good time in the process!

Whether you work for a large corporation seeking to supplement its advertising budget with publicity, a brand-new boutique in search of customers, a public library that wants to let job seekers know about its vocational books, a trade organization promoting natural and organic foods, or a committee opposed to school budget cuts, your task will involve hard work, skill, a sense of humor, and a pinch of luck. But when everything goes well and your story is on the airwaves and in print, that hard work and hard-earned skill will pay handsome dividends.

Publicity Defined

Now what, exactly, is publicity? It involves supplying information that is factual, interesting, and newsworthy to media not controlled by you, such as radio, television, magazines, newspapers, and trade journals. If you use slide shows, speeches, posters, brochures, newsletters, billboards, direct mail, and advertising, where you can control how and when a message is used, then you have become a promoter rather than a publicist. Michelle Rapkin, publicity woman at Bantam Books, explains the difference this way: "Publicity is the front cover of *Time* magazine. Promotion is the back cover."

Publicity is not advertising, since you do not pay for time or space. You have to earn coverage with interesting, timely material. Publicity is not public relations, either. Public relations is a broader task, which includes publicity, but involves promotion, public affairs, advertising, and opinion making as well. These are areas you might want to branch into later on, when you have mastered publicity skills. For now, your task is to learn how to do the best possible job of presenting your message to the public, via the media.

Making a Publicity Plan

Even if you have been doing some publicity for your organization, if you don't have an overall publicity plan, you should take the time to develop one. A carefully considered plan can save you many headaches and help you avoid bad publicity later on. But most important, planning will help you come out ahead in the competition for space in publications and air time.

Determining Your Publicity Goals

Your first step in the planning process is to list a set of goals for your publicity efforts. Write them down on paper because that makes them more concrete. These objectives will, of course, dovetail with your organization's overall goals. And they should be specific. It is not enough to say that you want your product, service, cause, or point of view to be well known to the public. That isn't specific enough to help your organization reach its goals.

Your publicity should help your organization accomplish one or more of the following:

- Inform people about how to choose, buy, and use your product or service.
- Persuade consumers to buy your product or service.
- Counteract misconceptions about your product, service organization, or cause.
- Get customers into your store.
- Get information to the public on issues your organization is concerned about.
- Bring people to an event or series of events.
- Increase attendance at your programs.
- Get people to volunteer.
- Recruit highly qualified employees.
- Get people to vote for a bond issue.
- Attract shareholders and support your stock's price.
- Protect your organization from frivolous lawsuits.

If, for example, you want more people to come to your clinic for family counseling, you could develop publicity that explains what family counseling is and how families with problems can benefit from it. On the other hand, you may have found that a lot of people are coming to your clinic for emergency family counseling on weekends, when the other clinics in town are closed. Your waiting room is jammed, there are not enough offices for your counselors, and on bad weekends waiting clients overflow into the street. Your staff tells you that 85 percent of the weekend problems could be solved on the telephone. How can you get people to telephone first? Well, you could develop a publicity campaign to let people know that they don't even have to leave their homes—they don't have to spend money for gasoline or carfare—your counselors are ready to help the moment they get a call.

Or perhaps your trade organization represents resorts in the Caribbean that are booked solid in high season, from January through March. Although the weather in the Fall and Spring months is magnificent on the islands, neither love nor money seems to lure North American tourists during these "shoulder" seasons. An opinion survey shows that most vacationers believe that during the "shoulders" the Caribbean is hot, humid, and unpleasant, with nothing interesting happening. How can you change their perceptions? Provide publicity about the lovely weather and exotic events during the shoulder seasons—and the hefty savings in store for Spring and Fall Caribbean vacationers.

You will be able to be more exact about some goals than others, but whenever possible, try to measure the results of your publicity. If a survey shows that only 12 percent of the vacationers you survey are aware of the lure of the shoulder season's balmy weather and stunning special events, your objective might be to increase that figure to 25 percent within a year. Setting concrete goals using figures will help you evaluate the success of your publicity program.

Establishing Priorities

Your publicity goals will help you decide which programs, events, and issues get priority. Whether you're a volunteer or a full-time paid employee, most organizations will have more requests for publicity than you can handle. Says the former publicist for Chelm General Hospital, "Working for an organization that has no publicity priorities is hellish. You have to respond to each and every request for publicity because you don't have any basis for turning people down. You don't really have enough time to do it all, so you cut corners, and your material is never first-rate. Now that I work for an organization with clear publicity policies, the results are much better."

You must be selective, for if you deluge the media with publicity material, you're like the boy who cried wolf. Nobody will believe you when you do have a major story. Overkill means undercoverage. Not all events call for a full-scale publicity campaign, and if you overemphasize a minor one, you may have trouble getting coverage for a genuinely newsworthy program that takes place soon afterward.

Mike Martin, the news director for KRBE-FM in Houston, Texas, puts it this way: "Remember, if you flood me with stuff that is not important, you're diluting my interest. Then I'll take anything you send me as probably not important. If you hit me with only important stuff, stuff I need, stuff I can use, that's important to the community, I'm going to pay more attention when I see your logo on the envelope."

And Gus Venditto, an Executive Editor of *PC Magazine*, explains "You get to know press agents, and you get a feel for which ones will sell everything equally. You tend to ignore them. The better publicists, on the other hand, know the difference between routine announcements and a really interesting product development. They get my attention."

Analyzing Your Audience

Publicity involves selling, and like any good salesperson you should analyze your audience before you start. You have to understand why people will or will not be receptive to your message. And as a publicist, your task of persuasion is a double one. First you'll have to convince journalists to run your material or cover your story. Once that happens, your approach, angle and information must be enticing enough to get the public to act.

Now I know that some of you who are involved in charitable, nonprofit and community organizations are saying, "Who, me? You want me to be a salesman? I think selling is immoral, and salesmen are the lowest of the low. After all, I work for a group with a worthy cause. We would debase it if we 'sold.' "

You can call yourselves persuaders, convincers, campaigners, or anything else you wish. I'm still going to call you salespeople. Because the reality is that you have to make two sales pitches *every time you do publicity:* one to the journalist and another to your audience.

Figuring out precisely whom you want to sell your ideas to is an important part of your publicity plan. Can you increase sales more quickly by targeting publicity toward current customers? Or should you aim your message at people who never use your product, and provide them with reasons they should?

Are you trying to reach only the people who agree with your stand on nuclear power? Are there people who are undecided, or even segments of the opposition who might be persuaded to join you, or at least engage in a dialogue? Who, exactly, are they?

As Robert Cummings, environmental reporter for the *Maine Sunday Telegram*, says, "The key to getting publicity is to have something to say, and then choosing who to say it to."

Using Misconceptions in Your Favor.   If you are specific when you identify your audience, you will probably be able to make a list of the misconceptions that audience has about your organization, product, service, or industry. It might even be worth doing a survey just to get detailed information about such misconceptions, for that can be a valuable resource. It tells you exactly what people need to know about you. So even if being misunderstood angers and annoys you, or hurts you deeply, pay close attention to those wrong ideas. For example, if you work with a group that is opposed to nuclear power and your target audience consists of trade-union members who support atomic power because they feel it will create more construction jobs, you will have to find the facts and figures to demonstrate that your alternative energy program will generate more jobs than nuclear reactors will.

Or if people say, "Oh!, what a nice job you have, running a recreation center and playing baseball with the kids all day," you can develop publicity material that tells them exactly what is involved in a recreation center director's job. It should be easy to place this sort of material in the media because the public is always curious about how people earn their livings, and job profiles are popular.

A good example of using misconceptions as the basis for publicity material is the following 60-second radio public service announcement (PSA) by the American Foundation for the Blind.

> *Robert Klein*: The meaning of words. As a child, certain things were always couched in certain ways. For example, my mother used to say, "Go visit Max next door; he's unsighted. He must be lonely."
> *Announcer*: The American Foundation for the Blind presents Robert Klein.
> *Robert Klein*: Now Max isn't unsighted. He's blind. And he isn't lonely, either. True, my mother meant well. But what she and a lot of other people don't understand is that blind people don't want to be treated like children; they want to be treated like people. I remember I once said, "See what I mean, Max?"

My mother almost fainted with embarrassment. And you know
what Max said? "Look how embarrassed your mother is!" Now
if he can use words like "look," don't go around saying
someone's unsighted.

Of course, you should not concentrate on the misinformation;
you should emphasize the facts. "To get rid of stereotypes," says
Mary Jane O'Neill, director of public relations at the New York
Association for the Blind, "I would stress the positive. I would not
talk about beggars with tin cups, for instance, which is the classic
stereotype of the blind person. I would just ignore that. Instead I
would talk about the blind lawyer who is on his way to becoming
the first judge in his district, or the blind insurance man who just hit
the half-million-dollar sales mark."

Motivating Your Audience.   You've already decided what you
want to tell your audience. Now you need to figure out why people
should listen to you. How can you make them want to listen? And how
can you make them want to do something after they've listened? What
benefit can you provide them from their point of view?

Linnea Crowe, program manager for KSTP-TV in St. Paul, Minnesota, explains it this way: "I think not only of who I'm talking to, but
also what my selling point is. Why do I want them to listen to me now?
Why should they listen to me? You have to give people a reason: that
it's going to make them feel better, that it's going to make them happier.
If you don't include that reason in your piece, you might as well not send
it out."

Audience motivation is an area where nonprofit and community
organizations, special interest groups, government agencies—and many
businesses—often fall down. But the advertising world does an excellent
job of pointing out product and service benefits. And whatever you think
of advertising, you have to admit that it works well. So if you work with
a nonprofit organization or a business that is not experienced in the ways
of advertising, it would be a good idea for you to study some advertisements that you feel are particularly effective. Ask yourself exactly how
these ads are able to convince you of the product's benefits. Then try to
parody the ads, substituting your product, service, or organization's
name for the brand in the original and creating parallel product or
service benefits to fit your organization. This should help you see
yourself differently and increase your ability to translate your message
into your audience's terms.

It is always best to be positive. And it will help you motivate your
audience if you avoid reminding people of their fears or dislikes. That

approach only makes them anxious or annoyed. Would you want to go to a Fourth of July picnic at the country club if you were told that children under 12 would not be admitted without an adult, no dogs were allowed, and ball playing, open fires, and barbecues were not permitted? Even if the publicity piece mentioned that there would be all the burgers and hotdogs you could eat and great old-time family games, that negative beginning is hardly alluring.

There's another trick to help you find the service or product benefits likely to appeal to your audience. John B. Rand, a partner at advertising agency Reva Korda & Associates, says, "The best discipline I know is to complete this sentence: This is the business or group or service that does . . . for you. You should promise a benefit, satisfy a need, or offer a distinctive service. The more you can make this something really unique and really different, the better. I know of no other way to do this except by doing your homework and finding out what other organizations have to offer. Then invent something you can offer that they don't."

We know that media exposure can sell products and even ideas, but can it actually motivate people to change their behavior? The answer, according to a case study discussed in *pr reporter*, is yes, if . . .

Despite "reams of research" that seemed to show that mass media can't change people's behavior, the Harvard School of Public Health ". . . announced plans in 1988 to insert 'designated driver' messages into [the] dialogue of popular TV shows like *LA Law* and *Cheers*, [and] then supplement them with a battery of public service announcements." Since 1988, between 95 and 98 percent of the designated driver messages in the media have been placed there by the Harvard project.

According to the *pr reporter* article, the Harvard researchers found that "randomly rotated, arbitrarily directed" messages are not effective. But when the researchers involved media people in a partnership right from the outset, drew on research-based principles of behavioral change, and committed to a long-term process, they found they could actually measure the impact of the campaign. A progress report they issued in 1990 said that "Seventy-eight percent of a national sample stated they'd noticed designated driver messages in . . . programming."

If you want a copy of the progress report, which contains a wealth of information on the project and the principles involved in "mass mediation" of messages, check the listing in Chapter 12.

Researching Your Marketplace

If you think for a moment, you will realize that no matter what kind of organization you work with, you do have competition. There will almost certainly be other businesses offering similar products or services; there may be other community organizations with different perspectives from yours; there's a likelihood that other nonprofit groups compete with yours. And there is always plenty of competition for peoples' time and attention.

So even if yours is the only library in town, the only health club with Nautilus equipment north of the tracks, the only company that makes ginger beer in the state, or the only place in the county that rents power tools, people may not be convinced that they should be reading library books instead of watching TV, working out instead of hanging out, guzzling ginger beer instead of sipping champagne, or renting tools instead of buying a ready-made bookshelf. You have to convince them. And to do that, you have to *know* your marketplace well.

This is especially true if you are publicizing a product. "The number one thing about product publicity," according to Bob Seltzer, executive vice-president of Porter-Novelli Public Relations in New York, " . . . is you have to understand the marketplace and what the competition is. You must know what has been said and done already. These days, if you have a computer and a modem, you have access to dozens of databases. So if you have a new contact lens cleaner, for example, you should be able to find literally dozens of stories that have been written on the subject of cleaning contact lenses during the last two, three, or four years."

If you have never used on-line databases before, you'll have to do some learning first. Some of the more complicated databases, like NEXIS®, offer one-day training sessions that teach you how to use their services efficiently. User skills are critical, indeed, when you tackle databases, because you are charged by the minute. And those charges can be quite steep. Before you start using any database to research your marketplace, be sure you understand all the charges for:

■ Membership, maintenance, minimum and monthly fees.

■ The actual time you're connected to the service.

- The actual time you're connected to each database within that service. Many desirable databases have additional access fees.
- Printing out or saving information.
- Time-sharing costs. Some databases have to be accessed indirectly through a time-sharing service like Tymnet or Telenet.
- Fees for "global" searching of more than one database at the same time.
- Any software you need to use the database.
- The surcharge for using a high-speed modem, if you have one.

This may sound daunting, but it really isn't. Publicists who have used databases for marketplace research can't imagine how they ever did without them. And you may find that you actually enjoy calculating whether it's more cost-effective to subscribe to a specialized database or use a "gateway" service to access it once in a blue moon, without paying subscriber fees. You can, for example, subscribe to a generalized database service like GEnie, and use it to access the Dow Jones databases. Information on some of the more popular databases is listed in Chapter 12.

If you don't have access to a computer with a modem, do not despair. You can still do marketplace research at your library the good, old-fashioned way. Sure, it will take longer, but it costs much less. And it gets the job done. You can also subscribe to one of the press clipping services listed in Chapter 12, and gather information about your marketplace, your competitors, and your industry from thousands of national and international publications. Or you can have the research services listed in Chapter 12 access and search databases for you.

Reaching Your Audience

Once you have chosen your audience, you have to decide the best way to reach it.

Less experienced publicists often use the shotgun approach and send publicity to every broadcaster and publication in the country. But if you want to get teenagers to buy your new line of acid-washed jeans, it would be a waste of time to direct material to a radio station with a big-band format and an over-40s audience. Why should a press release about workshops for young doctors establishing their practices be sent to a weekly community newspaper? Most readers of a community weekly will not be young doctors. This sort of release should go to a professional journal.

Says Teresa DiTore, community affairs director for WCBS-AM Newsradio in New York, "You would find it much more profitable if you took the time initially to do that little bit of research because you'd get more mileage out of your efforts. It is important to know who it is you are trying to reach, and go to that station."

You have to ask yourself several questions before you decide which media will be best for your material. The answers, of course, will vary from one piece of publicity to another:

- Which stations or publications will reach the specific audience you want?
- How much credibility do those media have with their audiences?
- Will their staffs be interested in your material?
- Will their audiences be interested in your material?
- How much lead time is required?

You should also keep in mind that media with large and broad audiences are the most difficult publicity targets. But specialized media often don't get enough material that fits their narrow focuses, so they may be very eager to use yours. Since they specialize, they know enough about your material to give it knowledgeable treatment. So it's worth searching for the highly specialized newsletters, magazines, trade journals, syndicated columns, and even specialized broadcast programs that reach exactly the audience you're targeting.

There are several ways to become familiar with the audience and format of media outlets. The directories listed in Chapter 12 are a useful source of such information and will help you send your material only to those publications and stations that reach your audience.

Remember that editors and broadcasters don't want you to send material they can't use. And media people respond better if you address your publicity material to them by name. A good set of media directories will give you hundreds and even thousands of names and titles. But you need to watch out for a pitfall here. Journalists and editors change jobs. And even the best media directories start going out of date the moment they are printed. So you have to check the most important names on your media contact list periodically.

That's only the start. Mary Jane O'Neill of the New York Association for the Blind advises that you should read a newspaper you are interested in and, "Find out the kind of stories it runs." KRBE-FM's Mike Martin says that, "The publicist should take time before he sends anything or calls, to make sure that the format of the station fits the subject he's dealing with."

The same principle applies to magazines. There's no good reason for a publicist to waste time and effort approaching a magazine that has no interest in his material. Yet it happens all the time.

"*PC Magazine* has a very clear focus," according to Gus Venditto. "We cover *products* for IBM-compatible personal computers. We're not really interested in anything else." That should be clear to anyone who takes the time to read through an issue or two. But Venditto, like many journalists, finds that, "We get a lot of calls from people who probably don't read the magazine. They often try to sell us stories about their users. We never run user stories. They're just not appropriate for us."

Selecting the Right Medium

To do this effectively, you will first have to become familiar with the wide range of publicity tools available to you.

If you are going to approach your audience via the printed word, your choices will range from simple community calendar listings to full-length feature articles, from one-page press releases to short attention-getting facts, in the form of fillers, about your organization, industry, product, service, or cause. Even letters to the editor are a good medium. All of these formats are discussed in detail in Chapter 4.

Should radio or TV be a more appropriate medium for your message, you can send out news releases and short features written especially for broadcasters, video news releases, public service announcements (PSAs), or community calendar listings. Techniques for putting these together are covered in Chapter 7. Appearances on special programs and talk shows, either in person or by satellite hook-up or telephone, are another important avenue for publicity, and Chapter 8 will help you prepare for them.

In addition, there are times when you will get the best publicity by having the media visit you, in which case you will want to plan a press conference or special event. Check Chapter 9 for tips on how to do this well.

The Nonprofit Advertising Dilemma

For nonprofit organizations, special interest groups, and government agencies, paid advertising and publicity sometimes do not mix well.

If your nonprofit organization pays for space or time, you may find it difficult to get free public service advertising in newspapers or public service announcements on radio and TV. "It's against our policy to run public service material if they buy advertising of any kind," says Harry O'Toole, public service director of KDKA-AM Radio in Pittsburgh. Running paid advertising will not, however, hurt your chances with news and feature material. Truly newsworthy material will still get coverage, no matter how much you advertise.

When the American Heart Association tried running paid ads in newspapers, the group found that after the advertising appeared, many papers, especially those that did not get paid ads, refused to give customary free public service advertising. To add to the confusion, dozens of radio and TV advertising salespeople began to seek paid advertising from the association.

Not all broadcasters and newspapers are that rigid, however, and you might decide that it's possible for you to run limited paid ads for your group. If a community theater company ran a small paid ad in the theater section of the newspaper, that probably wouldn't hurt its chances of getting free coverage at most media outlets. "We used to feel that if you had the money to advertise, then you didn't need us," says WCBS-AM's Teresa DiTore, "but often a group might have $300 and need more exposure than that can buy. We disregard paid advertising now."

You may conclude that it's so important for your organization to control when and where the message is used that you want to run paid advertising, even at the risk of losing those free PSAs.

Getting an Angle for Business Publicity

If you are involved with a profit-making concern, you need a different approach to get publicity. Nonprofit organizations can say "come to our clinic for counseling," and they'll get coverage; you probably cannot. But with the right angle, businesses can get news stories and feature material in the papers and on the airwaves. And even businesses can get public service announcements on radio and TV. Throughout this book you will find examples of business publicity that got good media play.

Sometimes your business will make genuine news that stands on its own merits. If you announce that your firm is marketing a new solar water heater that sells for $50.00, is easy to install, and can make enough hot water for a family of four, you will get coverage. Because that's news. That will have an impact on almost every person in the country.

But if you want people to replace their worn-out TV antennas with your new model, you've got a problem. While special interest and trade magazines often *will* print a straight announcement of a new product, general interest and mass appeal media are harder to crack. You have to develop a "service" approach. If you provide material to editors that tells people how to install antennas and how to solve TV reception problems, you're on the right track.

Judy Gail May, the principal of May Communications in Highland, New Jersey, did just that. Over a three-year period, she developed publicity material for the Winegard Company, including a regular newspaper column, TV interviews, public service spots, press releases, magazine articles, and speakers for radio talk shows. The result was a lot of coverage—*with the brand name mentioned.*

Virtually every business person can develop service material that will get media attention. After all, you are an expert on your product or service, so it shouldn't be too difficult for you to tell people how to choose, buy, or use it.

If you are the proud owner of a fine jewelry store, you might write a short radio piece on how to invest in diamonds. A mill that produces high-quality whole wheat pastry flour could provide the food editors at newspapers across the country with a recipe for quick and easy chocolate layer cake. Since most people aren't aware that you can make a light, tasty cake from whole grain flour, food editors will be interested. Where do you think those recipes in the paper come from? The food editor's test kitchen? Not likely! The majority of them come from commercial sources, just like you. And you will probably be surprised to find that folks are waiting for your advice. This is the "how-to" era, and short well-written material which can be read over the air or printed with minimal editing is in constant demand.

Testing and Evaluating Your Publicity

"How could they misunderstand that PSA?," moaned the publicist for the Chelm Public Library, holding his head in his hands. "It's perfectly clear. It says we have books that will help job seekers learn about the job market.

It doesn't say we have jobs." *Yet misunderstand it they did. Hundreds of people who were out of work heard "job seekers." They were so desperate for work, that's all they heard, so they jammed the library switchboard with calls, asking for applications for "the job." They poured through the front doors by the dozens, asking where they could apply for "the job." The librarian got some of them to look at the collection of vocational guidance books, but most of the callers and visitors were angry. They felt they had been tricked. Whether they had been isn't the point. The point is that the publicist should have pretested his publicity material to help avoid problems like this.*

Pretesting is especially important with public service announcements, but it's a good idea to pretest other kinds of publicity as well. Even the most seasoned publicist occasionally gets carried away and needs outside feedback to bring the earth back into contact with her feet.

That press release or PSA may make perfect sense to you, and even to your colleagues, but how do you know that your audience will actually get the message? After all, many people won't be familiar with your organization or your service, product, or cause. This is why you should try out your message on as many people as you can find who are not acquainted with your group. If they are cynical and unsympathetic toward your aims, so much the better. If you can communicate with unsympathetic cynics, you can communicate with anyone.

Of course, whenever possible, your test group should be made up of people in your target audience. The size of the group is up to you, but two dozen people will give you more accurate feedback than two or three.

Once you have sent out your publicity material and it has been used by the media, make an effort to evaluate its impact. Whether you are asking people to call for more information or a free booklet, place an order, visit your store or their nearest dealer, or attend a special event, sale or meeting, be sure you and your staff have a way to keep track of where people heard about you. It may sound simple, but there is no substitute for these data!

Press Clipping Services

Press clipping bureaus are an important source of information for publicists, especially if your publicity is getting picked up by wire services and syndicates and you're getting newspaper coverage in distant cities and states.

You might want to subscribe to one or two of the press clipping services listed in Chapter 12. Such services scan thousands of newspapers and magazines, and monitor hundreds of television talk shows and news programs, looking for mention of your product or organization. Or you can give them subject areas that are of interest to your group. They will supply you with clippings or broadcast transcripts mentioning the key words or names you give them.

You may wish to use one of the software programs or clipping services to develop reports that pinpoint the quantity of media exposure you receive, number of mentions of your product or organization name, the amount of favorable, unfavorable and mixed coverage, and the number of people your publicity reaches. One of the clipping services has the capability to index and store your clippings *and* the publicity materials that generated them on a high-density optical disk. Although this additional service is expensive, it can transmute file drawers of material into a package you can hold in your hand.

Whenever you use a clipping service, find out what *all* the fees are before you sign a contract. You'll probably pay a monthly reading fee, and a charge per clipping. Ask if there are any other fees, like minimum monthly charges.

Surveys

Counting clippings is a good start in evaluating your publicity program, but it measures quantity, not impact. Yes, it's nice to get a bundle of clippings from Peoria, Pecos, Portland, Pensacola, Pittsburgh, and Poughkeepsie, but the quantity of clippings should not be the only way you measure success. The real questions are what the clippings said about your group, how many people saw them, and what impact they had. Analyzing clippings is no problem if your publicity generates just a dozen or two. But if your organization is a major publicity player, you'll have to give some thought to how you want to organize and analyze that torrent of news clips—and how you want to measure their impact on the public.

To do this, you may have to run a survey. Surveys are most useful where you can use numbers to make a before-and-after comparison. For example, if only 17 percent of the senior citizens in your service area knew about your special insurance products for older adults before you started your publicity efforts, but 35 percent were familiar with them after six months of publicity, you have a concrete idea of your effectiveness. Unfortunately, it isn't always possible to obtain such neat figures. But even if you can't, surveys can still be useful.

It is possible for you to do a small survey yourself on the telephone or in person. Watch out for one common mistake: If you limit your questions to the customers of your store, the people who come to your anti-busing meetings, or the patrons of your library, you won't find out what non-customers, busing proponents, or non-users of the library are thinking. So keep these simple rules-of-thumb in mind:

- Unless you are seeking the opinions of a specialized group, such as doctors, senior citizens, or people with a Hispanic background, make sure your survey includes people who are a representative cross section of the geographic area you are interested in.

- When you are looking for a cross section, set quotas and make sure your interviewers fill them. Otherwise they will tend to interview the types of people with whom they are most comfortable.

- Always keep your questions short and make them specific.

- Allow time and space for unstructured comments; these can be most valuable.

- Limit yourself to one topic in an interview. More than that will only confuse people.

If you are conducting a before-and-after survey, be sure to ask the same questions both times. Otherwise, you will probably get different results from your two questionnaires, even without publicity.

If you don't know anything about doing surveys and you need more information to do them on your own, look at *Do It Yourself Marketing Research* by George Breen, listed in Chapter 12. Although it is geared toward marketing people in firms selling products, the basic techniques for doing surveys can be adapted by sellers of services as well as nonprofit and community organizations, special interest groups, and government agencies. If you don't have the time or the people to do your own survey or you need a sample that is larger than you can get on your own, you might want to contact one of the opinion research firms listed in Chapter 12. Many opinion research outfits have an "omnibus" plan, where you can cut costs by adding your questions to a regional or national survey.

Preparing Your Organization for Publicity

Another important aspect of your function involves setting up the structures and procedures that will make it possible for your organization to support your publicity efforts. If you are to work effectively, your authority must be clearly outlined and understood by the other members of your organization, and channels of communication must be set up between you and the rest of the staff and between your organization and the media. You also need to make sure that you have an adequate budget.

Defining Your Authority

Find out, first of all, exactly what your role within the organization will be:

- How much authority will you have?
- What kinds of decisions will need approval?
- Who will review your work, and at what point?
- Can you turn down requests for publicity by members or staff of your organization? Under what circumstances?
- Will you be able to write copy for publicity material yourself, or will that be done by a committee? Bear in mind that writing by committee is cumbersome and time-consuming, and you have deadlines to meet. It is possible to play four-hand piano, but four-hand typewriter is not practical. Try to arrange it so that only one person writes copy.

It is tremendously important that these decisions be made ahead of time and written down to prevent confusion later on. The answers to these questions may seem apparent, but many organizations do not consider what only becomes obvious with hindsight.

In most organizations, the publicist should be responsible to the executive director, president, or the vice-president of marketing or communications. In smaller groups that do not have professional staffs, publicists should report directly to the governing body. The only way you can know what you need to know is if you have a clear channel right to the top. Don't settle for less, or you may well find yourself hamstrung by complicated procedures for getting information and for approving your work. Complicated procedures mean time wasted. And publicists, who live by deadlines, can't waste time.

There is another reason why you need access to the top. "You can't fabricate publicity with some kind of machine. You can't publicize what isn't happening," says Harry Cohn, director of public relations for the American Red Cross in Greater New York. "So you should be involved in whether your organization is carrying out its programs and services well. Because if it's not, you're in real trouble."

Increasingly, innovative corporations are integrating public relations and publicity into their marketing plans. "Publicity is a marketing tool and I think it's very foolish to try to separate it from the ongoing marketing plan," says Bob Seltzer of Porter-Novelli Public Relations. Because this integration is a new strategy, some executives may not realize that they have to bring the publicist into the discussions up front, where you can make the strongest contribution. You may have to persuade them to include you.

Publicists also have to be concerned about public and media reaction to their organizations, industries and product lines, because bad public opinion will undermine the effectiveness of even the best publicity program. Since the publicist gets continual feedback on how the public views the organization or product, she should be considered an organizational resource and have input into policy making.

Setting Up Internal Communications

Make sure that there is a systematic way for the publicist to know what is happening in your organization, or business. The publicist has to know what everyone in the organization is doing, in advance. Nothing can undermine your credibility with the media faster than inaccurate or incomplete knowledge of your organization.

Another part of the publicist's task is to tell the staff, volunteers, and membership about the publicity plan and program. If the publicity effort is new, or if it has had a bad reputation in the past, you will need to convince these people that your efforts are worthwhile and worth supporting. Otherwise, you might find that the people who answer the telephone "don't know about" the program you just publicized, the sales staff have "never heard of" the free product literature and special offer, or the organization's staff or members make statements to the press that contradict yours.

Leslie O'Bergin, former reporter for the *Santa Cruz Independent* in California, puts it this way: "If the publicist is going to be contradicted by other people in the organization when I call for more information, she has no use whatsoever to that organization. She is, in fact, a liability."

Communication between the group and the publicist is not, however, a one-way street. The publicist should meet regularly with his or her supervisor or the governing body of the organization. Since publicity involves continual deadlines, fast responses, and occasional crises, there should be a provision for quick and sudden consultation.

Always tell your supervisor, key executives, or the governing body exactly what you are doing and why—before you do it. It is particularly important that they know beforehand about material that is to appear in the media. Otherwise, they might miss that television special you worked so hard to prepare, or, even worse, the media might call them for comment and catch them by surprise. Be certain that everyone in authority in your organization gets information from you first.

In the worst of all possible cases, the publicist for the Chelm Committee Against Nuclear Reactors invited the press to be present at a training session that was to prepare participants for the upcoming nonviolent occupation of a proposed nuclear reactor site. The publicist had been advised by several members of the group that inviting the press was permissible, but there had never been any discussion within the group about who could make this sort of decision. When the television crews appeared at the training session, the participants, who had not been told the media might appear, angrily turned them away. The result was some very negative publicity.

Setting Up External Communications

When your organization approaches the media, it should not speak with many tongues. Be certain your key executives, staff, membership, volunteers, and board all know that only one person should approach the media. Not only will this make it easier for you to develop working relationships and credibility with journalists, it will avoid the confusion so easily caused by having two or more spokespeople.

Journalist Leslie O'Bergin expresses the preference of many media people: "I expect to work with one spokesperson from the group. I don't like it when one person calls me this week and another contacts me next week. It indicates either total incoherence or conflict within the organization."

And John Canelli, news director of WAVI-FM in Dayton, Ohio, feels that continually changing publicists is, "the same thing as continually changing reporters. The reason why you like to give a reporter a beat is simply for the reason of contacts and knowledge. You have to build rapport and trust."

If it is absolutely necessary to split up the publicity work, try to have one person for newspapers, another handling radio, and a third working with TV. This will allow each person to develop ongoing working relationships and to learn over a period of time how to work best with individual contacts. If you decide on this plan, make sure that everyone involved communicates with the others on a regular, formal basis.

When the media come to you however, it is better to speak with many tongues. If the publicist or the executive director or the president is the only person who can talk to callers from the media, that person will be overburdened, and other people in the organization who may have the expertise to answer questions will feel left out. You should encourage those with expertise to answer routine media questions and then let the publicist know whom they spoke with and what they said. If there are any exceptions, such as controversial situations, disasters or emergencies, these should be spelled out—in advance.

Having more than one person available to answer questions from newspapers and broadcasters has another benefit. Says Fred Kirsch, a reporter for the *Ledger-Star* in Norfolk, Virginia, "A lot of times you'll call an office and there's only one person who is authorized to tell you something. And they're out for the day. That can get frustrating because we always need information *now*. Newspapers never give us enough time, so we're always saying, 'hurry up, we want the information!' The more people we can talk with in an organization, the better."

Still, there are some executive directors, board members, and officers who want the publicist to handle all calls from the media. And an occasional publicist will resent a reporter's request to talk with someone higher up. Cindy Loose, a reporter for the *Staten Island Register* in New York, explains why she needs to talk with an organization's officers: "Publicists often don't really understand the importance of quotes. You might call a public relations department and get some facts and figures. But if it's a pressing issue of the day, you have to quote somebody. You don't want to quote a publicist; you want to quote a president or a vice-president. I think publicists should be aware that sometimes, even if you've gotten all the information from them, you still need to talk with an officer of the organization because you want to quote them. It's not a slight of the publicist."

One final point. It's always wise to have written guidelines for staff, volunteers, and members on how they should deal with the media.

Staffing the Telephone

You sent out a fantastic press release on a major story, but no one from the media has called you about it. Or have they? Maybe they tried to reach you, but there was no answer. Reporters who really were interested in your story could have been discouraged by endless busy signals or eternal waiting on hold. Perhaps their deadlines came and went, and they couldn't run the story without some clarification. So it died, and it's being buried right now, in the landfill outside of town, with the rest of the rubbish. Or even worse, after they failed to reach you, the press *was* able to contact your competitors or your opposition. And they wrote a major story. Without any involvement from you. It happens all the time.

Jack O'Dwyer's Newsletter mentions just one media relations study in which 300 business journalists were interviewed. "According to the findings . . . 28 percent [of the journalists] said executives either did not return their phone calls or returned them too late."

But there's no reason *you* should lose important publicity opportunities just because journalists can't reach you! You can prevent problems with a good system for receiving and answering calls from the media. Your reputation with reporters depends on it. This is particularly important for small groups that don't have a staff or headquarters, and for larger businesses where reporters can get entangled in layers of bureaucracy and red tape.

Don't expect a busy reporter to keep calling you until you finally answer. Carol Rissman, news director for WBUR-FM in Boston, speaks for most journalists when she says that she is "likely to try again with a major story. But I am not likely to try again more than once, and I am not likely to try again on another day."

If you do not have an office, or if you staff it on a part-time basis, you need an answering machine or service. If your office is open full time during business hours, make sure that whoever takes messages from media people is clear and complete.

Try to have a direct telephone line that bypasses the switchboard, so reporters don't get caught in that quagmire. The person who answers that direct line should understand the constant deadline pressure media people work with. In fact, he or she should read this book, too. And whether your calls are answered by machine or in person, you will have to respond to your messages quickly.

Being prepared for calls from the media is only one side of the coin. The other side involves responding to calls from the public generated by your publicity.

Touting the new subsidized suburban industrial park with no taxes on new enterprises for the next 10 years, the Chelm Chamber of Commerce sent out a news release to every paper in the country. The release got tremendous press play, and thousands of executives read it. Unfortunately, the number in the press release was for a single telephone line, so most callers got a busy signal. And since the secretarial staff hadn't been told about the release, those prospects who did get through found that their questions weren't answered and the secretaries had not heard about the free booklet mentioned in the release.

If you expect your publicity to generate telephone calls, remember to have enough lines available to handle the response and to brief the people who will be answering those calls!

Making a Budget

Even if you plan to do all the work yourself, you still have to spend money on your publicity. You will need funds for copying or printing news releases, stamps to mail them, the lease payments for your word processor, photographers' fees, film and developing costs, telephone calls, and office supplies. If your organization does not have that money, you will have to raise it, or you won't be able to do a decent job of publicity. If you are convinced that publicity is important for your organization, you'll figure out where the money will come from.

It is a good idea to make a list of every possible publicity expense and then add 25 percent to cover emergencies like disasters, product recalls, controversy—or even more good news than you had planned for.

As you draw up your budget, try to project the rough cost of handling the response to your publicity. If you're sending out publicity material offering free pamphlets on how to choose, buy, and use your product, how much will it cost to handle the inquiries, print the pamphlets, and mail them? Will that cost be justified on your bottom line?

Of course there are times when your publicity's value just can't be measured. But when it can, you will have to design a yardstick that works in your situation. Before you start preparing your publicity budget, make sure you understand exactly how top management expects you to measure bottom-line success.

Success, itself, can be a problem. What would you do if every radio and TV station in town ran your PSAs for the new drug addiction treatment center, and hundreds of people showed up, all wanting immediate attention? Suppose the requests for that product literature you publicized nationally are ten times larger than you expected? What will that do to your budget? Will management look beyond the increased publicity expense and see the net result of increased sales? If they don't, you'll have to help them focus on the fattened bottom line, rather than the over-runs in your publicity budget. This isn't likely to happen often, but success on an unexpected scale has caused problems for some organizations.

If your publicity is going to reach large numbers of people, and you are asking for a personal response, " . . . you should always have a contingency plan outlining how you intend to handle large numbers of responses," says Harriet S. Schimel, Communications Director of the United Negro College Fund. "I think your basic concern, no matter how overwhelming the response, is that you want the public to feel that you're accessible . . ." You want to convey the message that even though you're temporarily overwhelmed by the response, you'll get to them as soon as possible—and deliver whatever it is your publicity promised.

If you work for a large organization, a carefully prepared budget will gain you management's respect and make planning easier. Your budget should probably be a functional one, that explains the purpose of major expenses, with specific goals your publicity program is moving toward, and how much each goal will cost.

The budget should include staff salaries. That helps management understand how much you're spending now, and why you will need more to accomplish additional tasks. You might also calculate overhead expenses at the rate of one dollar for every dollar spent on payroll.

Once you have established a budget, it's up to you to protect it. For example, if a top executive asks you to add to a publicity plan at the last minute, tell her how much it will cost. That might stop the addition dead—or get you an increased budget. And it's less likely that you'll be left hanging, expected to accomplish something without the dollars you need.

So far, we have looked at ways in which you can prepare your organization for the publicity effort. Before launching your campaign, you should also consider taking some precautionary measures. These include getting preventive legal advice, setting up emergency procedures in case plans go awry, and keeping good records of your own actions to protect yourself from unwarranted criticism after the fact.

Checking Legal Angles

It's a very wise idea to discuss your publicity plans with an attorney on an ongoing basis to see if there are any legal angles that might affect your campaigns. This is especially important if you plan to write material designed to influence legislation. In some areas, you might be required to register as a lobbyist, and there could be legal problems if you fail to do this. Your lawyer will also be able to advise you on model releases for photographs, the use of quotations from copyrighted material, and questions connected with libel and slander.

If you work for the federal government or an organization funded with federal money, ask your counsel how your publicity program will be affected by the act of Congress, dated October 23, 1913, that forbids government employment of public relations personnel. Publicists who work for government agencies or organizations that are funded by public money should ask how public disclosure or "sunshine" laws affect their publicity program.

There is an area where you must be *very* careful when you do publicity. Never comment on a case that is on trial unless you clear it with your lawyer first, or you might be held in contempt of court. While publicity can be a highly useful tool for winning legal battles, especially when it's important to explain legal issues to the public, you must work closely with your legal team.

A story reported in PR News describes one example of team work between lawyers and publicists.

"In 1988, Detroit-based Casey Communications Management, Inc. (CCM), Southfield, MI, made shareholders [of the R. P. Scherer Corporation (RPS)] aware of their own best interests and helped them win a bitter, court-contested proxy fight . . ." When RPS's Board of Directors refused to sell the company, brother and sister Karla and John S. Scherer, the largest shareholders, asked CCM to work out a ". . . communications strategy, targeted toward RPS's shareholders, securities analysts, and investment bankers . . ." And CCM did just that.

Working closely with their clients' lawyers, CCM used publicity to get their message across to shareholders, who often don't pay much attention to mailed stockholder bulletins. Since the story involved some court-room dramas in which the Scherers' lawyers battled the Company's Board, it received extensive coverage.

CCM helped tilt media commentary in their clients' favor ". . . by responding directly to reporters' questions and being available night and day to service the media. In contrast, the old guard of the company usually responded to reporters with a 'no comment.' As a result, media response was generous and articles giving . . . [the Scherers'] position usually appeared the morning after a late-afternoon release."

"The campaign literally paid big dividends," according to PR *News*. "After two candidates nominated by the Scherers were elected to the Board of Directors and confirmed, the Board voted unanimously to explore options for sale of the company. In May, 1989, RPS was sold to the highest bidder . . . for a price that doubled the value of the shares."

While the Scherers might have been able to force the old Board of Directors to sell the company strictly with a court-ordered action, using publicity to win shareholder support made it much more likely they'd achieve their objectives.

Media publicity can also be used to help ward off frivolous law suits. Joel Strasser, Senior Vice-President and Managing Director of Dorf & Stanton Technology Communications, explains how his firm helped inform corporations that challenging his client's patent was going to be fruitless.

"About every five years or so," says Strasser, "somebody tries to challenge Olof Soderblom's patent to the token ring technology." This is the main method of local area networking for personal computers, and a lot of people in the computer industry still think token ring was invented by IBM.

"It wasn't," according to Strasser. "Soderblom owns the patent. And he insists on royalties. But who wants to pay the bill collector?"

Although Soderblom's company, Willemijn Holding B.V., successfully sued three companies which were withholding payment, still another business tried to challenge the validity of his patent. In order to build support in the industry, the challenger was trying to get the trade press on its side. A number of negative articles appeared about how the Soderblom patents were going to be knocked down.

"To counter this inaccurate press coverage, we booked him on a very intensive U.S. media tour, aimed at data processing publications," says Strasser.

Below is just one of the press releases Dorf & Stanton sent out to dozens of high tech publications. In addition, Strasser issued announcements every time another large corporation signed a token ring licensing agreement with Willemijn. He provided the press with a backgrounder on Soderblom's token ring invention which described in plain English how it was developed and how it works. And he offered journalists interviews with the inventor.

The resulting coverage was extensive. For example, MIS *Week*, a prestigious data processing publication, did a major personal profile on how Soderblom got the patent, and what he's had to do to hold on to it. Because of this coverage, any corporation that is considering a suit to overturn the Soderblom token ring patent will realize that it is tackling a formidable enemy with a battle-hardened fortress. While it's true that you can't measure the number of law suits that won't be initiated, the savings in legal fees could be far higher than the cost of the publicity campaign.

Willemijn Holding BV
FOR IMMEDIATE RELEASE

CONTACT: Joel A. Strasser
or Jim Lawler
Dorf & Stanton
(212) 420-8100
1-800-223-2121 Outside NY
George Vande Sande
(202) 331-7111
Olof Soderblom
011-44-372-378538

WILLEMIJN EXPECTS PATENT OFFICE TO UPHOLD TOKEN RING RIGHTS

ROTTERDAM, May 24—Confident of a successful conclusion, Willemijn Holding B.V., owner of the Soderblom token ring patent, today indicated that it is expediting the reexamination proceeding in the U.S. Patent and Trademark Office relating to the Soderblom patent. The reexamination proceeding based upon the request by an anonymous party, was instituted last month.

Foregoing its right to file an objection with the Patent Office, Willemijn announces that it has instead requested that the reexamination be undertaken promptly. Willemijn says it is likely that the Patent Office will issue an initial rejection of some of the patent's broad claim. This, of course, does not in any way affect the enforceability of the patent. However, such a rejection clears the way for prompt submission of a full response by Willemijn's attorneys.

Willemijn Vice Chairman and token ring inventor Olof Soderblom said, "Given the utter lack of merit of the arguments put forth by the anonymous requestor, we are confident that the Patent Office will reaffirm the broad scope and validity of the patent."

Soderblom's patent, originally issued in 1982, was reissued in 1985 following Willemijn's invitation to potential licensees to file with the Patent Office whatever protests they deemed appropriate. Six such protests were filed but each was dismissed by the Patent Office in granting the broader claims contained in the reissue patent.

– more –   – more –

To date, more than 50 companies, including such household names as IBM, NCR, Hewlett Packard, Hitachi, and Toshiba have accepted licenses from Willemijn under the Soderblom patent. Since last June, three infringement suits have been successfully settled, each resulting in a license and compensation for past infringement. Consent decrees have been entered by two Courts, acknowledging the validity of the Soderblom patent.

# # #

A final word of legal caution. If your group is running a lottery, where prizes are given by chance for a consideration, most newspapers will not be able to give you coverage; postal regulations usually forbid them to mention this type of activity. Broadcasters, however, may be more helpful. Although many broadcasters may not be aware of this, the Charity Games Advertising Clarification Act of 1988, which became effective on May 7, 1990, permits them to mention lotteries as long as they are "not otherwise prohibited by the State in which . . . [the lotteries] are conducted." Since lotteries are heavily regulated by many states, you will want to check with your lawyer before mentioning them in your publicity, even with this new law in effect.

Preparing for the Unexpected

"People involved in publicity should be aware of *all* the things that can go wrong, so they can develop plans to cope with emergencies," says Harriet S. Schimel.

What plans do you have in case your carefully created publicity program for that super-improved widget is scooped by a competitor with an even better design? What if your volunteer publicist suddenly becomes ill? Do you have people standing by who will be able to pick up where your sick volunteer stopped? Suppose the governor calls a particularly important press conference and your previously arranged television and radio programs are preempted? Does this mean your event will fail? Or do you have an alternate plan for reaching the public? Part of planning publicity involves making a list of every possible thing that can go wrong, as well as what you will do when that happens. Merely drawing up such a list will help you design your plans to avoid the obvious problems.

Consider in advance who your opposition might be and how you will handle them. Let's say that your geranium fanciers' group wants to donate potted plants in bloom to the local hospital to cheer the patients. No one would object to that public-spirited act of charity, would they? Better think again! How will the florist across from the hospital feel about your idea? Does the proprietor have friends on the hospital's board of directors? He does? Well, you better start planning!

Now this is a deliberately extreme case. A geranium lovers' group is perhaps the least controversial organization possible. And that is the point. There is probably no organization that will not run into hostility and opposition at some time. Your publicity efforts will be vastly more effective if you think through your plans for handling opposition before it surfaces.

At a time when you least expect it, you will have to be ready to deal with "breaking" news: events that happen suddenly and that demand media coverage, such as fires, crimes, and accidents. San Francisco journalist Nancy Dunn explains, "Even with breaking news, you can be prepared to some extent. You should know media deadlines; you should know who to contact. And you should have the telephone numbers for direct lines to newspaper and broadcast newsrooms, so you can reach them when the switchboards are closed at night or on weekends." This is particularly important in crisis situations. If *you* don't provide information during an emergency, reporters and the public may speculate about what is really going on. And those speculations can be far more damaging to an organization than the facts.

You should also decide who in your organization needs to be told about a breaking news event. Reporters may call officers or board members for comment, and you will want to give your people the information they need and a chance to think through their responses.

Handling controversy and dealing with the unexpected are discussed in detail in Chapters 9 and 10. They are mentioned here because they should be included in your publicity plan.

Protecting Yourself from Criticism

You may find some important hidden attitudes emerging as you try to clarify your role and develop your publicity plan. If you are involved in a nonprofit organization, community or special interests group, or government human-services agency, your organization's executives and board of directors may look down on publicity. Says Richard Weiner, owner of a public relations firm in New York and author of eight books on public relations, "Sometimes . . . there is a feeling that public relations is sleazy, improper, and immoral, and that the organization shouldn't really be doing this."

A common hidden attitude among corporate executives is that the publicist can *make* the media print or broadcast anything—even self-serving puff and fluff with no facts, figures or news value. If you think your colleagues have either of these attitudes, even if they don't actually say so, make sure there is an honest discussion. Otherwise these prejudices will return to haunt and hobble you again and again.

In addition, there are some specific precautions you should take when you are serving as a publicist, no matter how much you trust the people you are working with:

- Get information for press releases, public service announcements, and other publicity materials in writing. This is a valuable way to avoid misunderstandings.

- Follow up all conversations, both within your organization and with the media, by writing confirming memos. This is yet another way to be sure that everyone involved in the publicity effort agrees on the outcome.

- If other people in your organization have to approve your publicity material, ask them to initial it. They will give it more careful consideration this way, and many problems can be avoided.

- Keep copies of everything you write, including memos and interview notes, particularly if you are quoting others.

- When you quote someone in a news release, be sure to send them a copy ahead of time. Include a note asking them to initial the release and send it back to you. If someone later says you misquoted them, you can put an end to that potential problem very quickly.

Questions about publicity material can arise several years after the material has been released, and by that time your memory might be pretty foggy. Suppose that two of your ardent supporters—or several disgruntled customers—turn against your organization and decide to seek revenge for a real or imagined gripe. They take you to court, alleging that you slanderously misquoted them in a press release five years ago. Your defense will be much easier if you still have the notes from your interviews and the copy of the release, with their initials on it, neatly filed away.

Keeping Expectations Realistic

No matter how carefully you plan and how hard you work, it is easy to expect too much from your publicity efforts, especially at first. Says journalist Nancy Dunn, "The amateur publicist is often marked by an unreasonable expectation about what one person in a media organization can or should do for his group."

Not every event is front-page material. And not every new product is a cover story. "If it isn't a landmark product," says *PC Magazine*'s Gus Venditto, a small product review is the best you can hope for. You should be grateful for it, because it's all you can expect."

Even if you get full cooperation from a reporter, and your group is covered in a front-page story with pictures, or on prime-time TV, many people won't read the paper or watch that channel that day. And those who do read the paper may not see your story; if they see it, they might not read it. If they read it or see it on TV, they still may not absorb or remember it. Because people are bombarded with communications in newspapers, radio, TV, magazines, direct mail, and billboards, it takes many messages to have an effect.

Creating publicity is like weaving a fabric. Each newspaper story, every radio public service announcement, each TV program, is another strand. It takes a lot of strands to make the yarn that weaves the cloth. And since the fabric is constantly unraveling, as people, following that all-too-human tendency, forget previous messages, you will have to weave rapidly and continuously.

"I don't think you can say 'this press release yields that amount of business,' " says Gary Blake of The Communication Workshop. "That's asking too much. Publicity sets the scene and indirectly leads to new business." But when your publicity is on target, it can be a fruitful scene, indeed.

You should now have a good idea of how to plan your publicity program. In the following pages you will learn the specific skills you need to get your organization the kind of publicity it deserves. There will be situations, however, when all the skills of Madison Avenue won't get you the time of day from the media. If your group is controversial or your product is new and innovative, you may find that the media ignore you. American newspapers and broadcasters are often heavily geared toward middle-of-the-road, noncontroversial material.

If your publicity material for newsworthy events is good and you get no play from the press or air time from broadcasters, you have an access problem. If this is the case, your task is more complex, but it is certainly not hopeless. Chapter 11 discusses the issues surrounding access to the media and what you can do about such a problem.

As you read through this book, you may find that there are examples of situations that don't seem to apply to you because your product, service, or cause is "different." Please bear in mind that the examples are selected to illustrate problems and principles that apply to all publicity programs, no matter who runs them. It will be a good exercise for you to translate the examples to fit your situation.

Small-town publicists will find their tasks are not as complex as those of their city cousins; media people will be easier to work with, and there will be shortcuts that just aren't possible for urban publicists. But the principles behind a good publicity program are the same in Clinton, Arkansas (population 2,080), as they are in New York City.

Checklist—Your Role As Publicist

1. What are your organization's publicity goals?
2. Have you written them down?
3. Do they include specific figures?
4. Have you set publicity priorities for your organization?
5. Do you have criteria for separating major and minor stories?
6. Who, exactly, is your intended audience?
7. Can you break it into subgroups?
8. What misconceptions do people have about your product, service, cause or issue?
9. How can you use these misconceptions in your publicity?
10. How will you motivate your audience?
11. If you're trying to change the public's behavior, can you make a long-term commitment to do this?
12. Have you made a list of your product, service, or organizational benefits for your audience?
13. Have you made a written list of your competitors?

14. Do you know what's been written and said in the media about your product, service, and industry in the last few years?
15. Have you explored the idea of using on-line databases to research your marketplace?
16. If so, are you aware of all the fees and charges for the database you've chosen?
17. Which are the best broadcast stations and publications for reaching your audience?
18. Are you familiar with their formats?
19. Have you included newsletters, trade and special interest magazines on your release list?
20. If your organization is not-for-profit, do you have a policy about paid advertising?
21. Is it based on feedback from the media in your local area?
22. If you are a business person, have you figured out one or more "service" approaches for publicity material that teaches people how to choose, buy, and use your product or service?
23. How will you pretest your publicity material?
24. How will you evaluate its impact?
25. Have you gotten management to agree on a bottom-line yardstick for measuring the results of your publicity?
26. Do you have a system for keeping track of where people read or heard about you?
27. Have you decided how you will gather and evaluate your press clippings?
28. How much authority will the publicist have?
29. Is the publicist's role in the organization clear?
30. Will you be involved in developing marketing strategies?
31. Does your organization have a written publicity plan?
32. Who will review the publicist's work?
33. Have you determined what decisions need to be approved, and who has to approve them?
34. How will the publicist know what is happening in the organization?
35. How will the publicist inform the staff, membership, board, officers, and executives about the publicity program?

36. Does your organization have a written policy about who can approach the media and who can respond to questions from the media?

37. How will you receive and respond to telephone calls from the media? The public?

38. Have you drawn up a publicity budget?

39. Does your budget include extra funds for emergencies and unexpected response to your publicity?

40. Do you have a plan for handling a larger-than-expected response to your publicity?

41. Do you have written emergency and contingency plans?

42. Have you arranged to consult an attorney?

43. Will your publicity arouse any opposition to your organization?

44. Do you have plans to handle possible opposition?

45. Have you developed a means to measure the profitability of each publicity effort?

46. Do people in your nonprofit organization have doubts about the validity of publicity?

47. Have you discussed these doubts?

48. Do executives in your organization believe that the publicist can "make" the media run anything, regardless of news value?

49. Have you addressed this attitude?

50. Are you keeping written records to document the information you use in your publicity?

51. Are you following up conversations with confirming memos?

52. Do you have initialed copy giving OKs, particularly for direct quotes?

CHAPTER TWO

Basics of Good Media Relations

Media people need publicists. Even the largest publications and broadcasters, with the largest staffs, can't be everywhere at once. So journalists count on publicists to help them cover the bases.

"There is no medium—not the *Journal of the American Medical Association*, not the editorial pages of the *New York Times*, not the columns of the *Catholic Digest*—that is off limits for the publicist," says public relations executive Richard Weiner. "Neophyte publicists may think that there are some areas where media people—namely columnists, editorial page writers, and radio and television commentators—do not rely on public relations assistance, or that they resent suggestions. That is absolutely not true."

Approaching the Media

Even though they need you, and even if your publicity material is newsworthy, well written, and properly presented, media people won't always use it the way you would like them to.

What happens to your material depends on the judgment and taste of the individual journalist, the editorial policies of the publication or station, and the other events that are happening that day, week or month. You do not control the media, and any hint that you would like to will surely raise the hackles of journalists.

Since raised hackles are most destructive to the publicity process, you should learn how to work effectively with media people. It may seem obvious, but when you visit journalists in person, ". . . you should be very careful not to smoke if it's a non-smoking environment," says Bill Howard, an executive editor at *PC Magazine*. And you have to watch your manners. "Occasionally," Howard points out, "an older PR person will call a woman a 'girl' or 'honey.' That will simply turn off many women . . ."

Good media relations also involves choosing the methods you'll use to contact the media. No one method is best—it depends on the situation, the newsworthiness of your material, and, most important of all, the preferences of the journalists you're working with. Some reporters love the phone. Others hate it. Some always want information by mail. Others prefer to get information by fax. You'll uncover these preferences as you build working relationships with journalists.

With today's explosion of information technology, you have quite a choice of distribution methods. You can mail your publicity materials, use an overnight courier service when the deadline is looming, send them by fax when the journalists you're contacting don't mind that, beam live appearances by satellite, use electronic mail to deliver your material right to an editor's computer, have a service bureau prepare a mailing for you, or pick up the telephone and handle it one-on-one. Check the listings in Chapter 12 to find out more about commercially available publicity distribution services.

Contacting the Media by Mail

The most common way to approach media people is to mail them your press release, tip sheet, public service announcement (PSA), or press conference announcement. Although this method often gets results, journalists get enough mail to set off a paper avalanche. Sometimes there are so many envelopes, they don't all get opened. And even if your piece is opened and read, it remains a piece of paper, unattached to any human being. You will not be able to make personal contact with all the media people you work with because you, and they, won't have the time, and because some of them will not be located nearby. So you will have to use the mail at times.

Some journalists want you to approach them by mail, at least at first. Even though he gets 40 to 50 pieces of mail a day, Gus Venditto of *PC Magazine* prefers ". . . to get information by mail. If they have . . . [a product] that interests us, I'll invite them to come give us a working demonstration. I get too many people calling me up and saying they sent me a press release. It's very annoying."

There is a trick that will give you some feedback on mailed releases and PSAs. Include a business reply (or stamped) postcard with your material. If you're a perfectionist, you can run off a duplicate set of mailing labels and place one on each of the cards, so your media contact doesn't even have to fill in her name and address. Ask people to check boxes to let you know the following:

■ If and when they used the piece.

■ If they want more like it.

■ If they want you to call them to supply further information. Be sure to leave a space for comments. The answers can help you evaluate your publicity material.

Contacting the Media by Telephone

If you are using the phone to make your initial contact, or if you are following up a mailed release with a call, find out first if the journalist is free to talk, and then be brief and to the point. Gimmy Park-Li, public service manager for KNBR Radio in San Francisco, says, "I appreciate someone who comes right to the point. I'm always pressed for time, but some people go on for five minutes. I have already determined in the first 90 seconds whether this is something for my station."

If you're calling a journalist about a story for the first time, your goal is to find out:

■ That you have reached the right journalist for your story.

■ If he's free to talk with you now.

■ Whether he wants to talk about the story on the telephone or have you send written material first.

When you make an exploratory call to a journalist, Bob Seltzer advises that you should "try to have three or four different story ideas so if the first one is shot down, you've got the next three ready to go. If you have only one door and it's closed, you don't have an alternative."

If you're following up on material you've already sent, be very careful. Journalists don't like to be asked if they "got that press release." On the other hand, if you have some new information you can offer them, there's a good possibility you can spark their interest. In fact, you might deliberately withhold some intriguing facts that aren't critical to your story, but will give it an interesting twist—and use them as bait when you follow up by telephone.

Whatever the purpose of your call, "always identify yourself when you're calling—even if you talked with me this morning," says Bill Howard. "Editors forget who you are very quickly, because we talk to hundreds of people. If someone just says 'hi, this is John Jones,' I can't remember if he's looking for a job, if he's a creditor, or if he's a publicist."

You might open a follow-up call like this:

> Hello, I'm Olga Statouras from the Plains City Real Estate Association. Is this a good time to talk, or should I call back?
> I'm calling about the press release on our new smart buyer program that teaches consumers how to inspect a home before they buy it. We just found out that Ajax Insurance Company is offering a discount on homeowner's insurance to graduates of our program. I can give you figures on the savings over a 15-year period, and answer any other questions you may have.

If you are making an initial call in a situation where you have not sent a news release, the journalist will probably ask you to send the material in writing. If you have already sent a news release, the journalist may tell you that it hasn't been received. Don't flinch! In either case, offer to send the written material. Ask about deadlines. If time is really tight, offer to send it by messenger, overnight courier, or fax. Then take care of it the instant you get off the telephone.

Sometimes when you call the media, you may not get a live human being on the other end of the line. According to Bob Seltzer, "The *New York Times* now has answering machines to leave messages for reporters. That's a lot different than just saying 'here's my phone number.' There is an art to figuring out what you're going to say in 60 seconds that will make that reporter think it's worth calling you back."

Contacting the Media by Fax

Using a fax machine to send your publicity material to journalists often seems very tempting, indeed. It's fast. It's cheap. And you'll know that your material was received in a matter of seconds.

The only problem is that many journalists don't like to receive uninvited faxes. They have a limited number of receiving machines, and a glut of unwanted releases can tie up their machines and keep them from getting important news. As Bill Howard puts it, "Don't automatically send faxed press releases. Many publications which don't handle breaking news dislike them. Faxed material should be sent by invitation only. You should be very careful of minding your manners."

But even where journalists work with hard, breaking news, uninvited faxes may not be welcomed. "Never send an unsolicited fax to the *New York Times*," explains Bob Seltzer. "They go nuts about it. For many reporters, it's an absolute policy, written in blood. We fax material to journalists if they have requested that material. The only exception is if we're faxing a media alert to an assignment desk."

When you are invited to fax material to journalists, take advantage of it! You'll be able to help them meet impossible deadlines. And your coverage should improve as a result.

There is one specialized area of publicity where faxing is an everyday practice. According to *Public Relations Journal*, "The fax . . . has emerged as one of the key tools . . ." used by publicists handling financial stories. In a 1989 survey cited in the *Journal*, 94 percent of the financial publicists said they use faxes to transmit their stories.

The reason for the extensive use of faxes by financial publicists is that publicly traded companies have to meet strict Securities and Exchange Commission regulations when dealing with information that could impact a stock's price. Publicists have to make sure that all investors will have the opportunity to act on that news at the same time, so no one has an unfair advantage.

If you work for a corporation with publicly traded stock, you'll have to examine your publicity policies very closely, indeed. News stories about new products, personnel changes, marketing campaigns, and emergencies, for example, can all impact the price of your stock. If your story could pump up or deflate your firm's stock prices, you'll have to meet minimum disclosure requirements. It is wise to discuss this question with your organization's lawyer and develop written guidelines for disclosure.

According to PR Newswire, (a press release distribution service), the New York Stock Exchange says a listed company is expected to release news that could bear on a stock's price by the fastest means possible, to at least the following information services and media:

- Dow Jones
- Reuters
- Moody's
- *New York Times*
- *Wall Street Journal*
- Standard & Poor's
- Associated Press
- United Press International

Since wide distribution of your financial publicity will help your corporation secure investors and lenders, you probably want to go beyond this list, as well. For example, you should include industry analysts on your news distribution list. They are often used as sources by journalists, so they are important opinionmakers, indeed.

Because of the timely notification requirement, you can't release financial news with a standard fax machine, which is too slow to deliver your news simultaneously. You probably need a fax service bureau or a newswire. Both types of services are listed in Chapter 12. Both fax services and newswires require a written contract in advance.

Before you sign on the dotted line for a fax service, you need to ask several questions. This is especially important since there are so many new operators in this industry.

Does the fax service have a mainframe computer? PCs probably don't have enough power to handle heavy traffic. How many faxes can they transmit at once? Will that be enough for your distribution list? Can the fax service store the image of your letterhead and signature in their computer? How many times will they re-try a busy fax number? For how long? If one of your recipients can't be contacted, how will they handle it? A reliable fax service can answer all these questions, as well as several more in the checklist at the end of this chapter.

Contacting the Media by Computer

If you're not comfortable with computers, and the information in this section seems like gibberish to you, don't worry about it. You can still whip up a major publicity campaign with just a typewriter and a telephone. Skip to the next section where we talk about human beings again.

If you are familiar with computers, you have several other options for contacting the media provided you're working with a journalist who is able and willing to receive your transmissions. Although some publicity prophets predicted that computer to computer transmissions to journalists would become the "in" thing to do, most media people don't feel comfortable with this method. They're concerned that incoming releases will swamp their systems. And for security reasons, they don't want outsiders to have access to their files and databases.

Especially in high tech industries, however, you may develop a working relationship with an editor who invites an expert who works for your organization to write articles and submit them by telephone, using a modem, directly to her computer.

With good communication software, the two of you can work on editing an article at the same time, using one telephone line for the data connection through the modem, and another one for your discussion. You'll both see the text and be able to follow the editing process on your computer screens.

The only problem with this is you have to remove all the "codes" that format your document before you transmit it. The editor or her staff will have to reformat the entire article after she has received it. But in special situations, direct electronic communication can be a very useful tool for meeting difficult deadlines.

A more common request from a magazine editor is to submit a by-lined article on a floppy disk formatted in the word processing program her publication uses. This can save a lot of time, since the copy can be edited and typeset directly from the disk. An offer of copy on disk might let the editor gain enough time so she can run your article despite a tight deadline.

If you subscribe to MCI Mail or a similar service, Bill Howard points out that ". . . you can often reach an editor by electronic mail . . . But you should check carefully to see what the editor's preferences are. Some folks love it but other folks hate it. We tell PR people never to use it for press releases unless we ask them to. We prefer it for queries like 'we want to come to New York on this date and show you our new product. Is that possible?' That's very much a personal communication, not to be confused with a boilerplate press release . . ."

Electronic mail lets you transfer computer files, data, worksheets, and even pictures. It does take skill, but in specialized situations, it can make a great deal of difference when you have to beat a tight deadline.

You can also use MCI Mail to cut your fax bill drastically when you have to send out a release while you're on the road—assuming you have a computer and modem with you. ". . . if you're staying in a hotel and you need to send 20 three-page faxes, they may charge $5.00 a page," Bill Howard points out. But assuming you've already gotten permission from your media contacts to send faxes, you could type one message on your computer, send it by modem to MCI Mail, and it will go out to all 20 recipients within 30 minutes.

Contacting the Media in Person

There are times when you will want to deliver your publicity material in person. You should do that with the media outlets that are most important to you, and with media people who don't object. When you start as a publicist, some journalists will be glad to spend time chatting with you. Randy McCarthy, city editor for the *Boise Statesman* in Idaho, says, "I always like to meet them in person, if they are local, just to see who they are. I like to give my scam to them: what I want, what I don't want." On the other hand, Fred Zehnder, news director for KTVU-TV in Oakland, California, says, "We're generally too busy to have conferences with people. We could not possibly talk to all the publicists who would like to talk with us."

It's almost a catch-22 situation. Sylvia Smith, assistant city editor for the *Journal-Gazette* in Fort Wayne, Indiana, sums it up: "Now it is sort of confusing because the person ought to be known to the reporter or editor, but we don't take real kindly to somebody calling up and saying, 'I'd like to meet you.'" You may have to start by using the mail and the telephone; later on, when journalists are familiar with your material and your voice, you may be invited to meet with them.

On the other hand, you might decide to use the approach advocated by public relations executive Ravelle Brickman. She suggests that, after journalists are familiar with your material, you "Call reporters and editors when you don't need a favor, to find out what they need and how you can help. I like to suggest a drink or lunch, so that I can get acquainted with the journalist as a person and find out what kinds of stories she's working on. She just might be planning a series where my organization can fit right in."

When you deliver your publicity material in person, be brief and to the point, especially if you are dropping in without an appointment. If you are approaching a city editor, you are apt to find him listening to the police radio, typing with one hand, and holding the telephone with the other. Wait until he's free, give him a twenty second summary of your material, and hand it to him. He will probably take a few seconds to eyeball it, and he may ask a question or two. Then, you should leave. If he has any further questions, he'll call you later.

Whatever you do, do not read the release to the editor. "Give editors and reporters credit for the ability to read," says S. Griffin Singer, city editor for the *San Antonio Light.* "Nothing irritates me more than for a publicist to bring in a release and then stand there and read it to me like a first-grade teacher. I think they're unconscious of just how annoying it is to us."

Answering Questions

Although you have delivered your publicity material to the media, your job does not end. A reporter, editor, or news director may need more information, and you should be ready to respond to his call. If he asks you for facts and figures, if he requests details, it's your task to get them for him.

"It is the publicist's job," says journalist Nancy Dunn, "to make things as easy as possible for people in the media. If you don't have all the information, you should say, 'I'll call you back. When would be convenient? When do you need it by?' If it turns out that you can't get the information, call back and say so. Don't leave them hanging."

If you don't help journalists with more information, your story may not get covered, and you will hurt your working relationship with media people. Says Tom Callaghan, staff writer for the *Birmingham News,* "I don't like the ones you call to get more information who don't have that information on hand or don't seem willing to go to any extra trouble to get it for you."

When you're asked to send a press kit or other follow-up material, Bill Howard advises that you ". . . stick a Post- it™ on the outside with a note like: 'Bill—as per our phone conversation Tuesday, here's the backgrounder on WonderCalc.' [This helps] trigger [an] editor's recall; if [a] high level editor's mail is opened by an assistant, [the note] assures that this is not an unsolicited mailing."

Avoiding Pressure and Observing Ethics

If you don't get a clear indication of interest, but you don't get turned down either, try to clarify the situation, advises Nan Hohenstein of Nan Hohenstein Public Relations in San Francisco. "Be very straightforward with journalists. Say, 'Are you interested, but just too busy to deal with it now? OK, then I'm going to call you back next Wednesday. I hope you don't think I'm pushing, but this has limited time value. If you can't get to it, quite truthfully, I want to shoot it on to someone else.' " Journalists appreciate and respond to that kind of candor.

The most important thing to remember is that you have to convince the journalist to give you coverage. "What I admire most is when I get a release that is written so that I want to cover the event," says the *Norfolk Ledger-Star*'s Fred Kirsch. And Ed Hinshaw, manager of public affairs and vice-president of WTMJ in Milwaukee, advises that "A friendly tone helps to keep the door of the mind open."

You need to be persuasive, persistent, and friendly, but not aggressive. Says KNBR's Gimmy Park-Li, "One of my pet peeves is publicists who are overly aggressive." And Fred Kirsch adds, "The main thing is to come across as a person. We can get the same information from various sources, but we just enjoy it more dealing with someone we like."

Whatever you do, don't waste time telling media people how hard you and your staff worked to put an event together. You will only annoy your contacts. The event must stand on its own merit.

Once you have telephoned or visited and presented your material, Nan Hohenstein advises, "Keep your distance. It creates an awkwardness to assume you have a relationship with a journalist. If you get one good story, then you begin to assume that they're all going to be good, and the journalist is going to start feeling put upon."

How do you make sure the journalist writes an accurate story once you've provided the material or finished the interview? There's usually not much you can do other than trust that he's a professional and will do a competent job. But even though reporters want to be accurate in their coverage, they have continual deadline pressure. They have to work on more than one story at the same time. And since many reporters are generalists, even at some of the trade publications, they often don't have as much technical knowledge as you and your staff do.

Most journalists bristle at even the slightest suggestion that you want to approve their copy, and rightly so. Remember, you don't control the media, and journalists cherish their independence. But there are techniques you can use to help make sure the coverage you get is accurate, especially in a controversial situation or when there is specialized or technical information involved:

- Give the journalist detailed, accurate written background information up front. If there are common misconceptions about your product, service, organization or cause, counter them in this material. Journalists will welcome and use this kind of material.

- If you have any inkling that you might get negative or mixed coverage, ask the reporter what unfavorable observations he has. This gives you the opportunity to state—or re-state—your point of view, and the result can be better coverage.

- Offer the reporter the opportunity to call you when the story is finished, to read direct quotes back to you so he can check for accuracy. Some journalists will agree to do this if you can make yourself available when they need you.

- If your story involves technical or specialized information, offer journalists the opportunity to review their finished copy with you for accuracy. Many journalists will welcome this chance, particularly if they are not specialists. Other reporters won't agree to it. But it's worth asking about.

Whether you decide to follow Nan Hohenstein's advice and keep your distance, or take Ravelle Brickman's working relationship approach, wait to make any friendly overtures until after your material appears.

Accurate, interesting, up-to-date information is what media people want from you. Liquor, tickets to ball games, and other freebies usually won't get you coverage. Many journalists resent publicists bearing gifts. They feel you're trying to buy their interest. In the summer, 1977 issue of *The Masthead*, the magazine of the National Conference of Editorial Writers, Millard C. Browne, editorial-page editor of the *Evening News* in Buffalo, New York, explains recent changes in journalistic ethics:

> "Journalism ethics have been going through a veritable revolution on the subject of 'freebies' in the past two decades. Practices that were once commonplace—papering the city room with free passes to movies and sporting events, for example—are long gone. So is all the free booze that used to pour in at Christmas time from . . . press agents.
>
> Now the rules in every reputable newsroom are being drawn tighter and tighter . . . .
>
> So free trips are out, for example. But what if a newsman has a chance to cover a bona fide story he can't reach except as part of a government or company sponsored trip? Does he stay home, or does he sign in and insist that the sponsor bill his paper for a reasonable pro-rata share of the cost?
>
> The *News*, along with more and more major metropolitan newspapers, does the latter in almost every case."

Ethical standards at newspapers, broadcast stations and many magazines have been tightened even further since the *Masthead* article was written. The Radio-Television News Directors Association Code of

Ethics mandates that members ". . . will decline gifts or favors which would influence or appear to influence their judgments." And concern about journalistic ethics is so keen now that there is a monthly newsletter devoted completely to news about ethical situations faced by journalists.

Talking Off the Record

No matter how well you know a journalist, even if you are friends, you should never expect to talk off the record. Says Nancy E. Karen, vice-president for marketing and communications at United Way of Tri-State in New York, "The press has a job to do. Yes, there are many journalists who can be trusted to keep what you say off the record, but that's a crummy thing to do to them. You're asking them not to do their job. Well, why tell them in the first place?"

Asking to go off the record can do more than annoy reporters. You may tell a reporter about the quality control problems you're having at your East Side Assembly Plant. Or the morale problem that's plaguing your clerical support staff. Sure, it's off the record—and an ethical reporter won't use your information directly. But you've given the reporter a clue to something she may not have known about, and she may find another source who is willing to talk for the record. Says Cindy Loose of the *Staten Island Register*, "I'll talk to anybody off the record, and I'll use that information if I can get it and confirm it from another source. I might get a lead I would not have had if they hadn't talked off the record. Also, I've got to agree before you tell me something that you want to be off the record."

Most of the time it just isn't wise to speak off the record, but when it comes to government agencies and organizations funded with public money, you cannot even make that request, except under unusual circumstances. Your money comes from the public, and you are accountable to the public. Reporters are well aware of this, and they may be even better acquainted with public disclosure laws than you are. Asking to go off the record implies that information which should be public is not. Since reporters depend on free access to information, they will be angered by a request to go off the record, and your agency or organization will look as if it wants to avoid responsibility for the information.

Taking No for an Answer

When you work with the media, there will be times when you will get no for an answer. Even if it's your major story of the year, even if you think you have the most amazing photographs, an irresistible news peg, and astoundingly important information, you will have to accept a negative answer. Remember those hackles! Don't argue with journalists when they've turned you down. You'll only alienate them.

Larry Kramer, managing editor for the *Trenton Times* in New Jersey, says, "I have no problem with somebody calling me and trying to pitch me a story; I have a problem if, once I decide one way or another, they keep trying to change my mind. We basically have an understanding here with most people we deal with. They can take their shot, and we'll do what we want with it. I don't admire anybody who can't be told no."

Ed Hinshaw, public affairs manager for WTMJ in Milwaukee, feels that this is an especially difficult area for inexperienced publicists: "They rarely recognize when a conversation has reached a natural conclusion in agreement or disagreement."

If you are turned down, ask the reporter or editor whether he might recommend anyone else at the paper or station who should get the release, tip sheet, or feature story idea. If he says no, your story is dead, at least at that media outlet. Don't try to circumvent him by going to another reporter or editor there. He'll be furious. And rightly so!

What you should do is put on your thinking cap, and see if you can dream up a whole new angle. Test it out on some colleagues and friends—and be certain it really is different. Then call the journalist who turned you down, say that you've just discovered a whole new angle on that story you mentioned, and make your pitch.

For example, if you've just been turned down on a story about your research on how high school sports influence female self-images, try a different slant. Instead of discussing how your research might affect the educational process, try describing the reaction male coaches and players had to your report.

Asking for Advice

If you start expecting too much from media people, you will have difficulty because they will feel imposed upon. This is particularly true when it comes to asking for advice about publicity. Public relations woman Nan Hohenstein puts it this way: "For the most part, journalists don't have time to give lessons. Also it's as if you're asking journalists to train one more pest. It's a bad idea."

"I wouldn't appreciate anyone asking me for advice," says reporter Cindy Loose. "They've got their job; I've got mine. If they don't know their business, they should go learn it and leave me alone. I'm not in the training business."

When you are working with reporters, editors, and news directors, you are trying to establish yourself as a reliable news source. Although there are some journalists who enjoy giving advice, asking for it undermines your credibility in the long run. So if you need advice about publicity, find other sources. Ask the journalism or public relations department at your local college if they can answer questions for you. Or, even better, join one of the professional organizations listed in Chapter 12. Then you can get to know other publicity people and you can share your questions—and solutions to publicity problems.

If you are asking media people for preferences, as opposed to advice, that's different. Says Nan Hohenstein, "I think you can ask them 'would you prefer to receive this in the form of a feature story, or would you prefer that I jot down the six issues you might deal with in your story?' " But, even with preferences, don't ask too many questions. You have to make decisions, and too many questions will make you seem indecisive.

Some reporters don't even feel that it's appropriate to discuss their preferences. Cindy Loose says that she expects a publicist "to give me something. I'll work from there. But I think it's their job to decide how to approach me. If they send me a press release and I'd rather meet with them, I'll call them and tell them I need a meeting."

There is one only exception. Public service directors at radio and TV stations are almost always willing to help nonprofit publicists learn. Some public service people run workshops and classes for publicists from community and nonprofit organizations; others work on a one-to-one basis. Asking public service directors for advice will not hurt your reputation, especially if you are a beginner, but even here, public service directors have limited time and an incredible work load, so be sensitive about how much of their time you're asking for.

You might think that if you send in public service material that is not up to par, the public service director will call to tell you. That does happen. Occasionally. But don't count on it. "We mean well," says By Napier, program director of WCCO-AM Radio in Minneapolis–St. Paul, "but there are other things to do. I guess our critique is expressed in how often we book them or use their guests [on our talk shows]."

Observing Format Preferences

One of the most important format requirements for any publicity material is that it be neatly typed and duplicated. Editors, reporters, news directors, and public service directors have to read dozens of press releases, tip sheets, backgrounders, press conference invitations, and PSAs every day. Even though virtually all of them are typed, reading them is still a difficult task, and it would become impossible if it involved interpreting handwritten material. (When you get to know some media people, ask to see how much publicity material they receive in a day or week. You'll be amazed!)

"I want it typed," says Bill Close, news director for KOOL-TV in Phoenix. And Joyce Michels, family living editor of the *Billings Gazette* in Montana, has this advice for beginning publicists: "Get a typewriter!"

If you can buy or borrow one, a word processor with a spell-check program will give you the most professional results.

If you must use a typewriter, be sure it's an electric typewriter that uses a carbon ribbon. A carbon ribbon will give you much clearer, darker type, and that is important if you plan to photocopy or print your publicity material.

If you have your choice of type styles, stick to standard types. Fancy typefaces, especially script faces, are hard to read and might convince a bleary-eyed editor that your piece should be entered in the "circular file." If you're using a word processor, be sure your printer has near-letter quality capability. Sure, the printer works faster in draft mode (where you can see the little dots that make up the letters), but the results don't command the same respect.

To duplicate your publicity material use a copying machine, photo offset printing, or an old-fashioned mimeograph. As long as the copies are clear and clean, the method is not important, although using carbon copies is considered bad manners. For an annual event, however, it is unwise to use a printed or photocopied form that you fill in each year, with only the dates changed. That format announces: Stale news. Nothing new!

The standard size for news releases, PSAs, backgrounder sheets, filler sheets, press conference invitations, and other communications with the media is 8 1/2-by-11-inch paper. Don't use legal-size paper. It is harder to handle, it doesn't fit into standard file folders, and it is too long to fit most copybooks used at radio stations. Use 20 or 24 lb bond; onionskin is too flimsy and difficult to handle.

At the top of each sheet of publicity material, include your name, your organization's name, address, and phone number, and the date.

Don't staple two-page press releases. The editor has to separate them, and that's a nuisance. Nor should you send two or three releases stapled together. If the editor doesn't like the first one, the others will probably be tossed out without being looked at. The best idea is to send each release in a separate envelope. They'll have a better chance that way.

Releases up to five pages long can and should be folded and sent in #10 business envelopes. If the background material accompanying your release brings the total to more than five pages, then you should use a 9-by-12-inch white envelope. Postal employees give first-class treatment to white envelopes—especially if they have a border of green diamonds—but automatically treat brown kraft envelopes as third class.

All mailed publicity material should be sent first class, of course. Don't give in to the temptation to save money by using your bulk-mail permit to send out press releases or PSAs. It's a sure-fire way to miss deadlines and make certain your material is dated before it arrives. And after all, you know what you do with "junk mail."

Further details on formats for different types of publicity materials are given in Chapters 4 and 7.

Working within Deadlines

When you work with journalists, you move in a world of continual deadlines, where time is tyrannical. "Sometimes the press seems arrogant because we have to have the information by an inflexible deadline. But that's reality," says Gus Venditto.

One of your first tasks as a publicist is to find out deadline times. Once you have made your media list, call each outlet and ask. You will find a wide variation. The public service people at a radio station may have three or four deadlines for locally produced programs and a four-week lead time requirement for PSAs. For the news director, it will be quite a different story. "Deadline time for me, for a radio news operation, is every hour at the top of the hour," says WAVI-FM's John Canelli.

At the newspapers, the city editor has a different deadline from the Sunday and feature editors. So you need to ask each person you'll be working with when his deadlines are. Then use this information—not only to get your material in on time, but also to avoid interrupting your contacts when they are too busy to talk to you.

Deadline Realities

You may have the most interesting story, but it will die if you miss the deadline. The deadline is when a reporter has to hand his copy to the editor so that it can be edited and set in type in time for the printer. In order for your morning paper to be on the doorstep or at the newsstand when you're ready to go to work, it takes the cooperation of many people, and it wouldn't be possible to deliver that paper on time if they didn't all have deadlines. Radio and TV people have similar requirements; they need to meet deadlines so their stories can be chosen, rewritten, and timed, so that visuals can be found to go with them, tape can be edited for broadcast, and everything put together to fill the air time exactly. Without deadlines, the six o'clock news might sometimes appear at 6:00 and sometimes at 6:45 or 7:00. And monthly magazines might appear every three weeks—or every seven.

According to public relations executive Richard Weiner, one common problem among nonprofit organizations is that "sometimes they will agonize over a news release for weeks, and miss the point, which is to get it out." But it's a problem even at many large businesses, where executives don't understand the realities of media deadlines.

The bottom line is stark and simple, however. No matter how worthy your cause, no matter how vital your story, you cannot be late when you are a publicist.

"Even advertising copy must be turned in by a particular time during the business day to be on the air," says KNBR's Gimmy Park-Li. "So if advertising people have to honor deadlines, I think publicists must honor them as well."

If you do not honor deadlines, you will undermine your credibility with media people. Carole Halicki, editorial director for WRAU-TV in Peoria, Illinois, says that she received a weekly newsletter from an area congressman touting the need to observe March 20 as National Agriculture Day. "The 'newsletter' was written on March 21, and I received it March 26. So even if I wanted to mark the celebration of National Agriculture Day, it was a week old and was by then probably National Pickle Day. I would think if a group goes to all the trouble to mail out their stuff, they'd do it so it would arrive before, not after, the suggested release date."

If you do miss a deadline and your material doesn't run, it is your fault. Don't try to blame media people for your failure. That may sound obvious, but journalist Nancy Dunn gives the following example: "Someone once called me at home and woke me up early on Christmas morning to berate me for not covering her event, which was submitted after the deadline. I was furious. I never could treat her seriously after that."

Allowing Enough Lead Time

You also need to know about lead time, that is, how much advance notice media people need. Lead time is especially important for feature material and special broadcasts.

The amount of lead time you will need to publicize your product, issue or event will vary, depending on the size of the publicity campaign, how much competition there is for air time and newspaper space in your area, the deadlines and lead requirements at the media outlets you'll be working with, and even the time of year.

For the Annual California Spring Garden Show, a major event sponsored each May by the Oakland Office of Parks and Recreation, planning starts during the previous summer. And when Oakland's Children's Fairyland celebrated its twenty-fifth anniversary with a seven-month-long festival that involved thousands of people from dozens of cities—as well as a score of foreign nations—and got worldwide news coverage, publicist Burton Weber made the first media contact six months before the festivities started.

There is another reason why you should not wait until deadline time or just before to approach media people. They are going to want some time to check on your material, to develop a story, to find background information. Gladys Adams, editor of the *Kansas City Voice*, says this about being approached at deadline time: "If you know anything about the operation of a newspaper, you would hardly do that. It really bothers us, especially if it's something we should be digging into, that would serve our community to know. If you call us at the last minute, our schedules are already full, and we can't do that digging."

Avoiding Last-Minute Panic

One problem for new publicists who have not planned carefully enough is last-minute panic. "Last-minute panic makes it hard to deal with a publicist," says Nancy Dunn. "Panic-stricken people tend to apply more pressure to squeeze things in after the deadline. Unprofessional publicists, either paid or volunteer, try to put responsibility on me to make the event successful. Often these are the very people who complain about bad coverage, when the real problem is they were badly prepared."

Media people generally are not sympathetic toward *any* publicist in the grip of last-minute panic. "Last-minute panic is really bad," says Mark Shepherd, feature writer for the *Columbia Daily Tribune* in Missouri. "My view is that if a person has a job cranking out releases and he doesn't get them out on time, I wouldn't have much sympathy for him."

So write this cardinal rule in big letters, and post it over your desk: "I must get my publicity materials in to the media in plenty of time so I avoid last-minute panic and I give journalists plenty of time to do a good job."

Showing Consideration at Deadline Time

You will generally want to stay away from your media contacts right around deadline time. That charming reporter who spent an hour interviewing you about your trade association's position on new zoning proposals will turn into a snarling beast, ready to bite your head off at deadline time. She has other things to worry about. She has to have her stories ready by the deadline, and that's all that is important to her. "I don't want to talk to anybody at deadline time," says WBUR-FM's Carol Rissman.

On the other hand, if you have a truly major story that is hard, breaking news, she won't mind being interrupted. Let's say, for example, that the Martians have just landed on your patio and they have chosen your organization to be their official Earth representative. That's news: that's big news, and it doesn't matter if you call the media at deadline time. In fact, media people will be upset if you *don't* call about major news as soon as it happens. "If it's something that's important, that's immediate, and I would like to know about it, I don't care if it's deadline time or not," says Jim Kemp, news director for WVUE-TV in New Orleans.

Introducing Yourself to the Media

If you are handling publicity for a new business, an organization that is not well known, or one that has never done publicity before, you will have to introduce yourself to the media. After all, anybody with a typewriter and some letterhead can send out a press release or a PSA claiming to represent an organization. Any reporter, editor, news director, or public service director worth his salt will want to check on your organization's background, history, and reliability. And, even if they're familiar with your organization, they'll want to make sure that you, the new publicist, are authorized to represent it to the media.

As Jim Kemp explains, "If I got something from an organization I didn't know about, before I'd do anything with it, I'd certainly want to find out who they are."

There are some media people who will call the publicist of an unknown organization to ask for more information. Others do not have the time or the inclination, so don't gamble that they will automatically get in touch with you or check into your organization's history or company's background. "We get so much material from organizations that we do know, unless a new group informs us as to what they're about, we would not use their . . . [material]," says Jules Moreland, public service and program director for KFMB-TV in San Diego.

The easiest way to introduce a new organization to the media is by pulling together all the basic information about your products, services, and track record into one convenient backgrounder sheet.

Providing Backgrounders

With every press release, press conference invitation, request for coverage, community calendar announcement, and PSA, you should include a backgrounder sheet on your organization. Says Sylvia Smith of the *Fort Wayne Journal-Gazette*, a backgrounder for a nonprofit organization ". . . should explain the purpose of the organization, when it was formed, who the people are on its board, where it gets its funding, and what it expects to do with its money."

A backgrounder for a business should include information about the organization's structure, capitalization, sales volume and a two- or three-sentence discussion of its history and position in the marketplace. But don't overdo it. According to Gus Venditto, "You can go too far with introductory material. One new PC company included an SEC filing in their media kit. They looked well capitalized. So that made me suspicious. Why did they include it?"

Even after you are well known, including a backgrounder is a good idea because journalists can use it to round out a story. Below is a typical backgrounder sheet.

Back to the Basics, Inc., 1535 Roaring Brook Rd., Plains City 00000. Contact: Dee Nominator, 999-0000

Purpose: To advocate the return to basics in education. To convince parents, teachers, and the public that reading,

– more –   – more –

---

writing, arithmetic, and self-discipline are the most important parts of education. To illustrate the problems faced by children who cannot read and write well, who cannot do simple arithmetic, and who have no self-discipline. To develop curricula and materials for teachers who want to go back to the basics, but have forgotten how.

Board Members: Linda S. Lurie, M.D., Director of Pediatric Services, Plains City Hospital; Lars T. Borgward, owner, Hill Street Restaurant; Mrs. Mary Kaapala, housewife; H. Michael Smith, member of the Plains City Board of Education; R. H. Asher, manager, Downtown Bookstore.

Membership: 775

Funding: Membership dues, 20%; contributions, 25%; grant from the Plains City Foundation, 55%.

IRS tax-exempt number: 99-999.

Plains City Fund-raising number: 675.

Budget: Staff and office, 30%; curriculum materials and development, 50%, publications, 20%.

Accomplishments: Back to the Basics, Inc. was founded in 1979. We have developed our basic reading curriculum and distributed it, without charge, to 1755 educators state-wide. We are about to release the third revision of our basic curriculum.

###

Sending Your Organization's Publications to the Media

Unless a media person has asked you specifically to include her on your subscription list, don't send her your newsletter or magazine. If it's written well and all the stories are in the right format, it would be easy for her to use one of them, but you're asking *her* to choose which one. There are two problems with that. She may not have the time. And *you* should be setting the priorities.

If you want the media to cover a story that will appear in your organization's publication, send out a release based on that story. Be absolutely certain to time the release so journalists get it with enough lead time to break the story just before your publication date. And be sure you let the journalists know you want to coordinate the release date with them. Then the media will have fresh news to work with, and they may, indeed, use it.

Don't send media people your organization's meeting agenda or minutes unless they ask you to. Agendas are notoriously dull, and the minutes will probably not seem interesting even if the proceedings are. If your meeting is newsworthy, write a news release—and make sure it has an intriguing angle and hard facts that a journalist can bite into.

Even a lovely new four-color brochure that tells all about your product line is not normally the kind of material you would send to the media, although there are some exceptions.

If you know a reporter or editor fairly well and you think he will file the brochure for future reference, then send it with a cover letter explaining that it is good background material.

You might, on occasion, be able to develop a news peg about the publication of the brochure. Send it along with a news release based on that peg. Here is a clever example by public relations executive Ravelle Brickman for the YMCA of Greater New York:

Consumer News Note

The YMCA of Greater New York has been running nonprofit children's camps since 1885.

Yet until this year, there has never been a single directory listing all the camps, sleep-away and day, serving the New York area.

Now the Y has put together a simple folder, listing rates, dates, hours and location of every camp in the five boroughs as well as its cluster of resident camps in nearby Port Jervis, New York.

To get your free copy of the directory, just "DIAL-A-Y," JU2-2000, any time of day or night, and ask about day camp.

Building Your Reputation with the Media

Reporters, editors, news directors, and public service directors know that your responsibility is to your organization and not to their newspapers or stations. They're not going to trust you completely until you establish a good reputation by proving that your facts are accurate, by keeping your promises, and by always meeting deadlines. According to Larry Kramer of the *Trenton Times*, "It takes a while to know someone well enough to know where their prejudices are."

You can never rest on your laurels. "A news source is only as good as the last time I used it," says Larry Badger, news director at KGW-TV in Portland, Oregon.

Being Known for Accuracy

A good news source provides information that is reliable and can be confirmed. KRBE-FM's Mike Martin explains that material from a publicist ". . . is of interest as long as he establishes the credibility of the information. It could be anybody calling. And I have to be able to check out the facts before I can use them as part of the news. So if he gives me enough to cover my backside with, I'm happy."

When a publicist is considered a good source, her job is much easier because reporters and editors seek her out. If her relationship with the media has become a two-way street, her publicity material will get more attention and interest. Since reporters and editors work under constant pressure, they will probably turn to their good sources first. As the *Norfolk Ledger-Star*'s Fred Kirsch explains, "I usually go to the sources that have been most cooperative in the past and seem to be able to grasp what it is I need. It's just tremendous to know that I can count on particulars, especially when I'm in a hurry."

With complete information and an honest approach, you are well on the way to earning that good reputation. "If they can give me all I need to know—if they know what they're talking about, and they haven't made me go to a lot of effort, they'll have a good reputation with me. Their reputation is as good as their information," says Randy McCarthy of the *Boise Statesman*.

A word of warning: Even if your facts are strictly accurate, media people will be furious if you try to fool them by leaving out crucial information. If your day-care center is operated by a religious cult and your release fails to mention the sponsoring organization, it doesn't matter that the rest of the release is completely truthful.

Tom Callaghan of the *Birmingham News* reflects the opinions of many journalists when he says, "We'd like you to be open and honest about who you are and what you represent." If the truth about your product, service, or cause needs to be hidden, you can't use a publicity program. You need a propaganda campaign.

"Reporters don't like to be manipulated," says journalist Nancy Dunn. "We have to work within an editorial perspective. We're not here to serve your goals; we're here to put out a newspaper."

Journalist Leslie O'Bergin feels the same way. "I don't like flim-flamming," she says. "Flimflamming is incomplete information, concealment of purpose. It's an insult to my intelligence. I have no intention of ever knowingly writing a publicity article—in a sense, a free ad—for an organization that is lying to me, no matter what their purpose, and even if I personally agree with that purpose."

"Sometimes flimflamming is intentional. Sometimes it is a misunderstanding of what publicity is all about. But in either case, I feel it indicates a mistrust of the validity of the organization itself. If the person in charge of publicity does not trust the usefulness of that group enough to be honest not only with me but also with the public, I think there's something worth investigating about the organization from an entirely different point of view," concludes O'Bergin.

Puffery is similar to flimflamming, and it's just as frowned upon. The publicist blows puffs of smoke that look interesting, bringing journalists running to see what's going on. When they arrive, the puffs of smoke have dissipated into nothing. But this puff is no magic dragon; it only makes media people angry. "If the event is different from what they said and they made something out of nothing in the press release, and I get there and it's not what I was led to believe, I would remember that. And I would probably bear a grudge against them," says Randy McCarthy.

Even if you're smart enough to put one over on journalists with puffery and flimflamming, you can't fool the public, at least not for long. Publicity cannot mask bad performance. "Bear in mind," says KSTP-TV's Linnea Crowe, "that the only thing you can do with publicity is to get people to sample your product or service. If it doesn't live up to your publicity, if you have a high return at the beginning and then it peters out, the service or product is not holding up to the expectations created by the publicity. And the people you are trying to reach are going to realize that sooner or later."

Being Able to Withstand Scrutiny

If you are going to have a good reputation with the media, your publicity efforts must withstand public scrutiny. Once that press release or PSA is sent out, you cannot take it out of circulation, and you can't control its use. It has been publicly distributed, and it is probably public domain under the copyright law. Anyone who has it can use it for any purpose.

It's a good idea to ask yourself the following questions about *each* piece of publicity material before you release it:

- How would I feel about defending it before a congressional committee?
- Would I be comfortable discussing it with an investigative reporter?"

If you have the slightest doubt, don't send it out.

Media people will often pick up on something that's not exactly as it should be. "Before a PSA goes on our air," says WCBS-AM's Teresa DiTore, "it is thoroughly researched. We even go out to community organizations and just drop in to see how they treat people. If someone sends me in copy that says 'fees based on ability to pay,' I want to know what that means. And very often, before we put it on the air, I call the organization. And I say, for example, 'I make $150 a week. I want to come in for psychotherapy. How much do I have to pay?' And if they tell me $50 per week, I say, 'Hey, now wait a second. That is not ability to pay.' Very often we have turned people down because of things like that."

That situation is damaging and embarrassing enough, but if it should happen after the information has been published or aired, you're really hurting your organization. For example, *The Columbia Journalism Review* awarded a "Laurel" to Sally Jessy Raphael, hostess of a talk show on New York's WMCA Radio, "for exercising firm control" when a guest, having billed herself as an ordinary person who had lost a great deal of weight, turned out to be a paid lecturer for a well-known weight-loss group. When Raphael discovered the deception, she told her listeners, "I'm gonna throw the lady off the show. I thought she was a civilian. I was misled. I apologize to you. We're going to continue the program without her."

A firm in Chelm built an expensive wastewater treatment plant that allowed it to recycle chemical pollutants, instead of discharging them into the river. It wanted to let the community know that its efforts were paying off, and the river was already cleaner. Unfortunately, it took publicity photos upstream from the factory, above the former source of pollution, because it was "more scenic" there. Even in Chelm, the firm got caught, and what a time the newspapers and broadcasters had with that one!

Keeping the Media Informed of Changes

There are certain procedures and taboos that must be heeded when you work with the media. Whether it's a weekly paper with a circulation of five thousand or a TV station with ten million viewers, if the time or place of an event changes, you must notify every media outlet that got your publicity material. Failure to do this can mean that you will never get publicity again, unless you buy your own newspaper or station.

Failure to notify the media of changes can cause other problems as well. The former publicist for the Chelm Recreation Department sent out a news release about an appreciation rally for the Chelm Soccer Team. But he got the time wrong. Instead of 8:00 P.M. he wrote 6:00 P.M. "What's the big deal?" he said to himself when he discovered the error. "So they'll sit on the grass for two hours and have a picnic. By the time the team arrives, they'll be full of vinegar. It'll make a good rally. Besides, it's too much trouble to call all those stations and papers, and I didn't make a list of them anyway."

The eager fans began arriving at 5:00 P.M. By 6:00, they were restless. At 6:30 they were pounding on the stadium doors, and at 7:00 a full-scale riot was broken up by the police. Soccer fans are generally not gentle folks. Dozens of people were arrested, and lots more were hospitalized. The stadium was a shambles, and damages were estimated at several hundred thousand dollars. Guess who was called on the carpet by the mayor the next day? The publicist for the Chelm Recreation Department quickly found himself in the market for another job.

When you send out publicity material about an event, keep a complete list of every media outlet you've directed it to. In the rare case of a change in time or place, call each station or newspaper and then follow up the call with a written note of the change. Journalists expect this, and they will be most unhappy if you emulate the ex-publicist of Chelm.

Jim Kemp of WVUE-TV says this about a publicist who doesn't tell him of last-minute changes: "It's not going to make him very popular. I'm going to forgive him once. After a second time, I'm going to get a little wary. And if it happens more often than that, I probably wouldn't take his calls." There are many journalists who won't even give you a second chance.

Your reputation with the media is one of your most valuable assets—or major liabilities. It will follow you from one organization to the next. Since media people know each other, exchange information, and relocate frequently, it may grow larger than life, and it could spread to other cities and states. A bad reputation can make it almost impossible for you to get coverage.

Checklist—Basics of Good Media Relations

1. Have you included a pre-stamped reply card with your mailed publicity material, so you can get feedback?
2. Have you practiced your telephone or personal approach to media people, so that you can be brief and to the point?
3. When you call, do you ask your media contact whether it is a good time to talk with him?
4. When you make follow-up calls, do you have some good additional facts or a new angle to tempt journalists to cover your story?
5. If you're making an exploratory call, do you have several story ideas ready?
6. Unless you're handling financial publicity, do you fax publicity material by invitation only?
7. If you work for a publicly traded corporation, have you consulted your lawyer and developed a written disclosure policy for news that could affect stock prices?
8. Have you included industry analysts on your media release list?
9. Are you prepared to answer journalists' requests for more information?
10. Does the fax service you're considering use a mainframe computer?
11. How many incoming and outgoing lines do they have?
12. How many faxes can they transmit simultaneously?
13. Can you send separate messages to different lists at varying times, and do this automatically?
14. Will they store and maintain your contact lists in their computer?

15. How many working days are needed to make list additions and changes?
16. How do they confirm that your faxes were received?
17. If one of your recipients can't be contacted, how many retries will the service make? Over how many hours?
18. If one of your recipients can't be contacted after repeated retries, how will the fax service handle it?
19. Can your letterhead, logo and signature be stored in their computer?
20. Can they generate cover pages that let your recipient know which person in their organization this fax is directed to?
21. Can you send them material to be faxed, by fax?
22. If so, how do they ensure that the image they receive will be clear enough for re-transmission?
23. Can you send them material to be faxed by modem directly from your personal computer to their mainframe?
24. Is there a set-up fee?
25. Are there minimum charges?
26. Is there a minimum billing time per transmission?
27. After the minimum billing time, is time billed in full minutes, or 30-second units?
28. What is the discount on overnight transmissions?
29. Do they supply a daily accounting of on-line time billed?
30. Have you asked the journalists you work with closely if they subscribe to an electronic mail service—and if that's how they want you to deliver your publicity material?
31. If you're thinking about delivering publicity material in person, have you made sure the journalists involved are receptive to this?
32. Do you tag all follow-up material journalists request with a short personal note reminding them they asked for it?
33. If you're not sure whether a journalist you've approached is interested in a story, have you called him to clarify the situation?
34. Have you prepared a backgrounder sheet for your non-profit organization?
35. Does it include your purpose, the names of board members, your funding sources and budget, and your goals and achievements?

36. Have you prepared a backgrounder sheet for your business?

37. Does the backgrounder include information about the organization's structure, capitalization, sales volume and a two- or three-sentence discussion of its history and position in the marketplace?

38. When journalists interview you or people who work for your organization, do you provide the reporters with written background information?

39. Is it prepared especially for the story you're working on with them?

40. Does it include material that counters common misconceptions about your organization, product or service?

41. Do you ask, during interviews, if the journalist has any unfavorable observations so you can respond?

42. Do you offer journalists the opportunity to read back direct quotes to you before their stories are finished?

43. If your story involves technical or specialized information, do you offer journalists the opportunity to review their finished copy with you for accuracy?

44. Do you understand why it's not wise to go off the record in conversations with journalists, even in your "special" situation?

45. Can you gracefully accept no for an answer?

46. If you were turned down when you first pitched an important story, have you worked at developing one or more new angles?

47. Do you avoid the temptation to ask journalists for advice about how to prepare your publicity?

48. Have you found a better source for advice?

49. Is all your publicity material on 8 1/2-by-11-inch paper?

50. Is all your publicity material neatly typed and duplicated?

51. Are you mailing all your publicity material with first class postage?

52. Is the material you're sending to the media in the correct format?

53. Have you made a list of the deadlines faced by all the reporters and editors you'll be working with?

54. Do you know the lead times at all the media outlets you work with?

55. Have you figured out how much lead time you need for your events and publicity campaigns?

56. Do you avoid contacting the media at deadline time unless it is really necessary?

57. Do you coordinate the release of stories that run in your newsletter and the press with the journalists involved?

58. Are you being straightforward about your organization or business? Have you given journalists a complete picture?

59. Are you sure your publicity will withstand public scrutiny?

60. Do you keep a record of where all your publicity material is sent in order to issue corrections, if necessary?

CHAPTER THREE

Keys to Newsworthy Publicity

Before going into the details of writing news releases, features, public service announcements (PSAs), and other forms of publicity material, let's take a look at the essential requirements of good publicity copy, in any format and for any medium—the press, radio, or TV.

One of the most important things you need to know is the difference between hard news, and feature, or human interest stories. Hard news has time value; it must be covered *now* or it will be stale. Disasters, crimes, layoffs by large companies, new medical and scientific breakthroughs and even major league scores are all hard news. Soft news is often related to hard news events, but it doesn't have the same urgency. The media can run it today, tomorrow, or next week. It usually involves more background information and often has a human interest angle. Because it will stay fresh for a long time, soft news is sometimes called "evergreen" material.

A feature story summarizing AIDS research during the past year is "evergreen." If it doesn't run today, it can run tomorrow. Or the next day. On the other hand, a news story about the discovery of a new, highly effective treatment for AIDS is hard, breaking news. It won't keep.

Your organization may continually generate hard news. On the other hand, most of your publicity may involve feature and human interest material. Or, like most organizations, you'll be somewhere in between.

Where your organization falls on the hard-soft news spectrum depends on three things:

- The type of product, service, or cause you're involved with. Bowling ball manufacturers make less hard news than oil companies.

- Whether or not your industry, organization or cause gets caught up in controversy or tied in with trends. If it does, you're more likely to generate hard news.

- Your ability to show the media that the material is newsworthy and backed up with facts, that it's related to what's happening in the news, that it has a unique and interesting angle or news peg and that you can be objective and informative.

You'll generate more hard news coverage if your publicity material meets these guidelines.

If you want to do a first-rate job of publicity, you must relentlessly pursue every opportunity, every possibility. Still, you have to be sure that the opportunities and possibilities are genuine and not false hopes that result in no publicity or, even worse, undermine your credibility with the media. You need to develop a sense of what is news—and what isn't.

Selecting Newsworthy Facts

Even Mary quite contrary would probably not make news these days if she didn't cultivate her message as well as her garden. When, where, why and how does her garden grow? These are the basic questions all journalists will ask.

Before you write a single press release you will have to work and rework your message until it is crystal clear.

First, make a list of the five *w*s and the *h*:

- Who is doing what for whom?
- When, where, and why are they doing it?
- How is it being done?
- What are the results?

For example, it's not enough to say that your product is an exciting new development based on years of research. Why is the product exciting? What will it do for buyers—save them time and money? Make them happier or healthier? How is it better than what's on the market now? What research was involved in developing it? What tests show its superior performance? Who is using it already? What are its specifications? How was the technology discovered? By whom? What was the *personal* impact on the team who developed it?

It's not adequate to say, for example, that your charitable organization has hundreds of volunteers who raise thousands of dollars for community activities. What are the activities? Who are the volunteers? Each of them is a living, thinking, feeling human being, and in every person there is at least one human interest story.

Perhaps you have a retired actress who volunteered to coach a high school drama group. She helped the youngsters raise money to buy costumes for their most recent production. A story is beginning to emerge. Probe further and you might find that the teenagers really enjoy someone who can tell them exactly what it was like working with Elvis. Much to everyone's delight, they are leaping clear across the generation gap. And one of the students, a quiet fellow, was cast in the role of a social butterfly. Suddenly, he is becoming more confident. His English grades were borderline, but now his schoolwork is improving. That story will interest many more readers than a dull list of fund-raising quotas.

You will also have to figure out how to present statistics in an interesting way. For example, if your company has developed a new, recyclable package for microwave food products, determine which facts and figures might have visual appeal. Even without photos, a good description can create pictures in the minds of readers or listeners. How many tons of waste will *not* end up in landfills or incinerators this year as a result of your new product? What would that waste look like piled high? Ten football fields 30 feet deep? 100 fields? More? How much paper and metal will the recycled packaging save yearly? How many books could be printed on that paper? How much energy will recycling save, and how many tankers of petroleum does that represent? The clearer and more descriptive your message, the better your media coverage will be.

Media people expect you to have clarified and developed your message before you approach them. "We don't know your organization. You know your organization," says KSTP-TV's Linnea Crowe. "And you should know what kinds of things you're trying to sell."

Editors, reporters, and public service directors want you to be specific because they need facts, not impressions, and focus, not fuzziness. "If there is a clear focus to the group, then it will be easier for their publicist to get my interest, and it will be easier for me to write about them," says journalist Leslie O'Bergin. "I couldn't even begin to count the number of people who thought their organization had a clear focus, but who could not give me the explanation I needed to write a thorough story."

Before you leap into print or onto the airwaves, ask yourself if you're prepared to be in the spotlight. "Don't publicize your organization or event until you're really ready," warns journalist Nancy Dunn. "If you're not fully prepared, you'll be stuck with an amateurish image that will be hard to live down."

Remaining Objective

The only time your publicity material should contain opinions is when quoting someone. "There's no way an opinionated release would ever see the light of day in our paper," says Brian Youmatz, news editor for the *Framingham Middlesex News* in Massachusetts. And although he might use the release as background material for a reporter-written story—if he thought the issues were important and he wanted to cover them—it would make him "think twice about the reliability" of that publicist's material in the future.

News releases are supposed to be objective, and that means they are written in the third person. A biased news release might do more than harm your reputation as a credible news source, since many journalists may assume you have something to hide. Such a release could, conceivably, set off an investigative reporting effort aimed squarely at your organization. Fred Zehnder at KTVU-TV comments: "An opinionated, biased news release or news conference will result in a very zealous attempt to get the other side. It would be a cue right off the bat that somebody has an ax to grind." No matter how passionately you feel about your product, the issues and the information, keep that passion under control. Give facts and figures. Leave opinions for quotes, which actually help your release by giving it color and life.

The following sample release tells you almost nothing about the product. The extreme hyperbole will turn editors off. Change the names of the company and the item, and it could be about almost anything! What do you do if your superiors won't listen to reason and insist you produce material like this? You could write two releases, one to satisfy them, and one designed to get media coverage. It has been done.

July 1, 1992   For Immediate Release
Very Big Widget Company   Contact: Ben Pupik III
1000 Easy Street   999-5000
Chelm 00002

Very Big Introduces High-Powered Widget That Anticipates Market Needs

CHELM, July 1, 1992—Executives at the Very Big Widget Company, in one of the industry's most impatiently awaited maneuvers, continue to demonstrate tangibly the corporation's pledge to develop cutting edge SOS Technology with the debut of the New, Improved HH-707 High Powered Widget which sets new standards for widget performance.

"The HH-707 High Powered Widget offers a higher output capacity, uses less power and ultimately gives its users a far lower cost per job," according to Chaim Trotskell, Product Manager for the 700 Series Widgets.

"With this powerful solution to the high cost of Widget usage, we have met the increasing demand for reasonably-priced Widgets. We have reinforced our worldwide pledge to become the global Widget leader," Trotskell continues.

With worldwide headquarters in Chelm, The Very Big Widget Company is a recognized trailblazer in Widgets featuring the latest SOS Technology, which takes full advantage of micro-miniaturization. The Company, with $550 million in sales in fiscal 1991, employs 1500 people worldwide.

###

If you are writing about your new French restaurant, it would be unwise to say, "Chef Andre Paté delights in leaving the kitchen to explain the composition of each delightful surprise to the anxiously awaiting customers." It would be much better if you wrote, "Chef Andre Paté often shares his recipes with the customers. 'I love to tell people how I make my pastries because they are so eager to learn,' he says."

The following release is an example of slanted material without factual backing. The opinionated words and phrases and undocumented information are italicized.

CHELM, September 30, 1991—After our *victory* in the Chelm State Assembly, the *struggle* to *break the back* of the *parasitic* head shop trade shifted yesterday to Federal Court, where attorneys for the drug paraphernalia industry pulled out a last-minute temporary restraining order in a *bold* attempt to protect the *multimillion-dollar profits* of their clients from going up in smoke.

This move lays to rest the *myth* that head shops are small, innocuous businesses making a few dollars on rolling papers and water pipes. This industry is *wealthy, organized, and powerful,* and it has the *money and the clout to hire high-priced* legal talent to protect its *vested* interests. In fact, a *huge war chest* was collected for their court challenges.

The constitutional issue is merely a *smoke screen* hiding a *vast empire built on the enhancement and glorification* of drug abuse. As one of the sponsors of the paraphernalia ban, I call upon the Governor of Chelm to lend maximum assistance in resisting any *cynical* effort to *manipulate* the law or prevent its immediate enforcement.

###

The following rewritten version makes better news for several reasons. First, it still contains many of the opinions in the original release, but they are now in direct quotes. Second, the opinions used are more selective, so they do not overwhelm the reader. Third, a key allegation is now supported by giving the source of the information, the Chelm Attorney General's Office. And finally, the use of proper journalistic format makes it read as news, not bombast.

CHELM, September 30, 1991—The effort to limit the "head shop" trade shifted yesterday from the Chelm State Assembly to Federal Court, where attorneys for the industry got a last-minute restraining order that will delay the State's enforcement of the new laws against drug paraphernalia.

"This move lays to rest the myth that head shops are small, innocuous businesses making a few dollars on rolling papers and water pipes," says Assemblyman Ed Tichnor. "This industry is wealthy, organized, and powerful. It has the money and the clout to hire the best legal talent."

The Chelm Association of Head Shop Owners has raised $785,000 for its legal defense fund in the past five months, according to figures obtained by Tichnor from the Chelm Attorney General's Office.

"The constitutional issue is merely a smoke screen hiding a vast empire built on the enhancement and glorification of drug abuse," says Tichnor, who formally asked the Governor to provide legal resources to defend the new laws.

###

Round Hole or Square, You Need a Peg

Another important news test involves uniqueness. If every other new widget has the same features yours does, if all the charities in town run garage sales and pancake breakfasts, if every other small business has crazy days sales in late August, then your business or charity won't get much more than an events calendar listing or minor media coverage. But if you come up with an unusual angle, you increase your chances for major coverage of an ordinary product or event.

With product publicity, you'll have to work closely with the marketing department to decide which aspects of their strategy will create the most usable news angles. Perhaps your new widget comes with a guarantee of satisfaction, while the other widget manufacturers "let the buyer beware." That's one way to separate your product from the crowd, give journalists a usable news angle, and get good coverage.

You can use the same approach with events, too. If your crazy days sale is the only one around to start with an old-fashioned tug-of-war in the middle of Main Street, just like they used to do before World War II, you have a better chance at good coverage. Should your group's garage sale feature a trunkful of historic pictures from the turn of the century, you're apt to get a nice spread in the paper if you offer to let the editor use any pictures she wants.

The most important thing in a news release is the peg. The peg is the focus, the angle, the main point, the unusual idea, the new material, the explanation of how the story will have impact on the audience. The peg is the justification for the news release. There are some standard techniques to create news pegs where none existed before. Americans love to celebrate holidays, anniversaries, seasons, and new world records for the biggest and the best. Tie your story to a celebration, anniversary, new record, or seasonal theme, and you have an instant peg that can make the difference between good coverage and no results at all.

Another standard technique for conjuring up a news peg is to create an award. "I've gotten coverage in the Business Section (which isn't easy to do) for an award I used to give out. I called it the Percy Award," says Gary Blake. "It's named after that awful phrase 'pursuant to your request.' I started the Percy Awards four years ago when I gave a mock award for the worst, most vague and antiquated memos, letters and reports. People heard about them on the radio and in *USA Today*. They submitted their favorite examples to me. And the Percy Awards became a regular feature, with a lot of newspapers picking up the story every year. Because of the Percy Awards, people began to identify me as a crusader for good writing. I can't say the Awards brought me business directly, but they did help my image," says Blake.

Adding new information to a major debate among consumers who buy your product, or in your industry, is another way to create a strong news peg. Copywriter Bob Bly sent out the following release, which discusses the most effective techniques for creating advertising aimed at engineers. Since this is a hot topic in publications specializing in advertising and public relations news, editors will welcome this material.

FROM: Bob Bly, 174 Holland Avenue, New Milford, NJ 07646
CONTACT: Bob Bly — (201) 599-2277

For immediate release

New Free Fact Sheet Reveals What Engineers Like (and Don't Like) about Industrial, High-Tech, and Business-to-Business Advertising

New Milford, NJ—If your most recent industrial, high-tech, or business-to-business ad campaign didn't generate the

– more –   – more –

results you'd hoped for, it may be because engineers—a key target for such campaigns—respond to advertising differently than "normal folk," according to New Milford, NJ-based copywriter and advertising consultant Bob Bly.

"Engineers look down on advertising," says Bly. "For the most part, they have a low opinion of advertising and of people who work in the field. As a result, advertising aimed at engineers must be informational and professional, not gimmicky or promotional. Avoid writing copy that sounds like 'ad copy.' Engineers will be quick to reject such material as 'fluff.' "

Among Bly's advice to industrial advertisers and agencies:

The engineer's purchase decision is more logical than emotional. "Certainly, there are emotional components to an engineer's buying decision. But for the most part, an engineer buying a new piece of equipment will analyze technical specifications," says Bly.

Engineers want to know the features, not just the benefits. "In consumer advertising classes, we are taught that benefits are everything, and that features are unimportant. But engineers are not content to know just the benefit. They also want to understand the feature that enables the product to provide the benefit," insists Bly.

Engineers are not turned off by jargon and technical language. "In fact," says Bly, "they like it. Use of technical language in ad copy shows the engineer that you speak his language and are not superficial in your understanding of his requirements."

Engineers and other technical specialists are attracted by visuals that reflect their area of expertise. "For instance, when illustrating ads aimed at electrical engineers, use circuit diagrams."

Engineers do not like a "consumer approach" to advertising. "There is a raging debate in business-to-business advertising whether engineers respond to a straight technical approach, a clever consumer-style approach, or something in between," says Bly. "Those who prefer the creative approach argue that the engineer is a human being first and an engineer second, and will therefore respond to creativity and cleverness just like everyone else.

– more –   – more –

"Unfortunately," adds Bly, "there is much evidence to the contrary." Bly says he has been involved in numerous tests of consumer vs. technical copy in ads and direct mail packages aimed at engineers, and that "the straightforward, low-key, professional approach will outpull the 'glitzy' ad or mailing virtually every time."

To receive a free copy of the "Marketing to Engineers" tip sheet, write to Bob Bly, Dept. ME, 174 Holland Avenue, New Milford, NJ 07646, or call (201) 599-2277.

Yet even though a news peg is critical for good publicity, many publicists send out pegless releases. "One pet peeve" about publicists, says Tom Callaghan of the *Birmingham News*, "is when they put out a release without any news focal point just because they think it's time to put out a release. That's just a waste of our time." And KTVU-TV's Fred Zehnder adds, "publicists may feel that providing coffee and doughnuts for reporters and cameramen is a good reason for us to cover an event. It isn't." Coffee and doughnuts aren't a substitute for a news peg.

Can you see why the following sample releases are pegless?

CHELM, June 16, 1992—On Monday afternoon, June 15, Acme Products in Chelm honored 38 National Sales Champions who each achieved astounding sales figures for the most recent period. The audience included the justly proud spouses of the honorees as well as key employees and suppliers.

In addition to awarding Sales Champion pins, Mr. Martin Puffer, President, delivered a brief farewell address, since he is retiring in June after 54 years of distinguished service to the firm.

Corky McCorkle, Vice-President of Sales, was the guest speaker. Ms. McCorkle gave an interesting and unusual speech praising and congratulating the Champions after she presented them with their Acme Achievement certificates.

Mr. John Gonn, Chairman of the Board, was very proud to have made his 16th annual presentation of the Acme Champions

– more –   – more –

induction ceremony. He extended good wishes to the honorees and thanked the entire staff of Acme.

The Chelm community should be very proud of their Acme Champions, since Acme's requirements are perhaps the highest in the nation. These employees are the key hope for Chelm's economic future.

CHELM, January 7, 1990—How lucky can you get? You couldn't better the winning odds at the First Annual Golf and Field Day held by the Chelm Chamber of Commerce on Thursday, January 3 at the Circular Club Golf Course, according to an announcement today by Chamber President R. J. Solfeggio.

Four hundred Chelm businessmen who attended the Chamber's popular all-day outing enjoyed a "big edge" in their chances to win. Twenty-five "superduper" awards alone, valued at $100 to $250 and more, were picked during the wind-up dinner, starting at 7:00 P.M.

The problem with the first release is that it is full of congratulations and self-praise. Yes, it is nice that 38 employees are Acme Champions, but what does that mean? How much did they sell? When, exactly, is the "most recent period?" And why is it news? Award ceremonies like this are held all the time. The story might be of interest to the families and friends of the honorees, but the recipient's names aren't mentioned.

We are told that interesting speeches were made, but not *why* they are of interest; we have no idea what the speakers said. In fact, change a few names and phrases, and this release could apply to almost any organization. If you came across such release anywhere but in this book, would you bother to read it? Of course not! It's "inside stuff," of interest only to the people involved, and even they may be bored silly by the ceremonial pomposity. Ceremonial pomposity is not news, unless some very well-known people are involved.

The second release is also inside stuff. If you are not one of the businessmen involved, there's nothing in it for you because this is not a public event. You cannot take part because you have not been invited, and the news was released after the event was over. So even though the piece may have a peg when it is run in the *Chelm Chamber of Commerce Newsletter*, that peg falls apart outside Chamber of Commerce circles. That's why private events are not usually news.

"We do not serve as a bulletin board . . . ." says Paul Neely, features editor of the *St. Petersburg Times* in Florida. "It is important to have some awareness of what news value is, what makes something unusual. A stamp club meeting is not unusual. A stamp club meeting where someone from out of town is showing a stamp worth half a million dollars is unusual."

There is an important question you should ask yourself before you send out any news release. If this story was about an organization you were unfamiliar with, would you be interested in reading it?

You may think that's all fine for other people, but your product is unique and wonderful—or your group is a charity with a worthy cause—and *you* should be able to get publicity just by asking for it. Don't believe that for a second!

You're not asking for publicity, you're providing journalists with a story they can use. As KOOL-TV's Bill Close puts it, "Never use the word publicity. Publicity is a profane, obscene word. Don't come in here and say, 'hey, we need some publicity . . . .' The least the publicist can do is make an intelligent effort to camouflage it by saying, '. . . we have a cute little angle we think will make a good feature for you.' It's a matter of intelligent salesmanship."

Creating Newsworthy Events

Sometimes you will want to create news by staging an event that is designed to get you coverage. "We've done a lot of special events in which we hope to draw 80 people," says Bob Seltzer. But that special event is in no way, shape or form directed at those 80 people. It's aimed at the media, who will then cover what you're doing."

Let's say your construction trades association has not been able to interest the local media in figures demonstrating that defense spending will only produce a few jobs in your state, but the same amount of money, if spent on rebuilding the state's infrastructure would produce work for many more people. Although the idea of a "Peace Dividend" has been discussed in the national media, there's never been a local angle story from your state.

You might get coverage if you stage an event that dramatizes the controversy. It's possible that you could entice news photographers and camera crews to a rally where, for example, a dozen people are gathered in a tight group wearing jumpers and caps that look like bullets. Completely surrounding the "defense workers" would be a hundred "construction trade workers" with equally interesting and photogenic costumes. Since large groups are hard to assemble and difficult to photograph, you might use one person to symbolize each hundred—or thousand—jobs, depending on the figures your research uncovers. Photographed from a bird's-eye viewpoint, that would make quite a picture!

Perhaps you're running a halfway house that helps ex-drug addicts become part of the community again after their release from residential treatment centers. The house is across the street from a neighborhood park, and although there has never been a problem, the neighbors are worried; they're even reluctant to let their children play in the park. You're worried, too. Your permit to operate the halfway house has been issued on a trial basis. The neighbors might challenge your application for permanent status at the upcoming public hearings.

You have to create a positive image. You decide to sponsor an End of Winter Festival for neighborhood families, with your halfway house residents serving as volunteers. Several of them have formed a band, so it will be easy for you to fill the day with live music, and there will be free hot chocolate, hay rides, and a snowball fight with the alderman— whose daughter is one of the residents.

Although skating season is over, the outdoor rink is still frozen. Hundreds of children and their parents are given buckets of tempera paint, and soon marvelous murals cover the ice, fading slowly into a swirled rainbow as the surface melts during the next week.

The ice paintings appear on the front page of the evening paper, as well as on two local TV news shows; no one has ever painted murals on ice before, at least not in your city. The neighborhood is buzzing. They've had a chance to see the halfway house residents as people, and they liked what they saw. They're proud that their area is page-one news, and they know that you created that news. You got good coverage because you provided interesting, highly visual material with human interest and a new, unusual angle. That is what the media want.

The Local Angle

Since national news magazines, as well as all-news television and radio networks, cover national news so thoroughly, many weekly and daily newspapers limit themselves to local news stories. This is especially true with suburban newspapers. And many radio and TV newsrooms also concentrate on local news because they rely on networks and wire services to cover the national scene. So it is often very important that publicity material received from out-of-town sources is of local interest.

Localizing news releases pays handsome dividends, with placement rates five to ten times higher than releases without localization. In fact, some stories *must* be localized to get media coverage. Only about a third of the material needs to be local, and local statistics can be just as helpful as local names.

If your corporation is headquartered in Plains City, for example, but you have dealers all along the Eastern Seaboard, try to get coverage in their media outlets as well by localizing individual releases. Using a word processor, you can customize lead paragraphs for each release, and include a paragraph or two about how a customer from each community has benefited from your product.

When your organization is making an announcement, you can send out different releases attributing the announcement to local spokespeople in each community. Or you can refer reporters to a local expert in their area for an interview that rounds out the material in your release.

The following is an example of the lead paragraphs from a localized press release. They would be followed by more information about your organization and its product. How do you get the localized information? With the help of local dealers, who stand to gain a lot from press coverage in their area.

PLAINS HEIGHTS, April 30, 1992—Plains Heights resident Mike T. Chen doesn't rake and bag grass clippings anymore—but his lawn is still neatly manicured and deep green. Thirty-eight-year-old Chen, a member of the Plains Heights Garden Club, mows his lawn like everyone else. But his new Mulch-O-Matic lawn mower transforms the clippings into a fine powder and blows it deep into the lawn where it quickly turns into high-grade compost.

"Plains City residents create about 1500 tons of grass clippings each season. With a $30.00 per ton fee at the Plains County Dump, grass clippings cost the City's residents about $45,000 annually," says Mulch-O-Matic's President, Melissa Fielding.

"That's a double shame," Fielding continues. "Perfectly good mulch material is going to waste. And the County Dump is running out of room."

If you are sending out localized releases, you will want to let editors know immediately that, despite the out-of-town address, the material will be of use to them. Mark your releases "local angle story" with a red marker. If you plan to send out a great deal of localized material, you can even have a rubber stamp made up. However you do the marking, it will be appreciated by news directors and editors.

"It really does help to mark a press release 'local angle story' if the material originates in another city," says Gladys Adams of the *Kansas City Voice.*

Whenever you can, include the name and telephone number of a local contact on your material. This is most important when the media outlet is far away from you.

You can use the local angle approach in another way. If the media are covering a national story of interest to your organization, you can call news directors or editors and offer a local angle on the story.

If there's national coverage on the dangers of toxic chemicals seeping out of garbage dumps and into water supplies, and your organization has solid information about that problem at a nearby landfill, call the local media outlets and offer your story.

Or, let's say Congress has just passed new legislation that you feel will make your widgets much more expensive—and give foreign widget makers an unfair advantage. You could call local journalists and offer your facts and figures on how that decision will affect local workers. Or, you could contact national media outlets and offer material on how the new widget legislation will impact your area of the country. If you act fast, before there has been any "grassroots" coverage on this story, and if your facts, figures and anecdotes are specific, you have the best chance of getting coverage.

"I would certainly welcome a call like that because we are interested in attempting to localize national stories," says WVUE-TV's Jim Kemp.

Journalist Nancy Dunn suggests that you might open a call about a local angle story by saying, "I'm working for so-and-so and I'm trying to get some coverage of blank. Other sides of this issue have been covered, but I've never seen it covered from this angle before." Or, "This has been covered in the national press, but I haven't seen the local aspects covered yet." Then briefly tell the reporter your angle and information.

Backgrounding a News Story

Let's say there have been a dozen train wrecks in your county in the past few months. The media are running a story about the official investigation that has just been announced. You might call reporters and offer your Defend the Rails Association's information about discriminatory tax policies that favor other forms of transportation and lead to slipshod railroad maintenance—and train wrecks.

According to an article in the Radio and Television News Director's Association magazine, background information is especially interesting to broadcasters because most of them do not have access to adequate data. Although computerized information banks may take care of the information squeeze in the broadcast newsrooms of the near future, for now, an offer of solid background information is often appreciated.

You can even make that offer on an ongoing basis, using several different approaches:

- Set up a fact hotline for journalists, and promote it regularly. Your promotional material should explain the resources you offer and your hours of operation. If it's possible, include a preprinted Rolodex® card to help insure that journalists can keep your number right at their fingertips. To make a hotline successful, you'll have to keep a healthy file of facts at your command, and have a fast way to retrieve the exact information your caller is asking for, as well as a method for quickly handling inquiries that require research.

- Distribute a file folder with a pre-labelled tab (Widget Fact File, for example), or a looseleaf binder, with factual material about your product, industry, or cause. Make sure that every journalist who might ever write stories about your subject gets a copy. And set up a program to update the file regularly.

- List your organization in the commercially distributed *Yearbook of Experts* mentioned in Chapter 12.

Publicity for Products

Product publicity may *seem* simple at first glance. But there's a tremendous amount of thought and strategizing involved in getting more than a mere product mention.

First you have to look at the product itself. There are two broad types of products, and you have to decide which category yours falls in. Many products are somewhere in between.

- Commodity products are like every other product of their kind on the market—they all have the same basic features.

Sure yours may come in color while the others are all black or white, but if all the other qualities are the same, you still have a commodity product. Packaged goods like soap, peanut butter, soft drinks and hair spray are typical commodity products.

■ Differentiated products have features and benefits different from the competition. Quality furniture, books, many toys, and most heavy industrial equipment are some examples of differentiated products.

If you're promoting a commodity product, there are several strategies you can use. "Identify product benefits that competitors have ignored—even though their products have them as well," says Don Levin, of Levin Public Relations Marketing, Inc., White Plains, N.Y. Buyers will begin to identify that benefit with your product, even if all your competitors offer the same feature.

Another approach is to tie your commodity product to issues and events that are of interest to consumers such as awards and sporting events. If you develop a clever angle and do your homework with the media, an award program can pay handsome dividends, even with a very Spartan budget. Tournaments and sports competitions are more expensive to plan, run, and publicize.

For non-commodity products, or products that fall in between, there are several options. You can ". . . identify either what is NEW about the product, or the most different, unusual, newsworthy or interesting feature or aspect of the product," says Bob Bly.

You can produce publicity material that teaches the public how to buy, choose and use your product. Or you can tie in to a hot issue very much on the minds of consumers of your product.

Paul Gourvitz of Sheridan-Elson-Gourvitz, a New York video production house, recently solved a tough publicity challenge with a very clever approach. Matchbox wanted to do a video news release about its new toys, R.C. Ripskate and R.C. Radskate. "They were clever toys," Gourvitz says, "but we needed to make the product newsworthy."

Gourvitz and his colleagues interviewed a national skateboard champion, who used the toys to demonstrate safety tips for young skateboarders. With safety as a peg, this became an interesting news story, and, with action footage of an actual skateboard competition, ". . . the video news release was well-accepted by news producers across the country," according to Gourvitz' account in *Playthings*.

A good news peg is only the start of effective product publicity. You have to provide solid information about your product. If you say that your product's performance is superior, you have to be able to back it up with solid facts. And, if you can provide data to support your claims from an independent source, so much the better.

When you write a press release announcing a new product, be sure you include all the significant facts in the lead. The following lead paragraph, from a release prepared for Sharp by Dorf & Stanton Technology Communications, gives an editor enough hard facts so he knows beyond a doubt that this copier is a breakthrough product.

ATLANTA, June 1990—A full-color copier which can produce seven-color copies on letter-sized plain paper at the rate of 7.5 copies per minute will be highlighted at this year's COM-DEX show by Sharp Electronics Corporation. The CX-7500 is currently being sold through Sharp's network of dedicated color copier dealers throughout the country.

Timing Your Product Publicity

The right timing for your product publicity is critical. In addition to media lead times, you have to determine if the marketplace needs to be "conditioned" ahead of time to accept publicity for a product people may not have even thought of. As public relations executive Bob Seltzer explains, "If you're going to come out with a new contact lens cleaner in six months, you would be very smart to get articles about the problems of cleaning contact lenses in the media—now. These stories don't even require that your product is mentioned. You're educating the market-place about a problem, so when your product launches, you've made your audience more receptive. Publicity does not work as effectively if you wait until the product comes out to build awareness."

You can also publicize a product before it's available to create a dramatic awareness that gets the media and the public looking forward to its introduction. Seltzer's public relations firm, Porter Novelli, ". . . launched the Gillette Sensor Razor with an announce-ment in October—even though it would not come out until January. The object was to build anticipation and expectation. Every year *Fortune* magazine does an article on the 10 best products of the year. The Gillette Sensor was actually named one of the 10 best products for 1989, even though it wasn't even introduced until 1990," accord-ing to Seltzer.

This worked well with the Gillette Sensor partly because the story behind the product is so dramatic. It took ten years to develop this new razor with 13 moving parts protected by 22 patents. Gillette spent about $200 million on manufacturing equipment alone, and planned to spend $175 million on a 19-country marketing campaign. The size of the effort and expenditures alone is big news.

The publicity campaign was coordinated in 19 North American and European countries, with the kick-off at an elaborate press conference in early October, 1989. A second wave of consumer publicity was launched in December and January. The campaign included:

- special story angles and materials for trade, consumer and business publications.
- Sensor gift packs for selected editors.
- results from a panel of 5000 consumers who tested and rated Sensor.
- a backgrounder on the history of the safety razor, which Gillette's founder invented and first manufactured in 1903.

The results of this campaign were also dramatic, with more than 800 placements internationally, including:

- feature TV segments on "Good Morning America," "CBS Evening News," Financial News Network's "Business Tonight," and European TV.
- hundreds of feature stories in major business, trade and consumer publications, including *Newsweek*, *Forbes*, *Elle*, and *Mirabella*.
- stories on all the major wire services, including three AP stories, UPI and Reuters.
- hundreds of feature newspaper stories, among them *The Wall Street Journal*, *Los Angeles Times*, *Boston Globe*, *Detroit Free Press*, *Philadelphia Inquirer*, and the *New York Times*.
- hundreds of European newspaper and magazine placements, including *Le Figaro*, *Milano Finanza*, and the *Frankfurter Allgemeine Zeitung*.
- a picture on the cover of *Fortune* and the caption ". . . literally on the cutting edge."
- A report by *USA Today* staffer James Cox, who tested the razor himself and announced that it ". . . maneuvers well . . ."

Recycling Your Publicity

Your press release has been written and distributed, you have organized and analyzed the clippings, and gotten some very nice comments from your colleagues, superiors, and even the board of directors. Your task is over, isn't it?

Not so fast! Now it's time to start recycling your publicity. Take a quick look at the possible return on your investment of time, and I'm sure you'll be convinced. There are two ways to do this:

- Use reprints of the most favorable clippings in your promotional material. They can give you far more credibility than even the slickest four-color brochure. In a large organization, you'll want to coordinate this effort with your sales and marketing department.
- Use reprints as the basis of further publicity, by taking detailed articles on how to choose, buy and use your product, repackaging them, and offering them as free giveaways. This works especially well with articles written by an insider like you or someone from your organization.

In either case, you need to get permission from the publication that first printed the article, since it is probably copyrighted in their name. But this is usually a mere formality—write them a note explaining how you'll use the reprint, and they'll reply with their approval.

Gary Blake explains that he uses "copies of articles about The Communication Workshop in packets of material I send to prospects. They round out a prospect's way of looking at you. It gives you a lovely chance to parade your credentials without seeming self-serving—and that's the wonderful thing about publicity."

Freelance copywriter Bob Bly used the second approach with an article he had written for *Business Marketing*. The following press release, which he sent to 60 advertising, public relations, sales and marketing publications, has resulted in 18 stories to date. Some were just small blurbs, but others were word-for-word pickups of the entire release, including one in *Nation's Business* that generated 400 inquiries. Bly didn't send his release directly to *Nation's Business*; they picked it up from elsewhere!

As a result of this recycling campaign, Bly has received 2000 requests for the booklet within six months. The inquiries have led to sales of hundreds of copies of his books about advertising and marketing, and generated several consulting assignments. His out-of-pocket cost for the publicity was under $100.

FROM: Bob Bly, 174 Holland Avenue, New Milford, NJ 07646
CONTACT: Bob Bly—(201) 599-2277

For immediate release

Free Booklet Reveals 31 Ways to Get More Inquiries from Your Ads

New Milford, NJ—A new booklet, published by independent copywriter and advertising consultant Robert W. Bly, reveals 31 strategies for creating ads that generate more inquiries, leads, sales and profits for advertisers.

The booklet, "31 ways to get more inquiries from your ads," is available free of charge to business executives, entrepreneurs, advertising professionals, and students. The cost to the general public is $1.00.

Bly said he originally wrote the booklet for companies and ad agencies that need to see more of a bottom-line return from advertising campaigns originally designed purely to build "image" and awareness.

"There's no reason an image campaign can't also generate leads as well as awareness," says Bly. "High-quality inquiries mean more sales and profits. And they also provide a way of measuring response. The booklet presents 31 ways to increase any ad's pulling power without destroying the basic concept or interfering with communication of the key message."

Some of the inquiry-producing techniques presented in the booklet include:

Offer free information—a booklet, brochure, catalog, price list, order form—in every ad you write.

Give your literature piece a title that implies value. "*Product guide* sounds better than *catalog*" notes Bly. "*Planning kit* implies greater value than *sales brochure*."

– more –   – more –

For a full-page ad, use a coupon. According to Bly, "This will increase response 25 to 100 percent."

Make the coupon large enough so that there is plenty of room for prospects to write their name and address. "Tiny coupons drive people crazy," notes Bly.

In a fractional ad, put a heavy dashed border around the ad.

"This creates a coupon-like appearance, which in turn stimulates response," explains Bly.

Offer something FREE—such as a free product sample, free report, free video or audio cassette, free analysis, free consultation, free estimate, free seminar, free demonstration, or free trial.

Says Bly: "By modifying existing ads using the techniques outlined in this booklet, advertisers can increase response to their ads 20 to 100 percent—without destroying the basic concept and theme of these campaigns."

To receive a free copy of "31 ways to get more inquiries from your ads," send a self-addressed stamped #10 envelope to: Advertising Inquiries, 174 Holland Avenue, New Milford, NJ 07646.

Bob Bly is a freelance copywriter specializing in business-to-business and direct response advertising and the author of 16 books including *The Copywriter's Handbook* (Holt).

###

Self-liquidating Publicity

It's often worth offering a free report, article, checklist or other inexpensive giveaway to get people to respond to your publicity so you can mail them promotions for your products or services. Sometimes, however, you can charge a small fee for the item, and defray the cost of your publicity campaign, making it "self-liquidating."

Gary Blake of The Communication Workshop has done this successfully with a series called "The Excellent Writer's Posters." "The first poster we publicized was called 'No Institutionitis,' " Blake explains. "It had hundreds of stuffy institutional phrases like 'enclosed please find,' and 'under separate cover.' *USA Today* picked up the story from our release and we got about 1,000 paid requests for that poster over the next six months."

"I think when thousands of our posters go up on bulletin boards all across the United States, we're building for the future. A number of times a prospect has told me 'I saw your name once before. Today I saw it the second time, and that's why I'm calling you.' In fact, that's how I got my biggest client." Below is one of the releases Blake has used to publicize The Communication Workshop's posters:

CLIENT: CONTACT:
The Communication Workshop   GARY BLAKE
217 East 85th Street   (718) 575-8000
New York, NY 10028
(718) 575-8000

For Immediate Release:

New Posters Help People Learn Punctuation "At a Glance"

NEW YORK, N.Y. APRIL 23rd—What's the difference be-tween a comma and a semicolon? A dangling modifier and a misplaced modifier? If you're like most people, you need a brush-up in the basics of punctuation and grammar.

To help people master the basics of punctuation and gram-mar, The Communication Workshop, a New York City consult-ing firm devoted to helping businesspeople and technicians improve their writing, is offering 2-color posters on each of these touchy topics.

The eye-catching posters ("Punctuation at a Glance" and "Grammar at a Glance") clearly differentiate the eight most im-portant punctuation marks and the six stickiest grammar glitches, giving rules and showing examples that are visually bold and can be understood "at a glance."

For a copy of each of these posters, suitable for displaying on bulletin boards, send $4.00 (including postage and han-dling) to The Communication Workshop, 217 East 85th Street, New York, NY 10028.

###

Checklist—Keys to Newsworthy Publicity

1. Have you determined whether your organization generates mostly soft news, hard news, or a mixture of the two?
2. Do you understand why your release is either hard or soft news, and how to develop an angle based on the news type?
3. Have you checked each piece of publicity material before mailing to make sure it has the who, when, where, why, what, and how?
4. Have you decided how to dramatize your statistics?
5. Are your news releases objective? Backed by facts and figures? Focused on one or two main ideas?
6. Are your news releases written in the third person, with opinions confined to quotes?
7. Is your organization ready to handle the media's questions—no matter what they ask about?
8. Is your news release unique enough to warrant media attention?
9. If this release was about an organization you were unfamiliar with, would you be interested in reading it?
10. Is there anything else you can do to make your product, service, or cause stand out from the pack?
11. What is your news peg?
12. Are there other pegs you might use to make your release, press conference invitation, or tip sheet more interesting?
13. Have you considered creating a news peg by tying your story to a seasonal theme, anniversary, award or new record for the biggest and the best?
14. Have you thought about creating a news peg by adding new information to a debate in your industry, or among consumers who buy your product?
15. If you're doing product publicity, are you working with the marketing department to decide which aspects of their marketing strategy will make the best news pegs?

16. Is your event open to the public? If not, why are you publicizing it?

17. Do you understand why you don't ask journalists for some "publicity"?

18. If your release or press conference is about a cause or controversy, have you developed a peg that makes it news?

19. Have you thought about how your organization can create newsworthy events to further its goals?

20. Is your organization ready to offer local angle and background material on fast-breaking national news stories?

21. Are you developing background approaches for "grassroots" local stories for the national media as well as local media?

22. Are you localizing press releases for out-of-town newspapers and broadcasters?

23. Are you using your dealer and distributor network or local chapters as sources for the information you need to localize stories?

24. Have you marked your localized releases "local angle story"?

25. How many ways can you develop to localize stories in addition to those we discussed?

26. Have you considered positioning your organization as an authority journalists can turn to for information on a regular basis?

27. Have you promoted this backgrounder service to all journalists who can use it?

28. Will you handle it as a hotline or a fact file?

29. Have you determined if yours is a commodity or differentiated product—or somewhere in between?

30. If yours is a commodity product, have you identified product benefits competitors have ignored?

31. To which issues or events can you tie your product for a strong news peg?

32. Have you provided solid information about your product?

33. Have you backed up claims about product performance with verifiable facts, preferably from an independent source?

34. Have you determined whether there is a need to "pre-condition" the marketplace to prepare it to accept your product?

35. Have you worked out a timetable for your product publicity campaign?

36. If you're considering publicizing your product before it's actually available, have you made sure that the story is dramatic enough to make this approach work?

37. Are you using reprints of your media clippings to bolster your promotion material?

38. Have you thought about repackaging published articles about your product or service as free giveaways, and using publicity to promote them?

39. Have you considered charging a small fee to make your premium self-liquidating?

CHAPTER FOUR

Writing for the Press

I f you're like most people, you have no emotional reaction to a blank piece of paper. But put that same piece of paper into a typewriter with your fingers on the keys, and you feel ice crystals forming in your innards and an intense desire to run away from home. Writing scares many intelligent, creative, dynamic people, and many writers, too.

But if you are going to turn out crisp, interesting, pointed publicity material, you have to write. There are tricks you can use and steps you can follow to make this task easier, but, most important, the great dissolver of the fear of writing, is this simple fact: You can't edit what's not there.

So, don't be afraid of that blank paper. Fill it up with words, no matter how awkward they seem. As you work on that first draft, don't worry about precision and correct grammar. That can come later. What you need to do is start, and you start by starting. That's the only way.

Writing for the press requires mastery of several different formats, each serving a particular function. The one you will probably use most frequently is the standard press release that announces news about your organization's activities, and is sometimes accompanied by a supplementary fact sheet. The feature article, which is longer and not necessarily geared to a particular event, is another good publicity tool. In addition, you should learn how to prepare fillers and community calendar listings and to write effective letters to the editor on behalf of your organization.

Press Releases

Press releases are the cornerstone of any publicity program. Write them well, and your business or organization will get its share of coverage. If poorly written, with cute leads instead of solid information, misspelled words and inaccurate data instead of precise information, they'll end up in the "circular file."

Editors across the country, at large metropolitan dailies and small suburban weeklies, all complain that they get too many poorly written releases, that they are engulfed in an avalanche of useless material, and that they have to spend too much time sorting out the few good releases from the mountain of drivel.

Yet press releases are used—and even relied on by journalists. A survey mentioned in *Public Relations Journal* showed that more than two hundred travel editors rely on press releases almost as much as they count on material from their staff writers. To round out its coverage, even the *Wall Street Journal* uses press releases from businesses.

Press Release Format

Try to put yourself in the editor's seat for a moment. If she works at a large daily paper, she gets hundreds of press releases each day. She may have only an hour to read all of them, so she'll be able to spend half a minute on each one—or even less. She'll have to make quick judgments based on a skim of the first paragraph or two, but she'll also judge your news release by its format. If it doesn't look like news, she may not even read it.

There are plenty of other releases that fit her format, will need less editing and will create fewer potential problems.

You might be tempted to run a release on flashy pink paper with purple ink to grab attention. Don't do it. Says S. Griffin Singer of the *San Antonio Light*, "We had some stuff come through here not too long ago on fuchsia and chartreuse paper. It really looked awful. And that turned me off. Sure, it got my attention, but it had a negative impact."

Most publicists do use flashy letterhead for press releases, but you shouldn't, for the following reasons:

- Journalists prefer plain 8 1/2-by-11-inch paper, and that's reason enough.

- If you use a letterhead, you won't be able to fit as much copy on the page, making a one-page release flow over onto a second sheet.

- If you use plain paper, your release will stand out—it will be one of the few on simple white paper.

"Using plain white paper on news releases is important from a physical point of view," says Brian Youmatz of the *Framingham Middlesex News*. "If the press release is on a letterhead, we usually tear it off and glue the release to another sheet of paper, which is time-consuming."

Here are basic press release format guidelines:

- Keep typed lines 50 to 60 characters long, including punctuation marks and spaces. This length is easy to read and allows margins wide enough for editing.

- Double-space the entire release. Some less experienced publicists double-space the first few paragraphs—or graphs, as journalists call them—and single-space the rest of the release. Not only does this look awkward, it doesn't allow the editor space to edit. That's what goes between the lines, and you can't assume that your material won't need editing.

- Indent graphs ten spaces rather than the standard five. That makes your copy easier to scan and edit, and editors will appreciate your thoughtfulness.

- To prevent typesetting errors, avoid using hyphens at the ends of lines.

- If your release spills over to a second sheet, try to end the first page with a completed graph, or at least a completed sentence. Type MORE across the bottom of the first page at least three times. Start the second page with a brief heading that includes the name of your organization, the date, and the topic of the release.

■ Mark the end of your release with the digits -30-, or the number sign, ###, repeated several times across the page. These are two versions of journalese for "that's all folks"!

Headings

Your release should start with a heading that includes the name, address, and telephone number of your business or organization and the name of a contact person. Believe it or not, one of the most common problems with press releases is the absence of a telephone number.

"It drives me nuts when I don't know whom to call. And please include a home phone number because I generally work until 7:00 or 8:00 at night," says Randy McCarthy of the *Boise Statesman.* That home number is especially important if your organization expects to be involved in hard, breaking news or controversy. The inclusion of a home phone number on your release means that you will have to be ready to respond to reporters' questions at any time. Yes, that means during dinner, in the middle of a shower, or at 3:00 in the morning. If the reporter is working against a tight deadline, he needs the information now. So to keep your credibility with the media, you'll need to have the information at your fingertips. And even if it's the most inconvenient time imaginable, keep it a secret. It's your job to sound cheerful, organized, and intelligent.

If you are doing regional or national publicity and your firm or organization has a toll-free 800 number, list it at the top of the release, just below your regular telephone number.

Next in your heading is the date. You should guess at the date you expect the release to arrive on the editor's desk and date your release a day or two after that. The news in the release may be fresh and hot, but if it carries yesterday's date, an editor may assume it's stale and throw it away without reading it. So lean toward the future.

The next words in your heading will usually be "for immediate release." Never write "for immediate publication." That looks as if you're commanding the newspaper to run your release.

The only time you would use a different wording in a news release heading is when you have a good reason for asking the editor to hold the story. You might be alerting him to a major story ahead of time, so he can do some preparatory work. Or you've mailed the release to different types of papers, and you don't want the dailies to run it ahead of the weeklies. In either case, your heading could read, "for release after 10 A.M., May 18, 1991."

If there are pictures with your release, use the phrase "with art," and add a word or two to identify each shot. The following is an example of how your press release heading should look:

September 18, 1991	Plains City Robotics, Inc.
FOR IMMEDIATE RELEASE	11011 Arkansas Avenue, NE
	Plains City 00001
With Art:	Contact: Linda Ramirez
1. Serving robot in tuxedo	Day: 998-5500
2. Robot parts look human	Night: 999-3737

Contributing Your Own Headline

Should you write a headline for your release? Some editors object to headlines, believing that press releases should be judged by their leads, and headlines only get in the way.

On the other hand, there are some compelling arguments for using headlines. Dan Schlesinger, associate promotion director of the Family Circle Press Service in New York, puts it this way: "Even if a newspaper picks up every word of your release, it probably won't use your headline. Even so, it still pays to use a headline on your release, unless you're positive the editor you're contacting hates headlines on news releases. The editor is conditioned to judge if something is worth reading by glancing at a headline. Much of what he or she reads on and off the job—including most news releases, newspaper articles, advertisements, magazine stories, direct mail pieces, newsletters, and posters— contains headlines. So chances are that if your headline doesn't immediately communicate that your release contains news or information appropriate for his readership, he won't read any further."

Bill Howard of *PC Magazine* confirms this when he says, "In sending out press releases, it's important to include a brief headline that tells the whole story, since most press releases are read and acted upon (which typically means thrown out) within ten seconds. Make the editor realize instantly that this press release is worth reading."

Howard even goes a step further. ". . . announce the announcement on the envelope," he advises. "Editors often scan envelopes to see which of the day's mail looks most promising." Since direct mail specialists have proven that a headline on the envelope increases response, Howard's suggestion is right on target.

Should *you* write a headline? If you're customizing your releases for each reporter, you'll be wise to take their preferences into account. If you're not customizing, it's smart to use a headline, since most press releases do have them. And if your material has a strong news peg and is well written, any editor worth his salt will judge it on its merits, no matter how much he dislikes publicist-supplied headlines.

Leave at least two inches between the heading (or your headline) and the start of your text. "We need the top third of the page left blank so we have room to edit and write in headlines," says Brian Youmatz of the *Framingham Middlesex News.*

Organizing the Copy

To make sure the important information stands out clearly, press releases are written in inverted-pyramid form. Imagine an upside-down pyramid, its base in the air, its point in the sand. The most important information is up in the air, at the base of the pyramid, in the first one or two paragraphs. Even if you take away the rest of the story, those first one or two graphs still include all of the important information. Each subsequent graph contains less important information, until you reach the least significant material at the end of the story. News releases do not have strong concluding paragraphs.

A release written in this form help reporters and editors spot the vital information. It is also easy to edit; if there's not enough space in the paper for the whole story, it can be cut at any point, and the surviving graphs will still give the reader the basic information. Furthermore, since most readers skim through the newspaper, reading only a paragraph or two of most stories, this format lets them find the most important information quickly.

The best way to write a press release is to first list all the information you want to include. Then arrange it in order of importance. Your first graph or two, called the lead, contains the most important material, usually the who, when, where, why, what, and how. Stress the points that are most newsworthy.

If it is important that readers call you, include your phone number in the lead; most likely at the end of the second graph. Don't assume that a busy editor will see your number in the last graph and keep it in when he does drastic surgery on your story. He probably won't.

As you write each paragraph, double check to make sure it really is less important than the one before it. And make sure that you are covering only one topic, one concept, and one story in your release. Too many angles make a maze.

When you get to the end of the page: Stop! Even if you have more material, you should stop writing—unless you have a major announcement that you are sure will be page-one news. Then, and only then, should you write an additional page.

"I would never send out a press release longer than two pages," says Nancy Karen of United Way of Tri-State in New York City. "I always give a number to call for further information; if they're at all interested, they do call. You can add a fact sheet, but keep the press release, itself, short."

Using Newspaper Style

In addition to following the inverted-pyramid format, limit the length of your sentences and paragraphs. Long lines of typewritten copy get squashed into shorter lines in newspaper columns, so long paragraphs seem longer. With no paragraph breaks, copy becomes hard to read. So limit your graphs to four or five lines, which make about one column inch of newspaper copy. Short sentences are easier to read. Rarely make them longer than 20 words. Many of your graphs will contain only one sentence.

It is most important that a press release communicates efficiently. Every word counts. Go through your copy and see how many words you can cut out. You may be surprised to see that whole phrases can be blue-penciled, yet the meaning will become clearer. Cross out as many adjectives as you can. And be suspicious of the word *that*. It often isn't needed.

Always use the active voice. Say "Mayor Fernandez announced" instead of "it was announced by Mayor Fernandez." The active voice is a stronger statement and it takes fewer words.

Instead of writing "additional topics that will be discussed in depth during the course include futures, options, and the bond market," you should write "the course will also cover futures, options, and the bond market."

The most important part of a press release is the information. Sure, clear writing helps, but fancy phrases and verbal fireworks turn reporters off. Save them for PSAs and feature stories. "I don't need cute, catchy writing. I just need the straight poop," says the *Boise Statesman*'s Randy McCarthy.

Avoiding Jargon and Double-talk

Many people think that long words and technical jargon make their news releases more official. If you listen to radio news shows, you'll often hear government officials and corporate executives make statements that sound eloquent—until you stop to consider exactly what they've said. More often than not, you can't tell. They've probably used such words and phrases as *instructional day, integral remediations, noncompliance, discontinuance of service*—or even *discontinuity in the integrity of the epithelial tissue*. Believe it or not, that means *cut, sore* or *pimple*!

There are even fad phrases, such as *impact upon*, that are replaced in a few months or years by other, equally unclear, but popular, buzzwords.

When you're writing a press release, say what you mean. Avoid jargon. Try to use short, ordinary words. As author Rudolf Flesch points out, the more syllables there are per hundred words, the more difficult the writing is to understand. If you write as if you were talking to someone and you say what you mean, your press releases will be more direct and forceful.

If you absolutely must use a technical term or two, explain them in your release. One or two specialized words, clearly defined, can add color to your material.

Here are several examples and rewrites of double-talk and jargon from press releases:

According to Sandy Schlepper, supervisor, this profile will include vocational interests and aptitudes as well as an interpretation of this data in terms of specific jobs. In addition, core staff will pinpoint behavioral and attitudinal deficiencies that impact upon vocational feasibility and develop remediation procedures.

This can be more clearly written:

Job-training supervisor Sandy Schlepper says, "We find out what each person's work interests are. We test them to see what usable skills they have. Then we figure out what kinds of jobs each person would do best. If people in our program have behavior problems that get in the way of finding and keeping a job, we can help them change."

The graph below is long-winded and confusing. A rewrite, with more directness and punch, follows.

"An overflow crowd is anticipated," says Hometown Hardware's Marketing Director Ivor Gorodnikov, "because our expectation is that these home repair convocations zero in on problem areas that impact upon participants and generate enormous emotional involvement."

"We expect an overflow crowd," says Ivor Gorodnikov, who planned this home repair how-to series for Hometown Hardware. "These sessions zero in on problem areas. People get excited and involved because we show them simple techniques they can actually use. There's always a lot of enthusiasm."

Translate the next two examples into plain English. If you have difficulty, read Rudolf Flesch's book *The Art of Plain Talk* listed in Chapter 12.

Generally we first identify whether the complaint is legally cognizable under existing consumer law and advise the inquirer of the rights and protections so accorded. An attorney assigned to the complainant may identify relevant cases, statutory and regulatory provisions, and suggest alternative strategies for dispute resolution.

An examination of the cases processed this year indicates that the average time between the receipt of a request for a fugitive's return and the issuance of a warrant is approximately three weeks. However, to ensure that fugitives are returned to the jurisdiction from which they absconded at the earliest possible time, I have directed that all extradition matters be processed by my office within 30 days of the receipt of an extradition request, unless additional time is required to insure protection of individual rights. Inordinate delays in extradition cases result in the unnecessary expenditure of funds by Chelm State and its localities for the housing and maintenance of fugitives from other states.

Writing the Lead

A lead paragraph might look like the following:

Six members (who) of the Plains City Rotary Club were awarded blue ribbons (what) for the best pies and cakes (why) at the County Fair in Marigold Heights (where) today (when).

Another way to write this lead, using the same information, but more in keeping with newspaper style, is:

Blue ribbons for the best pies and cakes were awarded today at the County Fair in Marigold Heights to six members of the Plains City Rotary Club.

Be certain you don't include irrelevant material in your lead. In the example that follows, it's hard to tell what the news is. It's certainly not the cyclone of gatherings and parties; that's simply boasting.

Amid a whirlwind of high-level meetings and champagne receptions to formalize an agreement to exchange information on Codson's Disease in Brussels, Mrs. Wentworth Mason was presented with the Platinum Medallion, the country's highest honor, at the Villiers Hotel.

Recently elected as the first woman president of the Chelm Codson's Disease Foundation, Mrs. Mason has been instrumental in establishing working relationships with European organizations seeking a cure for the disease.

This lead could be rewritten as follows, to stress the news:

The first woman president of the Chelm Codson's Disease Foundation, Mrs. Wentworth Mason, was presented with the Platinum Medallion in Brussels yesterday.

The award, the highest recognition the Belgian government gives foreigners, is for Mrs. Mason's role in establishing working relations with European organizations seeking a cure for the disease. Codson's disease societies from seven countries signed agreements to exchange clinical information at a meeting just before the presentation.

Now let's look at a longer lead and its rewrite. The first two paragraphs sound more like rambling concert program notes than journalese:

Amanda Anderson, the exciting young sitarist and first American to be invited to perform on the Classic Sitar at the Circular Club series, the unique set of concerts featuring that enthralling Indian instrument, will play a wonderful program of traditional Indian classical music. It will include a premire of Chester U. Corfu's incredible Ganges Suite which is based on an Indian classical theme and was written especially for Ms. Anderson.

The concert will take place on March 1 at 5:30 P.M. in the Louisa Harding Holly Auditorium, named for the late patron of the arts, at 1055 River Avenue in Chelm. The sitar series is presented by the Center for Indian and American Exchange in cooperation with the Circular Club and Far East Instruments.

The rewrite is more effective, better organized, and written in journalistic style:

Sitarist Amanda Anderson will play a program of traditional Indian classical music at the Louisa Harding Holly Auditorium of the Circular Club, 1055 River Avenue, Chelm, on Sunday, March 1, 1992, at 5:30 P.M. For ticket information call 990-0006.

The program includes the Chelm premire of Chester U. Corfu's Ganges Suite, based on Indian classical themes. The piece was written especially for Anderson.

Anderson is the first American to perform in the Classic Sitar series at the Circular Club since it started In 1977. The sitar, a stringed Indian instrument dating back to the period before Christ, has a sound like a cross between a lute and a guitar.

The concerts are sponsored by the Center for Indian and American Exchange and Far East Instruments in cooperation with the Circular Club.

The following lead is indeed confusing:

The deaf are not being overlooked in the state's coordinated effort to alleviate problems for workers and others affected by the loss of an estimated 3,500 jobs in the closing of the Cord Rotor Plant in Chelm.

Are there deaf workers at the Cord Rotor Plant? Is that because the plant causes deafness, or do they just happen to work there? Why do deaf workers need special attention? There may be good reasons, but they're not in this paragraph.

The lead paragraphs below, on the other hand, immediately tell us the news:

After several years of intensive research, Saab-Scania AB of Sweden has developed a new and revolutionary system, APC— Automatic Performance Control—that can offer a fuel saving of up to 8 percent while at the same time boosting acceleration up to 20 percent.

The system also allows an engine to be run on fuels of different octane ratings without special adjustments.

Volume production of Saab Turbo engines with the APC system is expected to start in about a year.

Analyzing a Press Release

The following is a complete, detailed news release that attempts to present the information. But it's not clear enough, and it would be easy for a busy editor to miss some major points.

The Highway 138 asphalt recycling project completed in 1990 has been termed highly successful, with significant savings in much-needed highway funds and benefits in energy conservation and reduction of air and ground pollution, according to Waste Reduction Systems, Inc. and the Plains State Highway Bureau.

Instead of discarding 120 miles of deteriorated pavement, the PSHB reused it. The old asphalt was milled or planed off Highway 138, hauled to an asphalt plant where it was mixed with fresh stone and asphalt, and used again to repave inside and outside shoulders of a 16-mile stretch of the Highway. The finished product was a hot asphalt shoulder mixture.

"If milling was compared to placement of conventional leveling course methods on Highway 138, the savings for the entire project would have amounted to 22 billion British Thermal Units

(BTU) or 165,000 gallons of gasoline," reports G. C. Hobday, coordinator of the PSHB Engineering Staff.

"Approximately 14,000 tons of milled material from the old pavement was extended to 27,000 tons through recycling and was used to repave the shoulders," says Hobday. "In conservation of material resources, the combined savings were 2,900 tons of asphalt, or 712,000 gallons of gasoline and 55,700 tons of stone aggregates. Waste Reduction Systems, Inc. can be proud of its role here."

This type of project, according to PSHB officials, permitted the recovery of all of the asphalt and stone from the old pavement and produced a substantial saving because the cost of asphalt cementing material has risen dramatically. Bituminous concrete contains from 4.5 to 7 percent asphalt, a product of the crude-oil distillation process, so a high percentage of fuel also was conserved by recycling.

The project was environmentally significant because the entire removal and recycling process is smoke-free and does not pollute the atmosphere. It is also difficult to dispose of old road material due to the shortage of landfill space.

The Bureau, according to Hobday, is recommending that the recycling program be continued on other maintenance and reconstruction projects because of the success of the Highway 138 project.

The important news is buried in this release, under a lot of repetition, some unclear information, dull quotes, and confusing statistics. And the release is longer than it should be.

Let's examine it graph by graph:

Graph 1: The release starts with some vague statements. Who has termed this project highly successful? Who are *they*? The Plains State Highway Bureau, Waste Reduction Systems, Inc., or both? How are the two organizations related? What are *significant savings*? With such dramatic statistics available, this graph could be more forceful.

Graph 2: There are three problems here. First, the reader has to stop and figure out what PSHB means. An acronym or abbreviation should be introduced immediately after the full name, and set in parentheses. Second, the words *milled* or *planed* don't tell most readers what was done to the highway. And finally, an alert editor will wonder why the old asphalt had to be mixed with new asphalt.

Graphs 3 and 4: The quotes here are hardly lively. There's actually no reason to have quotes at all, except that Mr. Hobday wants his name in the paper. The use of undefined technical language like *conventional leveling course* obscures the main point: the project saved an enormous amount of money and materials. Finally, we don't understand why Waste Reduction Systems, Inc. should be proud of itself. The role it did play in this project needs to be explained.

Graph 5: This presents a puzzle. We were talking about asphalt, weren't we? Now, all of a sudden we're talking about bituminous concrete. Perhaps they are related, but few reporters, editors, or readers will know that.

Graph 6: The copy here assumes the reader knows that regular repaving methods pollute the air, and the relationship between the difficulty of disposing of old road material and the shortage of landfill sites.

Let's fix this release so it presents the important information clearly and forcefully. First we'll list the major points, in order of importance, and, unlike the original release, which discussed what was done first, we'll start with the results, because the results *are* the news:

1. The project saved 2,900 tons of asphalt and 55,700 tons of stone.
2. Asphalt is a petroleum product.
3. The project saved enough petroleum to refine 712,000 gallons of gasoline.
4. The process was smoke-free and did not pollute the air.
5. There was no need to dump old road material.
6. There are only two dump sites in the southern part of the state.
7. The recycled material would have filled one of the dumps to capacity and thus forced its closing.
8. Twenty miles of cracked and pitted pavement was scraped off Highway 138.
9. Fourteen thousand tons of old asphalt pavement was mixed with new asphalt and stone to give it added resiliency and strength.
10. The new mixture was used to repave the shoulders of Highway 138.

Assuming that it *is* issued by the Highway Bureau, and Waste Reduction Systems, Inc. was the contractor who handled the project, the rewritten release might look like the following. Notice that it now has a heading, as well:

February 18, 1991   Plains State Highway Bureau
FOR IMMEDIATE RELEASE   675 Euclid Highway
                                            Plains City 00002
With Art: Contact: Samuel Driver
1. Pile of old asphalt   Day: 674-1100
2. Asphalt scraping machine   Night: 997-9952
3. Graph of savings

who
    The Plains State Highway Bureau (PSHB) saved 2,900 tons of asphalt and 55,700 tons of stone by recycling old pavement that would previously have been dumped, according to G. C. Hobday, coordinator of the PSHB Engineering Staff.
    Since asphalt is a petroleum product, the Highway 138 Asphalt Recycling Project saved the equivalent of 712,000 gallons of gasoline. And, unlike traditional repaving methods, recycling asphalt doesn't produce any air pollution.
    Had the old pavement been discarded, it would have filled the Martinsville Dump to capacity, thereby closing one of the last two remaining dump sites in southern Plains.
    "Waste Reduction Systems, Inc., the contractor for this project, scraped 20 miles of cracked and pitted asphalt pavement off the surface of Highway 138. This old pavement was mixed with stone and new asphalt to give it body and resilience. The new mixture was used to repave 16 miles of shoulders on the highway. The traffic lanes of the highway were repaved with concrete, which stands up to heavy use better than asphalt," according to Hobday.
    "We're extremely pleased with the results of the Waste Reduction Systems, Inc. technology. Because this is a new process, we're still trying to figure out exactly how much money we saved. But it's more than 3 million dollars. From now on we'll recycle all our old asphalt pavement. It's just plain good sense," says Hobday.

###

A Model Press Release

The release below reads like a news story, which is exactly the point. A good release will sound as if it's been lifted from the newspaper. The release is in proper pyramid form, so you can make sense of the part you're reading here even though most of the original has been cut. It was written for the Permanent Citizens Advisory Committee to the Metropolitan Transit Authority of New York by attorney Michael Gerrard, a former newspaperman.

Fires in the New York City subway system have more than doubled in the past three years, and escape is being hindered by locked car doors, the Permanent Citizens Advisory Committee (PCAC) to the Metropolitan Transportation Authority revealed today.

There were 653 subway fires in June, 1980, or an average of 22 a day, up 218 percent over the 300 fires in June, 1977, the transit watchdogs reported.

"This growing peril to subway riders is caused chiefly by the cumulative effect of years of too little maintenance," said PCAC Chairman Michael Gerrard, an attorney and daily subway commuter.

At the same time, the Transit Authority (TA) is making it harder to escape fires. The front and back doors on the new R-44 and R-46 subway cars have long been locked, but riders could use the emergency door switches to escape. The TA just disconnected these switches, claiming maintenance problems.

The switches and the signs labeling them are still there, however, so passengers may flip them in vain, trapped inside smoke-filled cars until help arrives. Several such instances have already occurred. The locks also prevent passengers between stations from fleeing muggers or telling train crews of seriously ill riders.

###

Editing Your Release

Whenever you can, let your press release sit overnight before you try to rewrite it. You will be able to see the rough spots better the next day, and your editing task will be easier when you are 24 hours removed from writing the first draft.

As you rewrite, aim to vary your use of words. Watch out for excessive use of the same word, and pay attention to the beginnings of your graphs. If two or more of them start the same way, change them. There's nothing more boring than reading four paragraphs that begin, "Mr. Brian said."

Cross out as many adjectives as you can, and blue-pencil the word *that*. Think of yourself as a sculptor; the first draft is a nice hunk of stone, but you have to carve away extra material to create the smooth, flowing lines of a statue.

Look at all the names in your release. Are there any unusual spellings? If you're writing about Melissa Briwn, for example, most editors will assume you've misspelled Brown. Write a small "ok" above any name or word that appears to be wrong even though it's correct: Briwn.

After a certain point in your rewriting efforts, you reach the point of diminishing returns. If you find yourself trying to rewrite the rewrite of a rewrite, you've probably gone as far as you can. So if a small voice inside you says, "Hey! You're really finished," listen to it.

Checking for Accuracy

"Accuracy is the lifeblood of a newspaper," says Brian Youmatz of the *Framingham Middlesex News*. "If a publicist gets the facts wrong, and we use those wrong facts, it's our responsibility. If a publicist makes enough mistakes like that, I'll consider him unreliable, and I won't use his material."

Imagine what could happen if you misspell someone's name in your release. The journalist, working under pressure, doesn't have time to check. The story appears with the name spelled wrong, and the victim makes an angry call to the publication. The call is routed to the journalist, who squirms while he makes an apology. All the while he is wishing evil fates on your head, and when he sees another release from you, he may well tear it to bits.

At some of the smaller newspapers, your material will not be edited at all. According to Harry Cohn of the American Red Cross, "If it's a service story, if you're just telling people they can enroll in a first aid course or what they can do to avoid boating accidents, most weeklies will use those stories without any changes."

So, if you're tempted to be sloppy about your proofreading, don't be! A busy editor might just use your copy verbatim, and the spelling errors and grammatical mistakes in your release will grace the front page.

After your release is duplicated, proofread it once again before you mail it. If you find an error or two, all is not lost. You can make clear, handwritten corrections, and as long as you have no more than three corrected errors per page, your material is considered clean copy. Of course, your aim is to have no errors at all.

Correcting Errors

Despite all precautions, you may discover an error in a press release you've already sent out. You'll probably sit there feeling like someone is practicing macramé on your insides. Snap out of it! It's happened to all of us at least once. Get on the phone and call every reporter or editor you've sent the release to. Do not offer profuse apologies; a quick, matter-of-fact "sorry about that" is all that's in order. Then do the following:

- Indicate what the error was.
- Give the correct information.
- Send out a corrected version of the press release by the quickest means possible. Fax it if you already know the journalist doesn't mind. Or send it by messenger or overnight courier. Sure, the costs can add up, particularly if you have to contact many media outlets. But protecting your organization's reputation with the media is worth money, too.

"Don't try to correct if the story has appeared—it's too late at that point," advises Harry Cohn. "When it's in, it's in."

Fact Sheets

Suppose your solar energy resource center is about to issue a press release on a new program to help home-owners install solar water heaters. You have a mound of marvelous material to give to the press. You know that press releases should be limited to one page, but what about all that wonderful information? The answer to this dilemma is to use a fact sheet to round out your news release.

A fact sheet can run for several pages and include historical perspectives, anecdotes, and data. You get the best of both: a short press release that quickly gives reporters and editors the essence of your story, and material to do an in-depth article. Fact sheets should be well written, with short sentences and paragraphs, and wide margins. The name and telephone number of a contact person should always be at the top of the front page. Each page should end with a completed paragraph, and "MORE" typed several times across the bottom of the page. The last page should end with the numerals "30" or the number sign (###) typed several times across the bottom.

The following is a shortened version of a fact sheet put out for the Northeast Solar Energy Center by Joel Strasser, former director of Hill & Knowlton's Industrial and Scientific Communications Services. Notice the historical, anecdotal and factual information a journalist could use for an in-depth story, as well as the tight writing style, with short sentences and paragraphs.

Historical Perspectives on Solar Energy

The current need to expand solar energy applications and save oil is the latest manifestation of man's historical use of the sun's energy as a natural and abundant resource.

Here's a thumbnail sketch of some of the efforts over the years to harness the power of the sun:

■ In prehistorical times, cavemen sought south-facing caves as dwellings to take advantage of the sun's heat and light, as well as to protect themselves from northerly winds.

■ In warfare, King Solomon's vastly outnumbered troops blinded the eyes of an attacking Egyptian army by reflecting the sun off burnished shields, causing the Egyptians to destroy themselves by falling into a hidden abyss.

■ Later, legend describes how Archimedes successfully defended Syracuse by incinerating an attacking Roman fleet with a solar reflector which concentrated the sun's rays with polished brass onto the sails of the Roman galleys.

■ During the French Revolution, the great French chemist, Antoine Lavoisier, used the sun for research purposes, and developed solar furnaces. Curved glass discs were fastened together at their rims, with wine filling the space between to focus the sun's rays enough to attain temperatures of about 3,000°F.

These high temperatures were used to discover the nature of carbon and platinum. He also developed the science of the solar furnace by heating samples in a vacuum and in controlled atmospheres, using quartz containers.

- Solar pioneers also capitalized on one of the oldest uses of the sun—food preparation. August Mouchot demonstrated a solar cooker at the World Exhibition in Paris in 1878. His units were simple ones with glass lids to let in sunlight and trap heat inside.

- Distillation of water became another practical way to use the sun. In 1871, a huge solar still was built by an American engineer, Charles Wilson, to convert locally available salt water into potable form at a Chilean copper mine high in the Andes.

Covering nearly an acre in size, the still could produce over 4,000 gallons of water daily. And like today's solar stills, it consisted of a shallow basin painted with waterproof black compound covered with a glass roof and shaped like an inverted and flattened "V."

- At the turn of the century, solar experimenters in the United States focused on the sun for pumping water. The most spectacular solar engines were those built in Arizona by an English inventor, A. G. Eneas. He obtained backing from Boston financiers to build a giant solar concentrator to generate steam at pressures up to 150 psi [pounds per square inch], to pump water at the rate of 1,400 gallons per minute.

- Solar water heaters also interested many inventors, and their research resulted in the technology existing today. Previously, these heaters were developed mainly for use in hot baths, and during World War I many large installments were made in Army cantonments. Thousands of these ther-

– more –   – more –

mosyphon water heaters are currently being used in Australia, Israel and Japan with a few in California and Florida.

Feature Stories

A news release is straightforward, with no fancy writing. It must contain the who, when, where, why, what, and how. Let a news release sit for a few days, and it is no longer newsworthy.

On the other hand, a feature story, though it must also be newsworthy in the broad sense of the word, is relatively timeless. It can run in today's paper, or it can be used next week. That's why feature material is sometimes called *evergreen*—it won't fade.

Unlike a news story, a feature can have a point of view. And it usually isn't written in inverted pyramid format. You can write news stories and features about the same material, increasing your chances of successful placement. The feature story is a valuable publicity tool and an ideal vehicle for helping people understand how to choose, buy and use your product or service.

The "angle" is the most important attribute of a feature story, which usually highlights an intriguing or unknown facet of an organization, product, cause, service or individual. While a feature may be related to breaking news, its appeal comes from its interesting perspective or unusual point of view, and it often helps bring dull facts and dry statistics to life. Unlike a hard news story, it doesn't have to be objective, and a feature story is often longer than a hard news story on the same subject.

Some Examples of Excellent Feature Stories

Drawing on a copyrighted article by Dr. Albert R. Milan in *Family Circle* magazine, Dan Schlesinger wrote the following feature for Family Circle Press Service. You might ask why a magazine would want to "give away" its material. The goal is to get potential subscribers to associate the magazine with interesting information, so they are more responsive when they receive a subscription promotion or see the publication on sale. A woman concerned about her health who reads an article based on this release in her daily paper may turn to *Family Circle* for health advice in the future.

A woman can feel the difference between harmless and possibly cancerous lumps in her breast as easily as she can feel the difference between the skin over her eyeball and the skin on her nose. That's the basis of a simple "eye-and-nose" test featured in a current *Family Circle* magazine how-to article, "The Best Breast Self-Examination."

Developed by Dr. Albert Milan, attending obstetrician and gynecologist at Union Memorial Hospital in Baltimore, this test is part of a comprehensive breast self-examination, described step-by-step in *Family Circle,* that only takes 10 minutes per month. The *Family Circle* feature is excerpted from the *Breast Self-Examination Book* published by Workman Publishing Co.

Women should examine their breasts once a month by using a "palpation" (examine by touch) technique, insists *Family Circle.* Palpate by using the flat surfaces of two or more fingers and gently press them downward so the skin is moved along with the fingertips over the underlying structures.

Studies have shown that women who examine their breasts once a month greatly increase their chances of detecting a cancerous growth early enough to effect a cure. The chances of a complete recovery are 85 percent to 90 percent if a malignant lump is discovered while it is still localized in the breast tissue itself. The cure rate plummets to 40 percent if the cancer has spread to other organs.

Here's how to give yourself the "eye-and-nose" test to determine if you have harmless lumps, or attached, possibly harmful ones:

Gently move the eyelid over the eyeball's surface, and you'll feel how slippery the eyeball is and how the eyelid glides smoothly over it. Then pinch your eyelid to lift it away from the eyeball's surface. Notice how it lifts freely and easily. These are

– more –   – more –

similar sensations to the ones you'll feel from touching normal milk glands and ducts of the breast and harmless, slippery breast cysts as well.

Now place the ball of your fingertip on the end of your nose, and try to move the nasal skin with your finger without moving the tip of your nose. It won't go, notes the article. It is fixed, and the tip of the nose moves with the skin. The next step is to try to lift the skin on the tip of your nose. Pinch it between your finger-tips—the same way you did with your eyelid. It can't be lifted. This is a very important differentiating feature, says *Family Circle*. If you feel any lump in your breast that doesn't move, that is attached to the skin or underlying structures and above which you can't lift the skin, it should be examined by your physician immediately.

Not all fixed lumps are malignant, so don't panic if you find one. But don't put off seeing your doctor. Also see your doctor about lumps situated deep in the breast tissue. These are difficult for you to differentiate by self-examination.

###

The following business feature story was written and released by John Guiniven for International Paper Company. It was picked up by about 50 editors across the United States.

A Good Business Letter Can Mean Money in the Bank

NEW YORK, N.Y.—The business letter, a basic and important form of communication, is in trouble.

That's the opinion of Malcolm Forbes. And he should know. As president and editor-in-chief of the respected *Forbes Magazine*, he receives over 10,000 business letters a year.

Most of them are "mundane," he says, and many others are "stultifying if not stupid."

– more –   – more –

Declining reading and writing skills have hurt all forms of correspondence. But bad business letters are more than literary outrages—they can have a dollar-and-cents impact.

In an effort to improve them, Mr. Forbes has added his expertise to an ambitious communication program sponsored by International Paper Company [IP]. The program, titled "The Power of the Printed Word," is aimed at improving the overall reading and writing skills of young Americans through a series of "how-to" ads and supporting classroom materials.

The ads will run in magazines reaching the youth market, and will include comedian Bill Cosby, who holds a doctorate in education, on "How to Read Faster"; *Reader's Digest* editor-in-chief Edward Thompson, "How to Write Clearly"; actor-lexicologist Tony Randall, "How to Improve Your Vocabulary"; and Mr. Forbes, "How to Write a Business Letter."

In his ad kicking off the program, Mr. Forbes notes that "a good business letter can get you a job interview, get you off the hook, or get you money."

He says the most important step is taken "before you write your letter. Know what you want, and write it down. List the major points you want to get across. If answering a letter, keep it in front of you while you write and check the points that need answering."

Among his other suggestions are:

- Be brief. Keep the letter to one page, if possible, with the first paragraph telling precisely what your letter is about.
- Be natural. Imagine the reader sitting across the desk from you. Write the way you talk, and avoid business jargon.
- Lean heavier on nouns and verbs, lighter on adjectives.
- Make it perfect. No typos, no misspellings, no factual errors.

In explaining why IP is spending $1 million on "The Power of the Printed Word" this year, chairman and chief executive officer J. Stanford Smith says, "Inadequate reading and writing skills among young people are a concern to all Americans.

      – more –   – more –

"As a company with an historic commitment to the printed word and a significant stake in the future of printing and publishing, International Paper decided to act on that concern," he added.

Public relations executive Ravelle Brickman prepared the following feature story for the Neighborhood Cleaners Association.

New Pamphlet Points Out Perils of Poorly Made Spring Clothing—Drycleaners Urge Consumers to Buy Carefully, Know & Exercise Their Legal Rights

With the cost of clothing zooming out of sight, it pays to know what you're buying—and to buy clothes that will not only look good on the rack, but will continue looking good, on you, after being washed or drycleaned.

Sounds obvious, doesn't it?

But for the average consumer—the John or Jane Doe without a Ph.D. in fabric technology—figuring out what will last and what won't is not as simple as it sounds.

Reading the labels helps. But not always. According to Bill Seitz, Executive Director of the Neighborhood Cleaners Association, a group representing 3,200 drycleaners in nine eastern states, "A lot of garments are mislabeled. They'll say 'hand wash only,' when the garment really should be drycleaned. Or they'll say 'dryclean only,' when, in fact, the garment can't be cleaned at all."

One solution is to be armed with the new edition of "HOW TO BUY AND CARE FOR YOUR CLOTHES," a pamphlet published twice yearly and available free from the NCA as part of its consumer education program.

Judging by the NCA booklet, this spring's fashions present more problems than ever before. Here are some of the things a smart shopper should beware of:

– more –   – more –

Shrinking Violets—Cotton Jersey and Cotton Knits

100% cotton knit dresses and tops are very popular today. They're cool, they're comfortable, and they're nearly always labeled "washable." Trouble is, cotton knit shrinks. And unless the fabric has undergone proper preshrinkage treatment (rare in the case of imports), your brand new T-shirt dress or top will come out of the wash at least two sizes smaller, and so tight that even a beanpole would be embarrassed.

Passing Prints

You've heard the expression "color fast." It applies to prints as well as solids. If a dye isn't "fast," it will run, bleed, travel all over the place or just plain disappear. This is a particularly serious problem with prints, since the pattern may be precisely what attracted you to the garment in the first place. Check the reverse side of the fabric to see if the print goes all the way through. A surface print (such as a flocked or painted design) is one that is literally pasted on, and it is bound to fade away—along with your hopes, dreams and clothing dollars—in the course of washing, cleaning or normal everyday wear.

Impermanent Pleats

Pleated skirts are the rage—in more ways than one. Many pleats are so transient that even a single washing or cleaning will banish them forever—leaving you in rage and your skirt outrageously pleatless. If you want pleats, make sure they're permanent: the fiber content must be at least 55 percent nylon, acetate or polyester. Avoid rayon blends and intricate Origami-style fluting.

Fading Glories

Designer jeans (even though they shouldn't) are designed to fade—especially if, as is often the case, they come in deep solid colors. That is because they're often made of denim or duck cloth, and most dyes cannot penetrate those tight weaves. Faded jeans are fine, but not if you wanted— and paid for—designer colors.

– more –   – more –

Sequins, Beads and Glued-on Glitter

All that glitters is not gold. Some of it is poorly dyed plastic. And a lot of it isn't even sewn on. That's why most of the trimmings that brighten "Disco" outfits are bound to lose color, melt, curl or fall off in water or drycleaning solvent. Anything, in fact, that's glued-on will come unglued in cleaning. Make sure those sequins and beads are sewn (by hand) and confirm that they're colorfast.

Silk—Pure but Perishable

If you've ever wondered why synthetics were invented, it's because silk, while pretty, is highly perishable.

The dyes bleed easily and almost anything—water, perfume, deodorant—will cause color loss or a ringlike stain. Worst of all, perspiration causes the fabric to rot.

The solution? Buy silk only for "special" occasions.

Buy loose-fitting styles (tight-fitting silk tends to split). Avoid the very thin fabrics (look for something with weight and body), use underarm pads—and don't cry if, after normal wear and drycleaning, it shreds or fades away. Glamor costs.

Know Your Rights

Okay. You've read the warnings, studied the labels, bought carefully and followed the care instructions exactly. What happens if the garment still proceeds to fade, pill, melt, shrink, stretch or just plain fall apart?

The answer, according to the NCA, is, "Take it back."

As a consumer, you have a right, by law, to expect every garment you buy to be serviceable. If it isn't, you're entitled to a refund.

Too few consumers, the organization feels, are aware of their rights. And fewer still bother to exercise them.

"If more people took the trouble to demand a refund, the problems would disappear. The stores would stop carrying poorly made clothes, and manufacturers," Seitz predicts, "would shape up fast."

– more –   – more –

To help turn that prediction into a reality, the NCA has included the "Consumer's Bill of Rights" in the spring-summer edition of "HOW TO BUY AND CARE FOR YOUR CLOTHES." Also included in the pamphlet are helpful hints on home stain removal, do's and don'ts for wardrobe care and a guide to garment life expectancy.

For a free copy of the pamphlet, drop in at your local NCA cleaner or send a stamped, self-addressed envelope to NCA, 116 East 27th Street, New York, NY 10016.

###

Fillers

If you've toured your local newspaper's offices and plant and watched the makeup people assembling pages from copy and advertisements, you may have wondered where they get the material they use to fill in empty spaces at the last minute. Some newspapers and magazines use syndicates that provide filler, or their own reporters and editors write brief blurbs that are kept ready to fill in news holes. But some of that filler material also comes from publicity people.

There are large publications that almost never use filler. They edit carefully, and their makeup people are precision artisans who take a great deal of care and time to make sure there is no need for filler. Other papers, small and large, might not have enough staff or resources to do that, and their editors may welcome a sheet of one- and two-paragraph items from you.

Before you spend any time writing a sheet of fillers, ask your target publications if this sort of material is of interest to them. If they are at all interested, it's time for a brainstorming session. Gather a group of your staffers, members, employees, or colleagues and make a list of brief items about your business, industry, cause, organization, club, product, service, association, or committee that will amuse, interest, or help the newspaper's readers. Let the list sit overnight. Then take your blue pencil and mercilessly cut out any dull idea. Try to imagine a reader coming across the information for the first time. Will he say "Wow I didn't know that!"? Or, "That's good to know!"? Or, "I think I'll try that little trick next time"? If you're not sure, drop the item.

Each filler should be 100 words or less, and 50 words is probably the best length. Several 25-word items might also be useful. Fillers should be in paragraph form, double-spaced, with wide margins. You can type several of them on a page. Following are three examples of interesting filler items. The first comes from the National Multiple Sclerosis Society, and the last two were written by Dan Schlesinger for Family Circle Press Service.

An estimated 500,000 people in this country alone suffer from multiple sclerosis and closely related disorders. That is more people than live in the city of Seattle, or Denver, or Pittsburgh, or Atlanta, or Cincinnati.

To prevent the tell-tale shine and crease from a previous hem when you're lengthening a garment, try this technique from the "Reader's Idea Exchange" in *Family Circle* magazine. Apply white vinegar to the wrong side of the fabric and steam press. Both shine and crease will disappear.

Within a year after having an abortion, most women have few regrets or guilts, according to the "Here's News in Medicine" column in the current *Family Circle* magazine. The magazine cites a recent follow-up study of 63 women who had abortions. Twelve months afterward, more than 75 percent had positive attitudes towards themselves and the event. More than one-third noted that having an abortion had been a positive learning experience that helped them to cope better with other problems in life.

Letters to the Editor

"Letters to the editor sections of newspapers are highly read. They are not used by publicists as much as they could or should be," says public relations executive Richard Weiner.

Although editors get dozens of letters daily, many papers make it a point to publish as many of them as possible. According to a survey in the *Masthead, The Detroit Free Press* runs about 20 percent of the letters it receives, the *Syracuse Post-Standard* and the *Fresno Bee* each run about half of theirs, and the *News-Journal* in Wilmington, DE, tries to run them all. In other words, newspapers take these letters seriously.

Always address your letter to "Dear Editor." If you start with "Dear Sir," and the editor is a woman, she may decide that you're not really writing to her.

Letters to the editor should be short—a maximum of three to five paragraphs. Sentences should be concise. Make only one point per letter.

If your letter is about a controversial situation, start with the name of your organization and the purpose of the message. Your next paragraph should convey some brief background material. Your opinion should come in the third paragraph, and the concluding paragraph tells your readers what you want them to do.

A typical letter to the editor might look like the following:

I am writing for the Plains City Library Council. We are concerned about the effects of inflation on our public library's budget.

During the past three years, the budget for the Plains City Public Library has been held to a bare-bones minimum of $750,000 per year, but book prices have increased an average of 17 percent yearly. That means our library can buy only half as many books as it could in 1988.

That's a disaster for Plains City. Business people can't find the information they need, students can't complete assignments, and do-it-yourselfers can no longer count on the library for the latest how-to books, at the very time when inflation has caused an unprecedented demand for them at the library.

There is a possible solution, however. If the City Council adds a $400,000 yearly library tax to the cable television proposal now being considered, the library could have a generous budget. The tax could not be passed on to subscribers, and the franchise holder would still earn a generous return on investment. I urge you to tell your Councilman to vote for Measure 19, and provide this much needed help for our library.

Sincerely yours,

Urhan Artebedian
President, Plains City Library Council

It is also possible to write letters to the editor to clarify misconceptions about or inaccurate coverage of your business or product. In fact, journalists expect you to do this.

For example, Jim Stott, the *Calgary Herald's* ombudsman, who wrote in the *Masthead*, explains that "The main avenue of rebuttal for readers who disagree with *Herald* editorials or columns is the letters page. The paper employs a full-time letters editor . . ."

It's wise to briefly mention the misconception or inaccuracy. Then spend the bulk of the letter presenting the correct information. Your last paragraph should draw a conclusion or ask for an action. Once again, limit yourself to between three and five paragraphs. Here's an example:

Dear Editor:

I'd like to allay a common fear, expressed in these pages last week, that the noise from widgets can cause hearing loss.

In an evaluation last year by the Industrial Safety Research Center of Central State University, 95 types of electric widgets were rated for noise output. Sound levels were measured with state-of-the-art electronic instruments.

All of them, including our complete line of six models, tested at under 70 decibels, even when running at high speed. A thunderstorm is louder than that! That's why our state's industrial safety code lists electric widgets in the totally safe category, with no protective devices needed by users.

Please let your readers know that electric widgets can sound raucous—so can teenagers—but they're not dangerously loud. They're real time-savers. And they're totally safe. Thank you.

Sincerely yours,

J. Maria Abogado, CEO
Arizona Electric Widget Corporation

Under special circumstances, you can also use letters to the editor to get your product mentioned. A letter like the one below would never appear on the editorial page of a daily newspaper, but the paper's home improvements editor might run it. And it would stand a good chance in a special interest magazine for home handypeople. Notice how carefully the product message is mixed in. Take away the product name, and the information won't be complete, since most editors and readers won't know how to find a soap with no moisture content.

Dear Editor:

I'd like to share a tip that will help home handypeople drive screws quickly by hand, even in hard wood like oak.

Simply take a bar of bath soap, make sure it's absolutely dry, and rub the threads of each screw on it. The coating of soap will lubricate the threads—and the screws will be much easier to turn.

Use a high grade soap with no moisture content, like Brandex, because even a tiny amount of moisture will swell the wood fibers and rust steel screws, causing possible problems later on.

Jason T. MacSweeney, Product Manager
Brandex Soap Division,
Conglomerate Household Products, Inc.

Checklist—Writing for the Press

1. Is your press release neatly typed on 8 1/2-by-11-inch plain white bond paper?
2. Does your release include the name, address, and telephone number of your business or organization, the name of the contact person, the date, the words "for immediate release," and a brief description of any photos?
3. Have you included a nighttime telephone number? Will you have someone at that number ready to respond to calls and answer questions?

4. Have you dated the release a day or two ahead of the esti-mated arrival at the editor's desk?

5. If you are asking editors to hold the release, have you in-cluded the words "for release after . . ." and a date?

6. Have you decided whether to include a headline on the release?

7. If you do include a headline, does it summarize the story *and* generate interest?

8. Have you decided if you want to include a headline on the envelope?

9. Have you left at least two inches blank at the top of your release?

10. Are the lines in your release between 50 and 60 characters long?

11. Is your entire release double-spaced?

12. Are your graphs indented ten spaces?

13. Do your lines end with complete words?

14. Have you made a list of all the points you want to cover?

15. Have you listed them in priority order?

16. Have you included all the *w*s and the *h*?

17. Are the most important points covered first, and the least important last?

18. If your release runs more than one page, can you cut it, or cover some material in a fact sheet or backgrounder in-stead?

19. If you have a two-page release, does the first page end with a complete graph? Have you typed "MORE" across the bottom of the page at least three times?

20. Does the second page have a heading to identify it?

21. Have you ended your release with the digits "30" or the number sign (###)?

22. Are you using more short words than long words?

23. Do you let your releases sit overnight before you start edit-ing them?

24. Have you cut out as many words as possible from your re-lease, especially adjectives and the word *that*?

25. Have you avoided the passive voice?

26. Have you translated jargon and technical words into every-day language?

27. If you have to use one or two technical terms, have you defined them?

28. Have you cut out fancy phrases and verbal fireworks?

29. Are most of your sentences fewer than 20 words long?

30. Are your paragraphs short, with an average of 4–5 lines?

31. Have you checked to make sure you don't have two or more graphs that start with the same words?

32. Have you avoided repeating the same words or phrases?

33. Have you double-checked all the information in your release to make sure it's accurate?

34. Have you written in *ok* above any unusual spellings?

35. Have you used your word-processor's spell-checker, or have you checked spelling carefully?

36. If it is important for readers to call you, is your telephone number in the first or second graph?

37. Did you proofread the release again after it was duplicated?

38. Do you understand the difference between hard news on the one hand, and human interest, feature, or evergreen material on the other?

39. If you discovered an error after the release was sent out, have you issued a correction to every journalist it was sent to?

40. Are your filler items fewer than 100 words long and preferably around 50? Are they in paragraph form, double-spaced with a wide margin, and typed on one side of the page only?

41. Have you addressed your letter to "Dear Editor"?

42. Does your letter to the editor focus on only one issue?

43. Is it limited to 3 to 5 paragraphs?

44. If it's about a controversial situation, have you identified your organization, stated your purpose, included brief background material, given your opinion, and asked for action, in that order?

45. If you're writing to clarify misconceptions, have you focussed on the correct information and then drawn a conclusion?

46. If you're trying to get your product mentioned in a letter to the editor, have you entwined your product's name in really useful information?

CHAPTER FIVE

Getting into Print

D espite the rumors of the triumph of television over the printed word, American newspapers are alive and kicking daily in more than 1,600 American cities. In addition, there are over 8,000 weekly papers and more than 6,000 consumer, trade and business magazines published in the United States. The magazine industry in America is booming. According to *O'Dwyer's PR Services Report*, there were 584 new magazines published in 1989.

American newspapers range from weeklies with one staff member and a few thousand readers, to New York City's *Daily News*, bought by more than a million people each day. There are national newspapers read from coast to coast, such as the *Los Angeles Times*, the *Wall Street Journal*, the *Christian Science Monitor*, and *USA Today*. Some papers, such as the *Minneapolis Star-Tribune*, read in Minnesota and parts of Wisconsin, Iowa, and the Dakotas, serve as regional publications. Others, such as the *Arkansas Democrat,* are read in most parts of that state. And of course, there are the neighborhood, small-town, ethnic, foreign language, college, and special interest newspapers, too.

Each kind of newspaper appeals to a different audience, and each approaches stories differently. The large metropolitan daily, with circulation in the suburbs as well as the inner city, may not carry much information about limited interest topics such as your scuba equipment store's new schedule of diving classes. But neighborhood weeklies will probably print your entire press release, and they may ask for additional material about instructors from their community. Each type of paper has a different focus, looks for a different angle, and reaches a different audience.

There might be an instance, however, in which a small business, like a dive shop, could receive much broader coverage. Let's suppose that the shop discovered and encouraged a couple of budding young inventors. With your backing, they have developed a surprisingly simple tankless diving system that uses artificial gills to gather dissolved oxygen directly from the water. The system has been tested and tried, and you've been granted a patent for it. Both of the inventors, a Hispanic girl and a white boy, are still in high school.

This is national news, and a *Big City Morning Star* science reporter will be most receptive to your announcement. He'll want to interview the inventors and get the complete story from a scientific and technical point of view. The *Star*'s education writer, on the other hand, will probably want to write a story about how the youngsters mastered advanced biophysical engineering principles at a time when so many students can't handle basic math and science.

The neighborhood newspaper might want to run a feature article profiling the youngsters, their families, and their ties to the area. And a Hispanic paper in your region could do a story about the inter-cultural friendship involved. This is just one example of how an organization that *seems* to have limited appeal can get coverage in large-circulation publications. We'll explore other options and methods in this chapter.

Knowing Your Newspapers

If you've never done newspaper publicity before, you may feel that you have to get your material in a big-city daily. Sure, that's nice, but it's hard to do. And it's not the only way to go. Don't underestimate the power of small community-oriented papers. "If we want reader response," says Harry Cohn of the American Red Cross, "those community newspapers are much more valuable than the large dailies. People trust the credibility of their local editor. If we are looking for funds or volunteers or we're trying to promote courses, we find we get much greater response from community newspapers."

When you do want to submit your publicity to a daily paper, you need to know exactly which editor or reporter to approach—either by name or job title. A release about a Jewish Book Week program will be wasted on the theater and film reporter. And, although the business editor might be personally interested in your diving classes, he will not write a story about them unless there's a business angle.

Compiling a Press List

As you learn how to work with the press, your first step is to make a list of those publications that will be interested in your business or organization. See Chapter 12 for an extensive list of media directories. You should also consult your local Yellow Pages to see if there are any new publications that haven't yet been listed in the directories.

Analyzing Newspapers

Newspaper policies vary widely, so you should try to read all the newspapers on your list for several weeks—or even months—and observe the kind of news they print. Are all the releases from community groups put on the family living page? Which papers have Community Events Calendars? Is there a reporter at the *Evening Moon* who specializes in feature stories about local people? Which reporter's by-line usually appears on stories about small businesses? What kinds of businesses get short blurbs, and which organizations have two-column spreads with pictures? What types of products are featured in the home and family living sections? Asking yourself questions such as these, and writing down your observations will help you understand which papers will be most likely to use your material.

Don't be unwilling to send your release to the *Morning Star,* even if they've only printed news from the competition, or the "other side of the tracks." Some papers will be eager for news from areas they haven't covered, some won't. But you'll never know unless you give it a try.

"Most newspapers have policies on what they'll print, and a call to the city editor could probably get you a copy if it's in written form, or a brief description if it's not. While I don't see anything wrong with sending material that doesn't conform to that policy, don't expect that it will be printed," advises Sylvia Smith of the *Fort Wayne Journal-Gazette*.

Taking a Newspaper Tour

If your local daily offers guided tours of its plant and offices, bring your note pad and be guided. You'll begin to understand how the paper works and who is responsible for what. Ask the promotion director about tours. He can also tell you if the paper has free publicity seminars for nonprofit and community organizations.

On the tour, you'll probably meet the city editor first. She is the most important person you'll work with, since she is responsible for all local news in the city where the paper is published. If you live in a suburb or another city, you may work with the local bureau of the newspaper instead of the city editor.

As your tour continues, make sure to do the following:

■ Make a list of all the editors and beat reporters. You will want to know the names of the reporters and editors handling areas important to your business, industry, organization or special interest group, since you will usually work directly with them. Here is a list of some typical specialty areas at a large metropolitan daily:

Art	Movies
Books	Music
Business	News
Dance	Real Estate
Editorial	Science
Education	Society
Entertainment (Criticism)	Sports
Entertainment (News)	Suburban Affairs
Events Calendar	Sunday Editor
Fashion	Television
Features	Theater
Food	Travel
Foreign Affairs	Women's Page
Home and Garden	

■ Ask if you can observe the makeup people at work. These are the folks with jigsaw puzzle minds who build completed pages from articles and advertisements. Although many of them now work with computers, the basic process involves trimming articles to fit tight space or calling for filler for that empty space on page four, top left. Watch them at work, and you will understand why your release may get cut in the middle. Once you see that process, you'll be more able to write material that communicates the essentials despite drastic surgery. This will endear you to the newspaper staff.

■ Ask your tour guide if the newspaper has a style sheet. This is a manual, ranging from a single page to a pamphlet, that sets standards for style and usage. If you can get your own copy of the style sheet, it will help you write more professional news releases.

■ If the paper does not have a style sheet or won't give you a copy, ask if it is a member of Associated Press (AP) or subscribes to United Press International (UPI). Both wire services issue stylebooks. Use the stylebook of the wire service your local daily is associated with.

■ Find out if the paper has a handbook for community groups and small businesses. This explains exactly what the newspaper wants when your organization gives it publicity material.

■ If you're involved with a nonprofit or community organization, inquire about public service advertising. At many newspapers you will get a blank look, shrugged shoulders, and a "nope, never heard of it," but there are some papers that add a small surcharge to commercial advertising. This creates a fund for public service advertising by nonprofit groups.

Approaching Reporters and Editors

You've just completed your survey of newspapers and magazines that you think will make good outlets for your publicity, and you're surprised that there are so many. Now all you have to do is get acquainted with all those reporters and editors, tell them about your fantastic products, superior services, or worthy causes, and they'll immediately start beating a path to your door, seeking out stories. Right? Well, not quite.

In addition to the general advice given in Chapter 2 about approaching the media, there are some things you should know about the likes and dislikes of newspaper and magazine people. We'll start our discussion with newspapers, and cover magazines later on in this chapter.

In some smaller towns and rural areas reporters will indeed seek you out, and your relationship may be quite casual and informal. But in larger urban and suburban areas, most reporters will not want to talk with you until you have a concrete story for them. "Have something in hand when you approach an editor," says Mary Jane O'Neill of the New York Association for the Blind.

Many reporters prefer that you approach them in writing first. "That way I can make some judgments about the validity of the material and decide how much time to spend talking with her when she calls me," says journalist Nancy Dunn. If a reporter has had a chance to look at your written material before you call, she will be more familiar with your story, and the discussion will be more fruitful and to the point.

Even at the smaller newspapers, even if you know reporters well, be careful about dropping in without an appointment. If you show up unexpectedly to deliver a press release, be brief and don't try to make a special case for your press release; let it stand on its own merits.

"There are many people who simply take the opportunity to drop it off, say 'Hi,' and leave, without trying to initiate a discussion about it or taking too much of my time. What is annoying is when a publicist brings in a press release and makes an obvious effort to get more favorable play for the story," says Sylvia Smith of the *Fort Wayne Journal-Gazette*.

Journalist Leslie O'Bergin puts it this way: "I personally detest having people drop in on me out of nowhere, unless something amazing has happened to them. It interrupts me. Just because I happen to be sitting at my desk does not mean that I am waiting for someone to come by and talk with me, especially if it could take place by mail or phone. Phone gives me the alternative of saying I'll call back. Or I can ask for written material. I really believe in the phone.

"On the other hand, she says, "if the publicist stops by with a well-written press release, makes a brief pitch, waits while I eyeball it, and then leaves when I'm finished, that's OK, except at deadline time. And I don't like people who attempt to intimidate or guilt trip me into writing an article. It hurts their chances immeasurably."

Joining Professional Organizations

A good way to build better working relationships with journalists without disturbing them at their desks is to join professional organizations for communicators. Says Sylvia Smith, "One thing that improves my relationship with PR people is to be involved with them in Women in Communications." There are publicists Smith gets to know through this group who she wouldn't otherwise meet. And that gives her a sense of how straightforward and trustworthy they are.

According to Sharon Haver, account executive at Public Relations Aids in New York, "Women in Communications not only has given me the opportunity to make valuable contacts on a personal level, but also provides insight from media professionals through lectures, round tables, and general open discussions. This networking builds vital personal working relationships."

The names and addresses of several professional organizations are listed in Chapter 12.

Contacting News Bureaus

Larger daily newspapers, and many large magazines, too, have news bureaus in major cities, where staff reporters cover news of interest to the readership back home. According to public relations executive Richard Weiner, news bureaus have also sprung up in the suburbs as the big-city dailies strive to cover suburban stories and develop a broader readership. These bureaus often have specialists in such fields as business, fashion, restaurants, and cultural activities.

Contacting news bureaus directly has several advantages. If an out-of-town paper is involved, you'll save money on telephone calls, and you'll be able to get your material to the bureau more quickly than if you mailed it to the main office. You'll have a better chance to develop a working relationship with a staff member at a small bureau than you would at a distant main office.

So if you're working with out-of-town or suburban newspapers, find out if they have bureaus, where the bureaus are located, and what their policies are. If there are only one or two papers involved, you can call them and ask. But if you're working with large numbers of publications, you'll want to consult *News Bureau Contacts,* by Richard Weiner, which is listed under media directories in Chapter 12.

Working with Reporters and Editors

If you are going to have a major event that will interest several reporters at a large paper, ask if the city editor or your favorite reporter will serve as the newspaper's coordinator for coverage. Emphasize that this will avoid duplicate coverage. If, for example, you supply publicity material to both the science and education reporters, and they do similar spreads on your Lions' Club science fair for high school students, the reporters will be furious, and you will have a hard time getting any further publicity from that paper. "It's a bad move," says Larry Kramer of the *Trenton Times*. "I think if any publicist is going to do that, he ought to let each reporter know that someone else is being clued on it. Because if both stories actually ran in the paper, it would be an embarrassment. And the last thing a publicist wants to do is put an editor in a spot where he's embarrassed. If a publicist did that and both stories ran, it would be bad times."

Even if you have two entirely different stories, with different angles and information, if they're about the same event, product or service, you must let each reporter know that another journalist at his paper is working on that material. Suppose that there has been a sudden surge in shoplifting in your community, and your merchant's association has decided to work with two angles. You've written a press release with information from your study of the typical shoplifter, pointing to the need for more parental responsibility. And you've written another story about the economic effects of shoplifting on neighborhood merchants. The family living page editor is interested in the first approach, while the business writer is open to the second. Even though they are different stories, with different news pegs, you'd better tell both reporters exactly what you're doing. They will compare notes. And if they think that both stories stand on their own merits as separate articles, they will write and run both of them.

If you're sending a release to a reporter and a duplicate copy to the editor of an events calendar, label each release, indicating who else has gotten it. By the same token, do not send duplicate copies of the same release to more than one bureau of the same publication unless you have a *very* good reason for doing so—and you inform everyone involved. Otherwise you may begin to arouse suspicions that you're trying to put one past the editors.

Timing and Deadlines

In this section we will discuss general rules about deadlines, but you should also get specific deadline times from every publication you work with.

For weeklies appearing on Wednesdays or Thursdays, the previous Friday at noon is often the cutoff point. Morning papers usually need their material by two o'clock the previous afternoon. Although there are fewer evening papers published each year, you may still be working with one of them. So you should know that evening papers often have morning deadlines. For special sections of the Sunday paper, the deadline can be as early as the previous Wednesday.

If your area still has both morning and evening papers, consider that an early-morning release time will meet the deadlines for both papers, as well as the evening TV news broadcasts. Or, you might want to rotate, with alternate releases timed for the morning and evening papers' deadlines.

On hard news stories of major importance appearing first in the morning papers, some publicists rewrite their releases, giving the evening editors a new angle, or additional information. For example, you could even plan a special event schedule that maximizes your press coverage. If you know that the *Evening Moon* runs color on the front page and your Rotary Club Midsummer Family Carnival includes launching three dozen hot-air balloons that will fill the sky with patches of pastel, make sure you launch those balloons early in the day, so you meet the *Moon*'s deadline.

Perhaps you're running a conference for utility executives on techniques for neutralizing citizen opposition to nuclear power plants. The science writer at the morning paper has been consistently against atomic power, but the *Evening Moon* reporter on the science beat is undecided. If your material is really persuasive, he might write a favorable story. In such a case, you could persuade a prestigious nuclear engineer to reveal the findings of his latest research on nuclear accidents early enough in the day to meet the evening paper's deadline. If the evening paper comes out with a fair or favorable story first, the morning paper is more likely to give your story adequate coverage, even if their writer is opposed to your organization's position.

When you're working with weekly papers, you may have to send your release to them before you send it to the dailies. "I send out the same press release to the weekly papers first, so they have it in time for next week. Then I send it out to the dailies a few days later, so they run it about the same time the weeklies do," says Harry Cohn of the American Red Cross.

Whenever possible, the best policy is to make sure your press releases are received several days before the deadline. Remember that you're asking for free space, and the editor may not have any room to juggle at the last minute. Yesterday there was a gaping news hole he had to fill with prepared copy from the wire services and the syndicates. If your release had been in his hands then, he would have used it and been grateful.

Don't go to the opposite extreme. Although most large papers and some small ones do maintain files of upcoming events, your release may get lost if you send it more then ten days ahead. "Don't send it too far in advance, or I'll forget all about it and blow it," says the *Norfolk Ledger-Star*'s Fred Kirsch.

When you send out press releases about an event, make it clear whether you are asking for advance publicity or inviting the press to cover the event. Of course you can do both. "But if you send out a press release ten days before the event, even if the newspaper runs that story, it doesn't mean they're going to cover the event. They've probably thrown the press release away by then. So, you have to send a request for coverage a few days before and follow up with a call the day before the event," says Harry Cohn.

Following up on Press Releases

You wrote a fine press release, and mailed it five days ago. But your phone seems to have lost its voice, and you've seen nothing at all in the newspaper. Should you call the editor or the reporter to ask if he's going to run your story? Yes. No. Maybe. This is a delicate area, and even seasoned publicists don't agree about how it should be handled. If you ask two veteran publicists for advice, you'll get three opinions.

There are many publicists who would never inquire about whether a press release will be used. Mary Jane O'Neill of the New York Association for the Blind explains that she "wouldn't call to ask if they're going to use a press release. Having been on the other side of the desk, I know the reaction of reporters who say, 'My God, I'm too busy to tell. I don't know whether I'm going to use it. I mean I sent it through. The editor is the one who decides whether to use it. I don't know.' "

Your story may have been edited, rewritten, typeset, and fitted into place, but at the last minute there was a spectacular twenty-car crash on the freeway, and it preempted your write-up just before the presses started rolling. That sort of thing is hard to predict, and many reporters and editors do not like to make promises they may not be able to honor. Don't pressure them.

"I have been extremely annoyed by people who call up to tell me they want to make sure their press release 'gets in,' " says journalist Leslie O'Bergin. "They don't seem to realize that there is limited space, and there is some editorial discretion involved in what gets printed and what doesn't. I tell such callers that they're taking their chances with everyone else, and I ask them what makes them different. I can't think of a time when anyone has convinced me that they were, in fact, different. And I have been known to take their item, already typeset, and rip it up. Now that's not laudable, but I'm not the only person who has done that." However, if the topic interests her, and the caller makes a polite offer of more material and information, O'Bergin will accept.

On the other hand, public relations executive Richard Weiner feels that it is not considered impolite or overly aggressive to inquire about the status of a press release: "Public relations people tend to be shy about calling up; they don't quite know what to say. They're reluctant to say, 'Did you get my news release? Do you plan to use it?' So it's advantageous to figure out something better than that. Find some significant detail that wasn't covered in your release. Then you can hold your head up high and not feel embarrassed about making that call."

"Sometimes," Weiner continues, "the editor may have thrown away the release, or forgotten about it, and he can be sold by the phone conversation. Sometimes he will ask you to send it again. Send it again!"

From the other side of the desk, Randy McCarthy of the *Boise Statesman* says, "I'd just as soon they didn't call to ask about press releases, even though a lot of times it saves my life if somebody does call up and say, 'hey, I sent this in and it hasn't shown up yet.' Then I will make an effort to find out what happened to the thing. If I've never heard anything about it, or if it's one of those I looked at, didn't see anything too interesting, and canned, if they can sell it to me on the phone, I'll ask them to send it again."

And journalist Nancy Dunn thinks that "It is useful to follow up your press release with a phone call, but keep it brief. Have the details ready: it is annoying to have to pull details out of a publicist. Be articulate. If you can't come to the point quickly, you're not going to be taken seriously."

The best approach for the beginning publicist is to call after you're sure the journalist has had time to receive and read the release. Ask if it has been received. If it hasn't, briefly resell the story and offer to send another copy. If the reporter or editor has received it, ask if he needs more information and have some specific, brief material you can offer on the phone that was not in the release. Perhaps the most important thing is to keep the anxiety out of your voice. Try to be warm and friendly. It's hard at first, but after you've played the role for a while, you'll find that you actually are relaxed.

Asking for Clippings

It is unwise to ask journalists for clippings of articles their paper has run about your group. "We have a clipping service," says Brian Youmatz of the *Framingham Middlesex News,* "and I would send them to that department. I wouldn't have any of my people waste their time getting them." Fred Kirsch of the *Norfolk Ledger-Star* adds, "If they are outside the circulation area, I find their request legitimate. If they can obtain the paper, I feel they're just being lazy."

"Stop and think for a moment how insulting it is to the editor of your local paper to imply that you don't buy or even read it," says public relations executive Ravelle Brickman.

Get those clippings yourself!

Keeping Advertising and Publicity Separate

Never discuss your advertising program with journalists. It's too easy for such a discussion to be misunderstood as a particularly nasty form of persuasion. At most large publications, your status as advertiser will have no bearing on your status as publicist. Although there are some small newspapers and magazines that give better coverage to advertisers, that isn't always the case. And, even if a particular publication does cater to its advertisers with expanded coverage of their activities, you will win friends among the reporters if you always approach them with good, solid copy, newsworthy material, and an interesting angle. They'll feel that you're treating them as professionals, and you'll quickly gain a reputation as more than a mere advertiser demanding his "due."

Thanking Reporters

Be careful about thanking journalists; never imply that someone has done you a favor instead of using good journalistic judgment. Some reporters even take pride in completely avoiding public relations people, or at least not admitting any contact. Don't thank reporters.

There are even journalists, such as Larry Kramer of the *Trenton Times,* who like to hear occasional criticism: "Sometimes I get worried when people thank us for stories. A good crusty editor will tell you that he's only happy when both sides don't like the story. But I'm not that way. If people think we're covering them fairly, I think it's fine for them to say so."

Sylvia Smith of the *Fort Wayne Journal-Gazette* says, "Although everybody likes to be appreciated, that's a real fine line. If a publicist has a personal relationship with the reporter or the editor, I suppose it would be OK. But in general, I would shy away from it."

When you express your appreciation to a journalist, the important thing is to let him know that the story was well written and perceptive and to tell him what sort of response you've had from the public. Public relations executive Ravelle Brickman takes this approach: "I'm a writer. Every journalist in America is a writer, too. When I call a journalist to say thank you, I'm not just saying the story was well written, but, 'one writer to another, you did a fabulous job.' "

The thanks, of course, should never be in tangible form. And it should never be elaborate. "I don't like a great army of people to march in with the president of the organization and the publicist to say thanks, nor do I like to be invited to a luncheon to say thank you. I just don't think that's necessary," says S. Griffin Singer of the *San Antonio Light*.

Working with Cartoonists and Editorial Writers

As you've read the editorial page of your large daily newspaper and looked at the cartoons and editorials, perhaps you've wondered why your organization couldn't convince the cartoonist or editorial writer to take a stand on your cause. If you have great patience and tact, you might do just that.

Cartoonists

Editorial and political cartoonists range from the completely aloof, anonymous cartoonist who says "I can't be approached. Period. You can't quote me," to David Norwood, political cartoonist at the *Baton Rouge Advocate* in Louisiana. "If they just came in the door and presented themselves in such a way that there was a gentlemanly exchange there, I would probably honor anybody," says Norwood. "Or they should call me up and make a suggestion. I would make a little rough of it and bring it to the editorial department. They decide if they can use it. The group I'm doing it for doesn't get to see the rough sketch unless they come down here and make a personal call. I'm actually interested in anything."

Norwood is unusually accessible and receptive. John Reidell, editorial cartoonist at the *Peoria Journal Star* in Illinois, speaks for most American cartoonists when he says, "I prefer to come up with my own ideas. I don't mind getting information, though. I'm open to hearing different views. But I wouldn't want to be expected to follow any particular line."

The following interview with Craig MacIntosh, political cartoonist for the *Minneapolis Star,* is a good indication of the point of view of most cartoonists.

> *Yale*: Are you ever approachable by special interest groups who want you to do a cartoon on their issues?
>
> *MacIntosh*: Most of the time I would shy away from that, unless it's such a gentle organization, so non-political that I could do it without any qualms.
>
> *Yale*: But let's say they wanted to approach you and take their chances. Would you prefer to be approached with facts, suggestions, or are you just not approachable at all?
>
> *MacIntosh*: I would probably just say no because I think I might somehow compromise my independence on the issues. Basically I'm unapproachable.
>
> *Yale*: Suppose they were to send you fact sheets and say, "This seems to us to be an interesting issue. Enclosed are some fact sheets. Do what you want with them?"
>
> *MacIntosh*: Yes. I've had people do that. Everybody from air bag proponents to the United Way. I suppose getting those kinds of things in the mail is part of the job. But I've never had a suggestion about doing a cartoon.
>
> *Yale*: So that, basically, the only way to approach you is with facts?
>
> *MacIntosh*: Yes. I think I probably could speak for most cartoonists in the country. That's pretty standard.

Editorial Writers

Approaching editorial writers is slightly less difficult than making overtures to cartoonists, but you will still need the patience of a saint and the tact of several diplomats. Before you let those ice crystals start forming in your stomach, remember that many publicists have successfully approached editorial writers about topics important to their businesses, industries or organizations.

Editorials are not the same as letters to the editor, although many people confuse them. Letters to the editor are written by the publication's *readers*. Editorials are usually statements of the *publication*'s official position on an issue. They are written by the publication's editorial staff.

Bear in mind that editorials, by their nature, have a strong point of view. Kerry W. Sipe, Public Editor of the *Ledger-Star* in Norfolk, Virginia, explains why in an article in *Masthead*, the publication of the National Council of Editorial Writers. ". . . readers say 'Your editorials are one-sided,' or 'Your editorial writer lets his bias show in his writing.' I often have to explain that criticizing an editorial for being biased is like criticizing water for being wet."

The major sources of topics for editorial writers are news stories and magazine articles. According to a survey conducted by *Masthead*, "Almost 80 percent of the respondents ranked the news as the number-one source of editorials. Book and magazine articles, reporters on their staffs, public officials, and experts outside their staffs are mentioned as important secondary sources by about a third of the writers."

Editorial writers usually do not like "duty" or "worthy cause" editorials that merely endorse charitable organizations. They want to write about current issues, not fund-raising campaigns. In an article in *Masthead*, David B. Bowes, editorial-page editor of the *Cincinnati Post*, explains why:

> 'Worthy cause' editorials are like phone calls at the dinner hour when the caller inquires after the condition of your storm windows. The first time you fidget but listen, the next time you invoke cloture, and the time after that you find yourself explaining to the children that yes, it's impolite to hang up on someone but life can come to that.
>
> Does the contemporary editorial page . . . attempting to reach new audiences, have the space to give each worthy cause 'our annual editorial' as so many charity groups so airily put it? The quaint belief that a campaign will fail unless it is singled out . . . on the editorial page is a myth that all of us are loath to dispel, but something's got to give.
>
> . . . We're finding less space for on-demand editorials of obviously praiseworthy causes. Their tidings may be news for news pages . . . but they aren't always candidates for commentary.

Provide editorial writers with compelling facts, and *you* could become one of their "expert" sources. You will often find them more receptive if you provide them with fact sheets and all the information they need to fully consider your issue or cause. And since editorial writers are news oriented, you might fare better if you approach them when your organization is making headlines.

"What you send to the editor of an editorial page is different from what you would send to a business-news writer," says public relations executive Richard Weiner. "It usually consists of background material and a letter which says that the enclosed material could be used as the basis for an editorial in the paper. Editorial writers, just like any other writers, are always looking for valid suggestions."

You may, or may not, want to send copies of your press releases to editorial writers. Your releases alone will not usually get editorial writers to write about your cause. But "It helps if we already know something about the organization before being directly approached. And to the extent that being on a mailing list for press releases serves that goal, yes, it's helpful," says Anthony Morley, editorial writer for the *Minneapolis Tribune.*

Whatever you do, you should not submit suggested editorials that you have written yourself unless an editorial writer asks you for them. You may be asked to write one at some of the smaller newspapers, but most editorial writers pride themselves on their independence, and they will be offended if you imply that they don't write their own material.

In fact, the National Council of Editorial Writers Statement of Principles specifically says that "The editorial writer should discourage publication of editorials prepared by an outside writing service and presented as the newspaper's own. Failure to disclose the source of such editorials is unethical, and particularly reprehensible when the service is in the employ of a special interest."

When you talk with editorial writers, show them that you are aware of other approaches to your topic. They may even ask you to tell them your opponent's point of view. You will have more credibility if they feel you take other viewpoints seriously, but don't be afraid to take a firm stand. "If somebody is an advocate, I expect advocacy," says Anthony Morley.

Since many editorial writers are more interested in your material if it has a local angle, and since it is easier for them to check out a local rather than a national organization, it would be wise for national organizations and businesses to approach editorial writers through their local chapters, distributors, dealers, or district offices.

Even if an editorial has been written that gives you solid support, keep your distance afterwards. If you're tempted to ask the editorial writer for a contribution or invite him to sit on your board of directors, bear in mind that a *Masthead* survey showed that 66.7% of the editorialists, themselves, agree that editorial writers should avoid involvement in partisan political organizations. "Management prohibition of political activity by writers has risen dramatically," *Masthead* concludes.

Approaching and Working with Feature Editors

Unlike editorial writers, most feature editors want written article suggestions. For example, Paul Neely of the *St. Petersburg Times* prefers to be approached ". . . early and in writing. I never want a complete article," he says. "I have people on my staff to write complete articles. If they send us a complete story, we're going to rewrite it anyway, so they might as well not waste their efforts. Some smaller newspapers prefer a complete article, though." So it is best to find out the preference of each editor you will be working with.

You will often work personally with the feature editor, or a reporter, to develop a feature article. This means that you should have anecdotes, information, facts, and figures ready *before* you approach a feature editor.

A good way to approach feature writers is with a letter that pitches and summarizes your story. Letters to feature editors should cover the following points:

- Tell the editor you are offering a feature story.
- Summarize the idea in one paragraph.
- Explain why the editor's audience would be interested.
- Emphasize the scope and importance of the story.
- Give a few interesting details.
- Suggest alternate approaches where possible.
- Describe picture possibilities.
- Enclose a prepaid return card with a toll-free 800 number, or an offer to accept collect calls if the editor is interested.

Following are two excellent one-paragraph summaries of feature material. Both are examples of the typical summary prepared for feature writers. They were written by Hill & Knowlton's Industrial and Scientific Communication Services. The first generated forty responses for the client, the American Iron and Steel Institute, while the second item produced 84 inquiries for client Frito Lay.

Garbage Power

Thanks to a process called resource recovery, 20 American communities are now converting municipal garbage into energy. Ames, Iowa; Madison, Wisconsin; and Hempstead, New York burn garbage to generate electricity, while Baltimore, Maryland; Nashville, Tennessee; and Saugus, Massachusetts convert garbage to steam for heating and cooling buildings. According to a recent report from the U.S. General Accounting Office, if all the resource recovery plants under construction, or in planning, become operational by 1985, the U.S. will realize energy savings equivalent to 48 million barrels of oil a year. (Details, background information, interviews.)

Survey Says Educated Women Snacked More Over Past Decade

The passion for snacks—such as potato chips, and corn and tortilla chips—has increased dramatically among women over the past decade, according to a new study conducted by Barry Popkin, Ph.D., professor of nutrition at the University of North Carolina, Chapel Hill. In addition to a 26 percent increase in women with increased education that ate snacks, there was a 27 percent increase in the number who consumed green and leafy vegetables. These conflicting trends as well as others this survey discovered have resulted in changes by food manufacturers as they enter the next decade.

But there's more than one way to skin a cat. *The Publicist*, a magazine with extensive coverage of the public relations field until its recent demise, describes another innovative way to approach feature editors:

> A public relations agency in Los Angeles placed substantial articles in daily newspapers across the country by arranging for the papers to interview its client by telephone.
> The client, a San Francisco doctor who had written two books for cancer patients and their families, was unable to tour the nation for interviews; thus the telephone technique . . . . A major side benefit . . . was the fact that the publicity cost far less than the usual book campaign.

The Bruce Merrin Organization telephoned the largest circulation newspaper in each of the 100 largest cities in the United States. After locating the editor most likely to handle the story, it launched into a full scale pitch then and there.

The agency then shipped him or her . . . copies of the books, a biographical sheet on the author, and a photograph of him. It was accompanied by a personalized letter expressing appreciation for the editor's interest, repeating the key points of the original pitch, and offering to arrange a telephone interview at the agency's expense.

About 10 days after each kit was shipped, the agency followed up by telephone. Dr. Rosenbaum blocked out certain times when he could make himself available at the telephone in his office, and the agency scheduled the interviews accordingly. Some lasted as long as an hour.

Why Features Are Exclusive

"If the newspapers in your area are engaged in a rather competitive situation with each other," says Sylvia Smith of the Fort *Wayne Journal-Gazette,* "it's important to know that it's bad form to take the same feature story idea to both newspapers."

Mark Shepherd of the *Columbia Daily Tribune* explains the situation in his area this way: "There's another paper in town, there are three television stations that have news programs within the market area, and there are some pretty aggressive radio news programs here. So it's a very competitive news situation. That's why I try to get exclusive news interviews, or at least set up interviews where I can deal with the source by myself, so I can ask my own questions."

Although journalists expect you to distribute news fairly, many of them assume that feature material is exclusive unless you agree otherwise. Even if you intend to send the material to publications in other geographic areas, or to other special interest publications with different audiences, be sure the editor understands this. If you fail to honor an exclusive commitment, you will badly damage your reputation in media circles. Reporters and editors talk about such foul misdeeds, and word about unreliable publicists can spread quickly in journalism circles.

"I wouldn't have much faith in what they bring me next time around," says the *Maine Sunday Telegram*'s Robert Cummings. "If we make an arrangement, I don't want it broken because then there's a complication with my editors. They like to run a fresh newspaper on Sunday. So if I start sending in stuff that's already been in the papers, it hurts both me and the group that wants publicity."

Instead of labeling your feature material "for immediate release," tag it "special to the *Evening Moon*" or "exclusive to the *Morning Star.*" Then everyone involved knows exactly what the arrangement is.

Approaching Syndicated Columnists and Wire Services

Wouldn't it be great if your firm's new line of cosmetics could be mentioned by one of the beauty and fashion columnists? Or if your engineering firm's report on new techniques for containing chemical leaks from dump sites could be discussed in an ecology column appearing in hundreds of newspapers? Or if your trade association's position on defense spending could be explained in a syndicated political column? It can happen. And since syndicated columnists are widely read and highly influential, it would be quite a publicity coup.

Public relations executive Richard Weiner advises that "Syndicated columnists rarely use news releases and other mass-distributed material. A well-written letter to a columnist, offering an exclusive and demonstrating a familiarity with the type of column, is much preferred to a phone call or a news release."

One problem with offering an exclusive to a syndicated columnist is that she may not answer you if she isn't interested. Since you have offered the material on an exclusive basis, you are not free to take it elsewhere, and, without an answer, your material is tied up. Avoid that problem by indicating that the exclusive basis is for a limited time only. You might say, for example, the material is available on an exclusive basis if it is used by September 15. It is also a good idea to enclose a stamped, self-addressed postcard with boxes the columnist can check off to indicate interest or lack of it. And it is helpful to let the columnist know that you will accept collect calls from her if she needs more information, or provide her with your toll-free 800 number.

How do you know where to send your material? Consult the directory of syndicated columnists, listed under Media Directories in Chapter 12, which lists several dozen writers, classified by specialty. The actual office of each columnist is listed, as well. This is important because although many columnists are distributed by syndicates, not all of them work at the syndicate's main office, and mail directed there isn't always received. Material sent to the columnist's working office is certain to reach her.

To interest wire service reporters, your material must really be of international, national or regional importance. Wire services, such as the Associated Press (AP), United Press International (UPI), or Reuters, can help you place publicity material in dozens and even hundreds of papers. The wire services serve broadcasters as well, so the impact of material picked up by a wire service can be tremendous.

Both the AP and the UPI have scores of news bureaus in the United States. These are very much like newspaper bureaus, and you should work with the bureau nearest to your town or city. A local bureau may have a city editor, science writer, business reporter, and feature editor, as well as other specialized reporters. Find out their names and contact them directly. However, if you have specialized or technical information, ask the local bureau if the wire service has a specialist at headquarters who should get the material.

If you're not sure where the nearest bureau is, some of the media directories listed in Chapter 12 list wire service bureaus as well.

Getting into Magazines

There are four basic types of magazines, and each has a different focus. Some are harder to work with than others, but the results are often well worth your time.

General interest consumer magazines, with broad appeal and a vast audience, are not usually interested in specialized material. Although it may be a challenge to get them to consider your material, their very large circulations can deliver a publicity message with stunning effectiveness. If you can possibly place material in them your message will reach millions, but you will have worked exceedingly hard to accomplish your goal.

Examples of general interest magazines include *Reader's Digest, Life,* and *People.* The larger general interest magazines have local bureaus and specialized reporters, just like a big city daily newspaper.

As public relations executive Richard Weiner explains, "It is much more difficult to get publicity of any kind in a [general interest] consumer magazine. . . . [they] are more selective, so it's rarely possible to get articles simply by sending a news release. Many publicists ignore . . . [general interest] magazines, figuring that they're too difficult and the batting average is too low." But there are techniques for approaching them that will work, if you have genuinely newsworthy material.

Special interest consumer magazines always focus on a well-defined topic. If you approach one with newsworthy material on its subject, it is likely to be interested. The variety of topics covered is amazing, from *Art & Antiques* and *Bird Watcher's Digest,* to *Classic Toy Trains,* some with circulations of a few thousand, and others that reach millions of readers.

Business magazines include both national publications, like *Fortune* and *Business Week,* and local magazines interested solely in business news in their local areas, like *Business Atlanta* and the *Indianapolis Business Journal.* They often have reporters who cover special topics, and some of the national publications have local bureaus.

Trade publications are written strictly for people in a particular industry, and the only news that interests them is material that will affect that industry. There are two basic types of trade magazines, those published by businesses and those published by trade associations.

Trade publications published by businesses accept advertising, and they are almost all listed in media directories. Examples include *PC Magazine* (the 16th largest American magazine), *Adhesives, Florida Grocer, Group Practice News* (a magazine for doctors), *Plastic Trends,* and *The Typographer.*

Journals published by trade associations are sometimes for their members only. This type of publication can be harder to find, and is not always listed in media directories. If you're having trouble tracking down the trade magazine that would reach one of your target audiences, consult *The Encyclopedia of Associations,* available at any large library. It lists thousands of trade associations, and their publications.

Choosing the Right Magazines

As with any media outlet, you have to be familiar with the magazine before you try to get coverage. You may be tempted to use the information in one of the magazine directories listed in Chapter 12 as the only basis of information. Don't. You need to know firsthand how long articles are, what topics have been covered recently, and the general tone and style of the magazine. For special interest and trade magazines that run short product reviews, you must know their formats, so you can write to fit.

"Start by looking at the last three issues of the ten most important magazines you're shooting for," advises Donald M. Levin. Read them carefully. Try to figure out which types of stories get full-length articles and which get mere blurbs or mentions.

As you examine a magazine, or *book* as we call it in journalese, it will help you to know that most of them are divided roughly into three sections: front of the book, middle of the book and back of the book. More important announcements, blurbs, and columns usually appear in the front of the book. Feature articles usually start in the middle of the book, and may continue into the back section. Less important material is usually relegated to the back of the book, but here is where the bulk of the advertising appears. Some ads are placed in the front of the book, with few or none in the middle.

A careful reading of your target magazines is worth the time. Editor Bill Howard says that "If PR people understand who we are and what we do, they will have a better chance of getting through to us." His colleague at *PC Magazine*, Gus Venditto, explains why. "There are three pages in the magazine, called the "New and Improved" section, where we use press releases as the basis for the articles . . . . That's the only place where we use photos from publicists. For this section, a photo does give a story a bit of an edge. Black and white glossies are best." The only way to find specific editorial needs like this is to become familiar with your target magazines.

Sometimes choosing the right magazines for your publicity is straightforward. Sometimes it's more complicated.

Let's say that your company markets equipment and supplies for cleaning up hazardous waste. If you send your publicity material to all the new publications in the environmental field, won't that get you enough coverage?

Probably not, according to Joel Strasser. "The companies affected by environmental problems often don't read or even know about the specialized environmental publications. A chemical company, for example, might look to *Chemical Week* or *Chemical & Engineering News* for information on environmental management," Strasser says. Furthermore, he points out that environmental problems are not always handled by the companies affected. "Who does an oil or chemical company turn to when they have a serious contamination situation on a piece of property they want to sell? Or suppose a company wants to finance a piece of property—that may be contaminated with industrial waste— for a new plant. They'll involve real estate brokers, lawyers, bankers and insurers in the assessment of potential environmental problems. That's why there is a high degree of interest in stories with useful environmental information from real estate, legal, financial and banking publications."

To reach the largest possible audience, you'll have to do some strategizing. Curl up with a media directory that lists magazines, and ask yourself whether there are additional publications that should be getting your releases and article queries. Sure, it's not exactly as gripping as a good "who-dunnit," but as you look at the listings for magazines and ask yourself if their readers could have any possible interest in your stories, you'll probably make some intriguing, and highly fruitful, discoveries.

Using Editorial Calendars

For most magazine publicity, make your first contact at least three months in advance, and preferably six. Weekly news magazines, of course, have shorter lead times. But even in the dead of winter, many special interest and trade magazine editors will be planning their late-spring and summer issues. You'll be left out in the cold if you don't plan as far ahead as they do.

How do you know, in advance, what topics a magazine will be covering six months from now? It's not as hard as it sounds. Virtually every consumer special interest and trade magazine publishes an editorial calendar, usually for a year ahead. It lists the major topics, and sometimes even the article titles each issue will include.

Some editorial calendars are very detailed, others are not. Some magazines are very helpful, and go out of their way to provide information for publicists. *PC Magazine,* for example, even has a monthly update to the editorial calendar that lists changes and gives details as the topics become more specific.

Editor Bill Howard explains "We set up our new editorial calendar around the end of August and publish it around the end of September. It's pretty much solid for the first half of the year. We might modify a quarter of our story items over the course of a year. The ones that do vary often slide by an issue or two, as opposed to being changed entirely."

Editorial calendars are usually yours for the asking. At most publications the receptionist will be happy to help you obtain one. Several of the media directories listed in Chapter 12 also include editorial calendars.

Finally, bear in mind that editorial calendars are used mainly by special interest and trade magazines, as well as some business books. But "Although there are certain seasonal and perennial topics, there's no such thing as an editorial calendar at the hard news books," says Bob Seltzer.

Approaching Magazine Editors

Once you've targeted the magazines you want to pitch to, your next step is to find the right reporter or editor. Journalists expect you to do this.

"I want publicists to approach the right person, rather than the top person . . ." says Bill Howard. At large magazines, there may be dozens of possible contacts. At a smaller one, your task is easier: sometimes there are only two or three journalists working there.

To locate the right journalist for your story, call someone midway up the ladder who has a lot of experience at the magazine. An assistant to the editor or publisher can often steer you to the right writer or editor. No matter who you talk with, be brief and to the point. You might ask, "Can you tell me who handles user stories on green striped widgets?" or, "Can you tell me which editor covers new products in the gizmo industry?"

When you approach a trade magazine editor, never assume that you'll get favorable coverage just because your organization advertises in that book. While ". . . the trade magazines have often been accused of pandering to their advertisers," according to an article by Kim Foltz in the *New York Times,* that is changing. There are more trade magazines, and they're competing with each other for readers. John Emery, President of the American Business Press, a trade organization for trade magazines, predicts that ". . . more magazines may turn to adversarial reporting as a way to enhance their reputations with readers . . . [and] advertisers. When times get tough, advertisers naturally want to be in the book that everyone thinks is the only one to read,' " says Emery in the Foltz article.

This means that more and more frequently, journalists at trade books—and even special interest magazines—will be asking you tough questions. They'll be testing your products independently, and reporting the results to readers, even if they are unfavorable.

The policies at *Skiing* are a good example of the new breed of trade and special interest journalism. The late Al Greenberg, former editor-at-large, explained "We decided that our magazine could not be objective if it simply took press releases from manufacturers, or even from industry-wide organizations. Realizing that public safety was at stake, we determined that the only way we could effectively judge equipment performance was to find out what made equipment safe or unsafe and then set up equipment tests based on this knowledge. And though it wasn't our primary intent, we did play a role in driving many inferior products from the marketplace."

Making the Pitch to Magazines

There are three basic ways to work with magazine editors, and each of them has advantages—and drawbacks.

The first way to approach magazines is by sending a press release with the hope that the journalist will write a story based on it. Although this takes the least amount of time, it is not always fruitful. However, if you're providing useful how-to information or addressing a hot issue in the industry, you're likely to get coverage. And with some publications, it's the only way possible.

For example, Joel Strasser explains, "Most environmental publications usually don't want to talk with you or interview an expert—they prefer receiving written material, which they sometimes run unedited. The computer trades, on the other hand, like to talk to the people who make the news, and write their own stories."

If you're sending a release to magazines, it's a good idea to send supporting material, too. In a survey of editors mentioned in *Public Relations Journal,* 71 percent of the editors said they found backgrounders and white papers helpful.

The second approach involves persuading the editor to assign a writer to do the article, starting with your material, and building on interviews and perhaps other sources, as well. This takes more time, but once an editor agrees, it's much more likely to produce results. And, you'll have more input as well.

When you want an editor to assign a writer to your story, first call the editor and make a brief pitch, or write a short query letter, and then call to see if she's interested. Either way, be sure you understand exactly what commitment the editor has made to you, what her deadline will be, and what information, materials, product samples, and interviews with experts she'll need.

This approach works well with the consumer magazines, when you're trying to get them interview your spokesperson. Bob Seltzer explains "For Estraderm, which is a skin patch that delivers estrogen to menopausal women on a continual basis, we've created an educational campaign to help women cope with menopause. Our spokesperson is the actress Shirley Jones. We've done really well with getting reporters to interview her. It's her task to get our educational messages into the interview. Then we all hope it will make it through the writing and editing process."

With the last approach, you can try to get the editor to agree to accept an article written by your organization's spokesperson, clients, experts, or you, the publicist. This takes the most time and effort, and some magazine editors won't agree to it, so you should make sure the editor will not find it offensive. Joel Strasser points out ". . . publications like *Forbes,* the *Wall Street Journal* and the *New York Times,* always write everything themselves. They won't usually accept expert-authored articles." And Gus Venditto warns that at *PC Magazine,* ". . . it would not be fruitful for a publicist to send us an article or a query for an article. We would never run anything like that."

But this method gives you more control than the other two approaches, and the most input, as well. Bob Seltzer explains "We've found that a lot of publications will accept an article with Shirley Jones' byline, in which we structure the message. This gives us a much better chance that our message will survive the editorial process. And that's because of Shirley's stature."

If you will be writing the article yourself, ask for a copy of the publication's guidelines for writers. This will give you valuable clues to the magazine's approach. Most magazines will be glad to send them. Once you have done that, you will want to find out which editor handles your topic, and call or write with a brief pitch.

A query letter to an editor might read like this:

Dear Mr. Edwards:

With the widespread concern about the harmful effects of poisonous chemical sprays on the environment, consumers are looking for options. And the nurseries that can provide alternatives will stand to make above average profits—*if* they know where to find these products and how to promote them. From our contacts with nursery operators, we know that *National Nurseryman & Grower*'s readers are eager for more information on this subject.

I'd like to propose a two-part article written by Dr. Linda H. Corning, the research director of Ecolo-Grow, and Lucy Czaloski, our marketing director.

Dr. Corning, who has conducted research for the Plains State University on pesticide-free farming techniques, is the author of six books on the subject. Ms. Czaloski teaches advertising at the Plains City College Evening School. Her 1990 co-op advertising campaign for Ecolo-Grow, which helped nurseries promote alternatives to poisonous spraying, won a gold medal at the Plains State Advertising Club Convention.

Part one of the proposed article will cover types of biological insect controls, insect and disease-resistant plant varieties, and non-poisonous sprays. In the second part, we'll include

– more –   – more –

complete information about buying these products wholesale from a variety of suppliers, as well as how to promote and advertise them.

Since most of your middle-of-the-book articles seem to run about 3,000 words, we propose a 6,000 word article in two equal parts.

We can provide you finished copy on 5.25″ diskettes in Word Perfect 5.0, Microsoft Word 4.0, or ASCII format.

I will call you next week to learn of your interest. I look forward to talking with you.

Sincerely yours,

Robert K. Dajminnish
Publicity Director, Ecolo-Grow

Once you have an editor's interest, you'll want to get his tentative acceptance. At that point, it's a good idea to offer to send a detailed outline of the article, discuss the outline over the phone, ask for suggestions, and see if you can get him to commit to a tentative publication date.

You'll need to know how long he wants the article to be, and if he expects it to be in manuscript form or on computer disk. If he wants it on disk, you need to know what word processing programs he has access to. If you have access to the same program, that's great—send him a disk in that format. If you don't have the same word processing program, you'll have to convert your files to ASCII, a universal format that almost any word processing program can read. If this sounds complicated to you, ask a friend who is familiar with computers. It should be a piece of cake for him, and once he shows you how to do it, it won't seem difficult at all.

Using Freelancers, Experts and Clients as Writers

If you've approached a magazine and they've asked you to supply an article, you should know about working with freelance writers, as well as using experts, customers and clients as writers.

Always set two deadlines for articles you're responsible for: the deadline you give your writers, and the real deadline, perhaps two or three weeks later—that you never reveal. If there's a problem or delay, you can still have the article finished and delivered by the real deadline.

What happens if you promise to deliver material and you miss the deadline? Gus Venditto of *PC Magazine* explains that when publicists fail to deliver at the last minute, they don't get covered. The space gets filled with other material. Your organization or business may get covered later, but you'll get less space because your news is not fresh anymore. Venditto is unusually easygoing. At smaller publications, with fewer journalists on staff, a missed deadline can be very serious, indeed.

What do you do if the article by one of your customers (or an outside expert or the company president) arrives at the last minute and it's not usable? One publicist for a software company, who prefers to remain unnamed, tells this deadline story:

> I was extremely disappointed. I had asked the most important user of our software to write an article. When it arrived, it was vague, badly written, and dull. Now I had talked with this client many times, and I knew the article did not reflect her experience with our product and her insight into her industry. I also knew that I'd never have another chance at that trade book again if I blew this deadline—and it's the most important publication for our industry. The deadline was only two days off. It was a tight spot for sure!
>
> I took a deep breath and called her. "The article is great," I said, "but it needs just a little bit of fleshing out. Can I put you on speaker phone and start my tape?"
>
> Once she started talking, I knew there would be no problem with the material. She knew her stuff, but she just couldn't write. I taped her for two hours, and when we were finished, she was even more enthusiastic about her article.
>
> I called my wife to say I wouldn't be home at all that night, ordered Kang-Pao Chicken delivered from my favorite Chinese restaurant, loosened my tie, took off my shoes, and started transcribing the tape. I polished our client's words until they sparkled, took her best quotes, and used them to rewrite the piece. At 4 A.M. I faxed it to our client for approval, and went to sleep on the office couch.
>
> The client loved the rewrite. I sent it to the editor by Federal Express. It ran in the center of the book, as he had promised—under our client's byline, of course.
>
> Was it worth it? You bet it was! The reprint of that article became our company's most important promotion piece. And it led to a nice promotion for me, too.

There are some important ethical considerations in working with a freelancer. As Richard Weiner points out, "when we work with a professional freelance writer . . . [and] the writer is being paid solely by the magazine, there is no ethical problem. Sometimes we commission a writer to do an article, and then the writer sells the article to a magazine and gets paid from both ends. If the magazine knows about it, there is no breach of ethics. But if the magazine is not aware of the double payment, then there is an ethical problem. It can be questioned whether the writer or the public relations source breached the ethics, and this is one reason it is a gray area.''

The best way to avoid such problems is to have a clearly written agreement with a freelance writer. Good writers prefer that arrangement; many of them will not work without a written contract. Make sure your contract specifies how much the writer will be paid, and whether the writer is barred from accepting payment from the magazine involved. Specify that you're buying *all* rights to the article, and any other material the writer develops during the course of the assignment, otherwise the freelancer owns all rights to the material, and all you've bought is the right to use it once, in that particular magazine. If that's the case, he is free to resell and reuse the article anywhere and anytime— and you've lost control of the material you paid for.

A serious professional writer should be able to explain several possible angles or pegs for his story, and discuss why this subject interests him. He should really understand your product, service, industry or cause, and be able to explain—in his own words—the technical material he will have to deal with when he writes that article for you.

You should also ask if the writer is a member of a professional organization, such as the International Association of Business Communicators, or the American Society of Journalists and Authors. Not all professionals belong to such organizations, but membership is a sign of a serious writer.

Finally, ask a freelance writer for some clips. Look over the samples of material he has written. Does he write well? Is his style alive? Does it seem he will be able to capture the essence of your business or organization? If you're not sure after reading the clips, you probably shouldn't work with him.

Sometimes a freelance writer may approach you, explain that he is interested in an aspect of your business or organization, and ask your cooperation so he can write an article, which he will then sell to a magazine. Caution is in order.

You should also keep in mind that there are many would-be writers who can't produce the goods, let alone get them accepted by a magazine. Before you make a commitment in such a situation, ask him whether he has a firm written assignment from a magazine. If the writer does not, he is working on speculation, and there is no guarantee the piece will ever be used. Moreover, an amateurish writer who has no working relationship with the publication can make *you* look bad—and hurt your reputation with the publication.

Seminars for Editors

In some industries, editors at the trade books are experts in their fields. In others, particularly new industries like environmental management, many editors are good journalists, but they're not experts on the subject matter. The computer industry was like that, too, in its early days. If you're involved in such an emerging industry, or your discussions with trade editors convince you that their knowledge is limited, you could offer your company's expertise to them in a regular seminar.

If you run a seminar for journalists, be absolutely sure your speakers are experts in their fields, and polished presenters as well. Talk with journalists, and ask them what topics they need to know more about—or send out a survey to find out—and use this information to determine your program. Make sure there are no industry events like trade shows conflicting with the date and time of your seminar. And, be sure to invite journalists six to eight weeks ahead of the seminar date, so they have plenty of time to work it into their schedules. It's a very good idea to give every participant an evaluation form, and speak with as many attendees as you can. That will help you make the next seminar even more useful to them.

Joel Strasser of Dorf & Stanton Technology Communications set up an annual seminar for his client, Hart Environmental Management Corporation. Strasser explains why: "In an emerging business like the environmental management industry, the laws and the techniques are changing fast. A lot of editors recognize that they don't have the full background and up-to-date information on everything that is going on. We've been holding seminars for editors for the past three years. We take a look at industry events during the past year and our client's experts project what will happen during the year ahead. We hold them in November because it's a good time for publications doing year-end wrap-ups as well as projections for the upcoming year."

Strasser's latest editorial seminar for Hart was called "Outlook for 1990: Environmental Issues and Prospects in a More Demanding Decade." The topics, of keen interest to environmental editors and reporters, included what New York City's new administration has faced environmentally during 1990, the 10-year timetable for upgrading millions of underground storage tanks, and EPA's aggressive program for corrective action at active hazardous waste sites.

Seminar speakers included Fred C. Hart, President of Hart Environmental Management Association, a former commissioner of air resources for New York City, and Vice-President Lawrence B. Cahill. These two men are leading experts in their field. Hart is the author of numerous technical papers on environmental management issues, a speaker at national conferences, and a Registered Professional Engineer in New York State. Cahill, the principal author of a book, *Environmental Audits,* and a national lecturer on that topic, is trained as a mechanical engineer. With speakers like these, it's not hard to see why journalists are eager to attend the Hart seminars.

Checklist—Getting into Print

1. Do you understand the different editorial needs and focuses of daily, weekly, neighborhood and ethnic newspapers?

2. Have you checked several media directories, as well as the Yellow Pages, to compile a press list?

3. Are you balancing your media list with neighborhood, ethnic and suburban papers, and not just limiting yourself to the big city dailies?

4. Have you familiarized yourself with the newspapers you'll be supplying with material by reading them for at least several weeks?

5. Have you tried to get a copy of the editorial policies for each newspaper?

6. Do any local papers offer tours of their plants? Have you taken one?

7. Have you made a list of the specialized reporters and editors at the larger publications?

8. Have you tried to get a style sheet from a large daily paper? If not, have you bought the AP or UPI stylebook?

9. Do any of the papers in your area have a handbook for community groups and small businesses who want publicity?

10. Have you asked about public service advertising at your local papers?

11. Have you decided the best way to approach reporters and editors in your particular situation?

12. Have you considered joining a professional communicators' organization?

13. Have you checked to see if there are any local news bureaus you should be working with?

14. Have you determined which publications want you to approach their local bureaus, and which ones want you to direct publicity material to their main offices?

15. Have you asked the large newspapers to name a staff coordinator for major events?

16. Have you avoided sending duplicate releases or pitching the same story to more than one reporter at the same publication? Have you labeled duplicates where they are necessary?

17. Do you understand why you need to send separate requests for advance publicity and coverage of an event?

18. Are you delivering your releases several days *before* the deadline whenever possible?

19. Have you made a list of the deadlines faced by all the reporters and editors you'll be working with?

20. Have you planned events or release time to take strategic advantage of media deadlines?

21. Have you decided whether you want to make follow-up calls about press releases? Do you know how you'll handle the calls before you make them?

22. Do you have more information you can offer during your follow-up call that wasn't in the release?

23. Are you avoiding any mention of your advertising program when you talk with journalists?

24. Have you considered sending fact sheets on your special interest or cause to editorial writers and cartoonists?

25. Have you decided whether to include editorial writers on your release list?

26. Have you thought about asking for a conference with editorial writers about your cause or special interest?

27. Have you considered whether and how you want to thank journalists? Do you think this through each time?

28. Have you found out which feature editors want summaries and which ones prefer complete articles?

29. Have you written a letter that includes your feature summary? Does it cover all eight essential points?

30. Have you considered using the telephone interview method to place features in out-of-town papers?

31. Have you made a clear arrangement with the editor about exclusive rights to your feature story?

32. Have you considered approaching syndicated columnists with exclusive offers of material?

33. Have you put a time limit on the exclusive material you've sent to a columnist? Did you include a stamped, self-addressed postcard?

34. Before you send publicity material to a wire service, are you sure it involves a *national* story?

35. Do you know which wire service bureau and reporter is the right one to receive your story?

36. Do you understand the difference between general interest, special interest, business and trade magazines?

37. Have you realistically evaluated the possibility of getting publicity in the general interest consumer magazines and the large-circulation business publications?

38. Have you read several issues of each magazine in which you're interested in placing publicity, and *written down* your observations about the types of articles they print?

39. Have you thought about which publications in related areas of interest may be reaching your target audience?

40. Have you looked at the editorial calendars of the magazines you're interested in to see where your article ideas might fit in?

41. Have you determined if the editors at your target magazines want press releases, phone pitches, or tip sheets?

42. If you're sending a press release, are you including a backgrounder and supporting material?

43. Before you offer a completed article, have you determined whether the editor uses outside writers?

44. If you'll be supplying the article, have you asked for a copy of the magazine's guidelines for writers? Did you enclose a self-addressed, stamped, legal-size envelope?

45. Have you reached a clear understanding with an editor before you spend time writing an article?

46. Do you know how long the article should be, and the editor's preferences for manuscript or computer disk formats?

47. Has the editor approved a detailed outline?

48. Did you get a tentative publication date?

49. If you're working with a freelance writer, do you have a written contract?

50. Have you set two deadlines, one for you and one for your writers, whether they're freelancers, clients, organizational spokespeople, executives, or staff members?

51. If a freelance writer has approached you, does he have a written assignment from the magazine? Have you looked at his clips? Is he a member of a professional organization?

52. Have you worked out any unanswered questions about double payment of freelancers? Do both the writer and the editor understand the arrangement?

53. Does the writer fully understand your product, point of view, or cause? Are the news pegs he suggests really interesting? Does his approach excite you?

54. If you're planning a seminar for editors, have you used a formal or informal survey to determine what information the journalists in your field need to know?

55. Have you chosen expert speakers who are also good presenters?

56. Have you double-checked to make sure there are no industry-wide events that could conflict with your seminar for editors?

57. Have you mailed your invitations so the editors get them six to eight weeks ahead of the seminar date?

CHAPTER SIX

Getting Pictures Published

Maybe your bakery has just put the last touch of frosting on the world's largest cookie, or your company is celebrating the 50th anniversary of your founder's invention of the widget. Perhaps your Elks Club chapter is presenting a citizen of the year award. You know that when a newspaper or magazine story has a picture along with it there's a better chance people will read it—so you'd like to snap a few shots and send them along with your press release, query, or feature article. Before you load that film cartridge in your handy-dandy instant camera, there are more than a few things you need to know.

Some publications use publicity photos more often than others. Large dailies, general interest magazines, and business and trade publications that can afford their own photography staffs generally prefer to cover an event themselves, but many smaller publications do accept publicity photos. You have to find out the policies of the publications you'll be working with.

PC Magazine, for example, ". . . almost invariably takes its own photographs, with the exception of three of our 200 editorial pages each issue. We want to have a consistent look," explains editor Bill Howard, "especially since we primarily do comparative [product] reviews. It would be almost impossible to get 12 publicity photos that would look the same."

There are two ways to get that photo published. For magazines, you would work directly with the editor who covers your type of story, letting him know in your first or second contact exactly what the photo possibilities are. At the larger newspapers, you can try to interest either the photo editor or a reporter in your story. How do you know which to approach? The rule of thumb is to call the reporter who covers that beat for a specialized story. If it's really a photo essay—more visual than verbal—pitch it to the photo editor.

You can also submit really first class photos directly to newswires like the Associated Press, United Press International, or Reuters. "At the wire services," advises Bob Seltzer, "you absolutely have to go through the photo editors" with a photo story.

Once you've decided whom you are going to approach, call him and make a brief pitch on the phone, with a description of the photographic possibilities of your event. Even better, send him a photo tip sheet, including the good old who, when, where, why and how, along with a description of the visual possibilities. Then, after you're sure the journalist has had a chance to read your tip sheet, you can make a follow-up call. Your goal is to find out two things: if the publication is interested, and if so, do they prefer to shoot their own photos.

The second way to get that photo published is to shoot it yourself. Smaller publications will frequently depend on you for photographs, but there may be occasions when even a sophisticated large daily with a big staff will use your publicity shot. "In some cases, publicity photos are useful because there's no way we can get a picture quickly ourselves," says one newspaper's photo editor. But, he goes on to say, "I think the rules for pictures we accept from publicists should be the same as the rules we impose on our own staff photographers." In other words, your publicity picture has to be as good as the shots taken by the publication's regular photographers.

There is a third way to get pictures published that will work if you have a very expensive—and photogenic—product. "We offered to loan Audi cars to photo editors," says Bob Seltzer. "Some of the travel magazines which do a lot of outdoor shots accepted our offer, so an Audi is shown at sightseeing attractions in *Alaskan Highways*, for example."

You might also be able to use this technique with houses, home furnishings, jewelry, boats, and other high ticket or luxury items.

Here is an example of good visual planning for an event which press photographers and television cameramen were invited to cover:

> The popular director of a neighborhood recreation center in Plains City was leaving after five years on the job. The children were having a hard time accepting his coming departure, and some of the younger ones simply could not understand it. He felt that a ceremony would help the kids cope with their feelings and understand what was happening.
>
> On his last evening at the center, the staff hung a large sheet of paper on the wall and asked the children to help make him a giant good-bye card. With the card in the background, the director sat in a chair while two staff members shaved off his long, curly beard. As the children watched, a new man emerged from beneath the beard, and while a band played farewell songs, he walked slowly to his car. The children held a purple ribbon across the hood. The ribbon was cut, the drummer rolled the drums, and the director drove off into the sunset.
>
> Because it was so photogenic, the ceremony was covered by almost every newspaper and TV station in town.

Here are some tips that can be drawn from the story above. If you do invite the press, plan your ceremony so it will be visually stimulating. Spend time talking with photographers to explain what is going on, and let them know of any unusual visual angles. Tell them what to expect, and at what points in the ceremony you think the best photo possibilities will be. Sometimes a photographer will ask you to rearrange your program, so he can get the best shots fast. If that's possible, do it, because he may be on a tight schedule. If you can bend to meet his needs, you have a better chance of getting really good photo coverage.

Photos of Events

Journalists call news pictures *art*. Not art in the sense of museum pieces, but communication art. Good news photographers think through their pictures before they shoot, and they take their work very seriously. Publicists, unfortunately, usually give pictures short shrift.

As Larry Kramer of the *Trenton Times* points out, "art from businesses is notoriously bad. So a good business item with an interesting handout picture stands a better chance of making it. And there are stories that make page one because there was art with them."

The same is true for art from nonprofit organizations, trade associations, and government agencies. The photo editor quoted above amplifies on this: "Publicity photos we get are staid and unimaginative. That's why they seldom get in the paper. Ninety-nine percent of the photographers who take publicity photos have not had newspaper experience and don't know what we want. We want good action photos. Since publicity photos are often advance shots of things happening in the future, there's nothing going on in them. They're posed pictures of people doing nothing."

There are five standard pictures that most publications won't touch because they have become clichés:

- The check pass.
- The shovel dig.
- The handshake.
- The ribbon cutting.
- The plaque pass.

All of the above usually share the same problem: lack of context. You can't tell what the ceremony is about. If you don't know the people, it could be any ceremony, anywhere, anytime.

"Instead of shooting an award ceremony," suggests Phil Douglis, director of the Douglis Visual Workshops, publicists should "ask themselves who will benefit from the award or check or medal. Then go shoot the benefits. Instead of taking a picture of a man who set up a therapy center for mentally ill people getting a medal for his efforts, good public relations people will go to the therapy center, shoot real people involved in real benefits, and sell the idea to the press. This is the ultimate value of publicity pictures—to sell news, features, benefits—instead of superficial awards and ceremonies."

If you must take pictures of a ceremony, try to have your photos capture the feelings of the people taking part. Aim to show why the ceremony is important: what it *means*. Ask yourself why this ceremony is different from every other ceremony and how you can show that difference on film. Another question to ask yourself is why you want these pictures. What message are you trying to convey to your audience? How will these pictures carry that message?

A good technique for ensuring that your photos get your message across is called photo illustration. That's ". . . where you go out and construct a picture to illustrate a concept or situation," says Andrew

Yale, a freelance editorial photographer based in Sandstone, W.V. "Although most publicists don't use this technique, it's a good bet because it's dramatic and unusual. And since it's a recognizable, familiar style, most editors will use it."

Several examples of powerful photos created with the technique of photo illustration are described below.

■ In the middle of a long corridor, the publicist for a hospital lined up all the paper work required to admit one patient. On either side were all the people who had a part in doing that paper work. The lens used gave the maximum depth to the picture, so the lineup looked longer than life.

■ A piece of art for an organization concerned with over-population showed a standard highway sign that read "Los Angeles City Limits." Hanging from that was a hand-lettered cardboard sign reading "No Vacancy."

■ A photo by James Visser, photojournalist for Six Flags over Mid-America, showed a woman touching a static-electric generator. Her hair, standing straight up and lighted by an electronic flash, looked like a giant dandelion gone to seed. It's an unusual image, and it rivets the reader's attention.

■ Daniel E. Dahlberg, editor of the house publication for All-state Insurance Company's agents, wanted to remind agents forcefully that their customers might need million-dollar lia-bility insurance, even if they don't sit on the board of direc-tors of a large corporation. Dahlberg stacked a million bucks in bundled bills on the front of a boardroom table and had photographer Chris Kattson shoot a photo with the loot looming large in the foreground. In the far background, slightly out of focus, two executives confer. The almost empty boardroom with the two men strongly suggests a cri-sis or unusual situation. Combine that with more money staring the reader in the face than he's likely to make in a lifetime, and his curiosity is piqued.

There are a number of important elements to consider when you compose photos of events and people.

Include action in your photos of people and events whenever possible. Good stop-action shots can be dramatic if they are done well. (They are almost never used by publicists.) Capture the spirit of the occasion. What is most important in an ideal publicity photo, according to George Waldman, assistant graphics director for the *Detroit News*, is ". . . a unique viewpoint." Waldman means more than choosing a unique camera angle or special lens. What he's looking for are photos that tell you something interesting about the people involved.

Natural poses make the best photos. As you arrange the people in the photograph, talk with them. Laugh, joke, frown, stamp your foot, and do whatever you must to get them relaxed and looking natural. If they're too aware of the camera, try telling a story, and as soon as they've forgotten about the camera, snap one without breaking your narrative. This technique works with all but the most self-conscious people. If you're not a ham, or if you're photographing an activity where your song and dance would distract people from their tasks, an alternative is to be as quiet and unobtrusive as possible. You hope that people are so involved in what they're doing that they'll forget about you.

As you shoot, ask yourself what the focal point of the photo will be. Every publicity photo should have one and only one point of interest. That's the spot in the photo that draws your eye first. From there your attention travels to the less dominant parts of the picture. If you have two, three, or more competing points of interest, the shot will seem confusing because people won't know where to look first.

The way you arrange the people in your art will have an effect on the point of interest, so position people carefully. "If you've got a line of people, that detracts from having a strong point of interest," says newsman Robert Asbille. That lineup of people can look like a picket fence.

Phil Douglis says that "Boring picket-fence pictures . . . do nothing for anybody—the subjects are wooden, ritualized objects lined up in rigid horizontal rows. It is relatively easy to improve on this kind of cliché. The easiest way to do it is to simply relax the subjects, group them informally and in depth, vary body size via vantage point, and get much, much closer to the subject."

Douglis, writing in *IABC News*, published by the International Association of Business Communicators, advocates that you arrange the people in your photos so some are in the foreground and some farther back in the picture. A person in the foreground appears larger and gives the picture a focal point. The eye moves back from her into the picture.

Many publications have rules of thumb that encourage pictures with fewer than five people in them. "The more people there are in a shot, the more difficult it is to compose a good photo," says photographer Andrew Yale. So unless you or your photographer understand how to photograph large groups, avoid them in your publicity shots.

In general, the people in your art must not have their backs to the camera, and they must be identifiable. But if you're taking pictures of people in a confidential situation, such as a clinic or a hospital, it is OK if you can't see their faces.

Choosing an interesting angle can help make your art more compelling. "To the beginning photographer . . . all 'news' takes place at a distance of six to ten feet from the camera, and is always viewed from shoulder height. Because such photographers always assume the same position in relationship to their subject matter, all their pictures look the same. . . . To fight such redundancy," Douglis advises, "photographers must seek variety in vantage points. . . . The key to winning the battle against visual redundancy is to forcefully and emphatically shift camera position."

Shoot from a balcony or stand on a ladder. Group your subjects on a stairway and shoot from below or above. Take a shot from the side, crouch down, or even lie on the floor. If you're working with a hired photographer, suggest these viewpoints to him.

If you can't change your vantage point, change your lens. For example, make sure that you or your photographer knows the difference in effect between a 28mm and a 135mm lens. The resulting photos can be stunningly different. "Take many shots; film is cheap. Try different cameras, lenses, f-stops, depth of field, lighting, poses," advises Donald M. Levin in an article in *pr reporter.*

Consider the background. If your pictures must be shot against a busy background, use the depth-of-field adjustment to blur that backdrop to make it less distracting. "The background should not distract from the main action in the picture," says Andrew Yale. "You should especially avoid a strongly patterned background or repetitive architectural elements which can pull the eye away from the people and the action." "Don't shoot in front of a window," he continues. "If you really can't move, then draw the drapes or the blinds."

Whenever possible, include a banner, poster, or other item that identifies your firm or organization in the shot. But don't let it compete with your main action.

Make sure everyone looks his or her best. It may sound obvious, but to one publicist in Chelm it wasn't. People in publicity photos must be presentable. The Chelm publicist sent out 8 × 10 glossies of the president of the Circular Club making an important announcement. There was a large, clearly visible stain on the prexy's shirt, and the pictures weren't used. The publicist still hasn't figured out why.

If you're not sure about the quality of your publicity photo, show it to someone who is unfamiliar with your organization or business and knows nothing regarding the event. Ask them what the photo is about. The more they can tell you, the better the photo.

Keep in mind that photos need editing, too! Sometimes, by cropping, you can save a piece of art. Ask your camera shop to print 4 × 5 proofs for you. Then use pieces of plain white paper to blank out parts of the photo that are dull, not relevant, or compete with the photo's focal point. As you move these "cropping sheets," around on a photo, you may suddenly see an ordinary shot take on focus and impact. Once you've decided which parts of the photo you want to crop out, you can use a waterproof marker or a grease pencil to make marks right on the proofs so the film laboratory knows exactly how to print the enlargements. If you're not familiar with the process, ask your camera store for advice.

What Makes a Good Product Shot

While the technical requirements for product shots are similar to photos of events and people, the visual approach is quite different.

Freelance photographer Jerry Pozniak explains, "It's important to hire the right photographer for product shots. A newspaper or publicity photographer will probably not have the right skills or equipment. A photographer who specializes in product shots, on the other hand, will know how to make your product look its best."

The quality of your product shots is less important in newspapers, more important in magazines, and most important when the photograph will be enlarged. Especially if you send the same shot to many publications, you should shoot in both color and black and white. Some publications want product shots with people in them, others do not. So, shoot your product art both ways and either find out the editorial preferences or send both types of shots.

A camera that uses large sheets of film, called a view camera, is essential for product shots, advises Pozniak. "You need large format (4 × 5 or 8 × 10) transparencies to hold more detail and give better reproduction. A view camera also allows you to correct for distortions, which won't be apparent in photos of people but will be magnified in product shots."

Even if you're working with a top-notch pro, you'll have to be involved in the shoot. The photographer will need to ask you about lighting, positioning, angles, and all the other considerations that go into creating the photograph you want. Some photographers will shoot test photos with a Polaroid® camera after each shot is set up and ready to go. That gives you a chance to see what the finished art will look like, and do last-minute fine tuning.

Product photos should have simple, plain backgrounds in neutral colors. Seamless photographer's paper gives you a continuous background that doesn't distract from the product. The background should contrast sharply with your product, so the item seems to pop right off the page. "Greys, off-whites and pastels work better than bright colors. You can't go wrong with a grey. Black, on the other hand, does not work as well. And a very bright background may overwhelm your product. If you use an off-white background, you can make the product seem to float in space. Off-white also minimizes shadows, makes the shot easier for an editor to crop, and lets her run type across it," says Pozniak.

Good lighting is also critical for product shots, since deep shadows will distract from your product. "Make sure the lighting is even and diffused so there's no glare. And keep lighting simple," cautions Pozniak. "Use a single main light source and perhaps a background light to keep the background from fading into darkness.

It's sometimes difficult to judge the size of products shot against a plain background, since there's nothing to refer to. If it's important for readers to know the size of your product, you may have to include a recognizable item in the shot, like a coin, for example.

There are some important techniques that photographers use to make products look their best in photos. Sometimes it's to your advantage to have a model made of your product, rather than shooting the actual item. "Mass produced merchandise often has small flaws that you don't want reproduced and magnified," explains Pozniak. "For example, many items are not quite square, especially cardboard product containers. It's often cheaper to make a model than to retouch the photo."

If you have a shiny product, like a cardboard box printed on glossy stock, be especially careful about glare. You might want to make a non-shiny model or spray your product with a matte lacquer spray to cut the glare. But your photographer must be an expert in this case.

When you photograph food, use a food stylist who knows how to prepare and arrange each dish so it looks appealing on camera. Since the photographer's lights generate heat, the stylist will have to continually replace food as it wilts or dries out. Good food photography is expensive, but the end results are worth it.

Technical Requirements for Photos

You may have the publicity shot of the century, with great content, a strong point of interest, and an arresting image, but if it's not well done technically, it will find a home in the wastebasket instead of on page one.

Your publicity photographs should be shot with a professional camera. Instant cameras often have plastic lenses, and the images are not crisp enough to reproduce well on newsprint. And Polaroid® shots are generally frowned on by photo editors. "Most of the time we don't like to handle them because they don't reproduce well," says Robert Asbille of the *Des Moines Register and Tribune*. "They're always a hair out of focus. We have used them now and then for somebody who has been killed, when that's the only picture available."

The standard for newspaper publicity is the 8 × 10 black-and-white glossy. Don't send out color pictures to newspapers unless you check with your contact there first. If you have a color transparency, such as a 35mm slide, include a brief note with your black-and-white shot, letting the editor know that a color transparency is available.

"If you're speaking generally about magazines, I would say that it never hurts to include two or three black and whites and maybe even one color transparency, with an offer of more photos by overnight courier," says Bill Howard.

At most newspapers that do use color photos, they can be run on only a few selected pages. The editor may have a news hole on a black and white only page, which he'd love to fill with your story. If you've sent only a color shot, he can't.

Your publicity art for newspapers should have strong contrast, since a lot of its sharpness will be lost when it is transferred to newsprint. And since newspaper columns are narrow, your pictures should be shot in a vertical format so they can be reduced to fit one column, if necessary. You can include some horizontal shots as well, in case the editor really likes your art and decides to run a shot across four columns, but the vertical shot is the basic one.

If you're submitting photos to magazines, ask the editors you work with whether they prefer vertical or horizontal shots.

Your photos must have a white margin. This is the space where the photo editor at the newspaper puts his crop marks to let the printers know exactly which part of the photo to use.

Don't write on the back of a photo. The pressure of your pencil or pen can cause indentations in the surface of the shot that will show up in reproduction. Write or type any necessary information on a label, and then attach it to the back of the art. Never use paper clips on photos because they, too, can cause indentations. And always handle photos by the edges. That fingerprint you can hardly see, right across the president's face, may show up vividly when the picture is reproduced in the newspaper.

If you're going to submit the same shot to a number of newspapers, use copy prints instead of individually made enlargements, since they are less expensive in large lots. A few phone calls to photo laboratories will get you exact prices, so you can make your own comparison.

The requirements for magazine photos are more exacting, particularly if they are printed on slick paper. Because this paper has a special coating on it, photos reproduce better than on newsprint, and they show more detail. So the photos you submit have to be larger and even clearer than photos for newspapers. For slick magazines, handmade enlargements are necessary because too much detail is lost when copy prints are made.

Since the quality of pictures reproduced in major, mass circulation magazines is very high, they must have an 8 × 10 photo to work with, since a smaller photo will not reproduce well enough to meet their standards. Besides, groups of people as well as scenery and location shots look their best in an 8 × 10 format. If your photo includes only one or two people, or a simple object, you can submit a 5 × 7. And you can drop the size of the photo down to 4 × 5 for head shots.

Hiring Your Own Photographer

If you don't want to take on the job of photographer yourself, and there is no one else within your organization who is qualified, consider hiring a moonlighting press photographer. This is a good way to get publicity shots of events and people that will interest the press.

Call a newspaper, ask for the darkroom, and briefly tell the person who answers what you want. Even if he says he's not interested or he doesn't know anybody who can help you, ask him to take your name and number just in case he hears of somebody. He may call you back after he's finished work. Bear in mind that if the darkroom is dark at the moment, he won't be able to write down your number. Ask if he's developing, and find out when you should call back.

If your photographer does not have press experience, be sure that he can work fast enough to meet newspaper deadlines. It is wise to specify in writing that the photographer is an independent contractor. In that case you probably won't be liable for social security, unemployment, and workmen's compensation taxes.

Unless you specify otherwise, in writing, the photographer owns the negatives. You buy only the actual physical photographs he provides you, and even those can be used only for limited purposes. You cannot, for example, use a publicity shot in advertising without the photographer's permission. If he's any sort of businessman, he will charge you an additional fee for advertising use, so if you want to buy all rights and the negatives, be sure you have a specific written agreement.

Advise your photographer when you hire him that he will not be able to have credit lines with his work. "Most publications don't like to give credit lines to outside photographers," advises the American Red Cross's Harry Cohn. "Usually the only credit lines they give are to their own staff photographers. Why even imply you want a credit line when you know the policy of the paper is against it anyhow?"

Photo Captions

When you send out those publicity pictures, be certain to include captions. Otherwise, how will the photo editor know who is in the photo, what's taking place, or what the story behind the product is? Assume that your press release will not be used at all—that only the picture and the caption will be run. That's why it's a good idea to make your caption a summary of your story, with all the important information included. Repeat the obvious, rather than leaving potential questions unanswered. Identify everyone from left to right, with first and last names, or at least first initials and last names.

Include the name, address, contact person, phone number, and release date on your caption. You can type your captions when you view the proofs, send them to the lab when you order your full-size shots, and have the lab shoot them so they actually become part of the photograph. If you handle your captions this way, they won't get lost, and the editor can see both the picture and the caption at the same time. Or, you can tape typed captions to the back of the photo.

Two examples of good picture captions follow:

2,000 Heads Are Better Than One. XYZ Food-O-Rama manager Dale Johnson presents a week's supply of lettuce to Red Cross Disaster Relief coordinator Kcaj Nodrog. The 2,000 heads of lettuce will help make a mountain of sandwiches for people left homeless by the recent tornado in West Plains State.

XYZ Food-O-Rama

385 Rock Street East

Plains City 00001

Contact: Marie Tinaka, 998-3300

July 16, 1991

Contact: OR
Diana Tedesco   Bruce Cleverly
Suzanne Jones   Gillette North Atlantic Shaving Group
Porter/Novelli   (617) 421-8492
(212) 315-8000

A patented, easy-loading system makes blade changing with the new Gillette Sensor shaving system virtually foolproof, and its convenient organizer fits comfortably in the hand. The cartridges feature ultra-narrow chromium platinum-hardened blades, individually mounted on highly responsive springs, and an open-backed, flow-through design which allows for easy rinsing and cleaning.

Model Releases

You should have a signed model release from everyone in each of your publicity photos. This standard form, available at most camera stores, says that the person in the picture gives his or her permission to use that shot for any and all purposes.

For example, someone in a shot might decide the photo is unflattering, or change his mind about appearing on page one. It's not possible to have people sign all their rights away, but chances are if they have signed a model release, you won't have any problem. This is especially true if you are involved in a controversy, but in any case, you and your lawyer should discuss model releases for your publicity photos. Although model releases still don't make you 100 percent legally secure, they will help if somebody in one of your pictures tries to sue you.

"If you're doing publicity on a Hadassah dinner, for example, and you get a shot of the chairman and the woman who is doing the cooking," says Robert Asbille of the *Des Moines Register and Tribune*, "they've agreed to the picture. If it gets into a controversial area, or if somebody is being photographed in an institution, then we do want a model release. There have been lawsuits on invasion of privacy, and these are real tricky areas now." Also, if there's a child in the picture, it's a good idea to make sure you see the actual release, signed by the parent.

Permits

If you schedule a special event—or even just a quick publicity picture with two or three people—in a public place, you might think you don't need a permit. Find out first; you don't want your work or photo session interrupted by the police. In many cities you will need one or more permits to hold special events or just to shoot pictures in public places.

Submitting Photographs to the Press

Your photographs should be sent with sturdy cardboard stiffeners inside the envelope so the art can't be bent in the mail. If you bend a photograph, the surface may crack, and then it can't be reproduced well. Don't skimp on cardboard or postage. After all, you've put a lot of time and money into those shots, and you want them to arrive safely. They should, of course, be sent only by first-class mail, messenger, or overnight courier. Some of the newswires listed in Chapter 12 can transmit photos. This can work well in a tight deadline situation if the publications you're sending photos to are on the wire service's network.

If you are submitting photographs to a publication unfamiliar with your organization, be prepared for questions. "Of course we don't accept photos from new organizations until after we have checked them out," says one photo editor. "Otherwise it can get very sticky."

Some small newspapers charge an "engraving" fee when you submit a publicity photo. You should call and ask them about their policies for publicity art. Don't mention the possibility of a fee; wait to see if they bring it up. If the fee is minimal, it will be worth paying because it's probably a great deal less than the cost for the same amount of advertising space.

Don't expect your photos to be returned. Editors are flooded with photos, and they will either file them for future use or, more likely, toss them in the trash if they can't use them. They do not have the time to return them to you, and you'll only annoy them if you request it.

Finally, if the art accompanies a feature story, find out if the editor expects exclusive rights to use those shots. Be certain you honor that commitment if he does. This is especially important at magazines, although it is a good idea to ask newspaper reporters as well.

Checklist—Getting Pictures Published

1. When you approach an editor with a story idea, are you ready to suggest photo possibilities?

2. Have you found out the policies about using publicist-supplied photographs at the publications you'll be working with?

3. Have you prepared a photo tip sheet for your event and sent it along with your request for coverage?

4. Have you tried to get the larger publications to assign a photographer to your story?

5. Have you planned your event so it's visually interesting?

6. If you make or sell luxury products, like boats, houses or cars, have you offered to lend them to photo editors at magazines?

7. If you are shooting your own publicity art, have you avoided the five standard clichés in publicity pictures?

8. Do your photos of people show something about the relationship between them?

9. Do your photos of events and people show some action taking place whenever possible?

10. Have you captured the meaning of the ceremony to the participants?

11. Have you considered showing the benefit rather than the ceremony?

12. Have you considered using photo illustration to construct a picture that illustrates a concept?

13. Can someone who knows nothing about your organization and the event shown in your photo tell you what's going on without a caption?

14. Are you avoiding "picket-fence" shots by grouping your subjects imaginatively? Are you keeping your groups small?

15. Do your pictures have only one point of interest?

16. Unless you know how to photograph large groups, do your photos have fewer than five people in them?

17. Have you included an object that identifies your organization in the shot?

18. Are you getting variety in your vantage points by shifting your camera position?

19. Are you using different lenses, f-stops, depth of field settings and lighting arrangements to get shots with a range of effects?

20. Unless the shot is of patients in a clinic or similar situation, are all the people in the art identifiable?

21. Are you avoiding backgrounds that detract from the important part of the picture? Have you avoided taking photos in front of windows?

22. Are you editing and cropping the proofs before you have your final art printed?

23. Have you hired a photographer with product shot experience who knows how to make your merchandise look its best?

24. If you're sending product photos to a variety of publications, are you shooting in color as well as black and white?

25. Are you shooting your product both with and without people?

26. Is your photographer using a large-format view camera?

27. Do you go to the photographic shoots so your photographer can have your input?

28. Does your photographer shoot sketch shots with a Polaroid® camera so you can see what the final shot will look like?

29. Are you using simple, neutral backgrounds like grey and off-white for your product shots?

30. When you look at your sketch shots, do you check to make sure there's no glare, and the background is well lit?

31. Have you talked with your photographer about the need for a model of your product?

32. Have you checked with your photographer to make sure that your product doesn't need antiglare treatment?

33. If you're shooting photos of food, have you hired an experienced food stylist?

34. Are you using a professional 35mm camera rather than an instant camera?

35. Are the pictures you send out to newspapers black-and-white glossies? Are they at least 5 × 7 inches, or 4 × 5 for head shots?

36. If you're working with newspapers that run color, do you know which pages the color runs on? Have you checked with an editor to see if there's any possibility your story can run on a color page?

37. Does your art have strong contrast?

38. Are most of your photos for newspapers vertical rather than horizontal?

39. Have you asked the magazine editors you work with if they prefer vertical or horizontal art?

40. Do your shots have white margins?

41. Have you avoided getting fingerprints on photos, writing on the back of photos, or using paper clips on them?

42. Have you determined if you can use less expensive copy prints, or are hand-made enlargements necessary?

43. Have you considered hiring a moonlighting press photographer to shoot your art for newspapers?

44. Can your photographer meet tight media deadlines?

45. Have you specified in writing that your photographer is an independent contractor? Have you made a written agreement concerning rights, ownership of negatives, and credit lines?

46. Have you included captions that tell the whole story, identify everyone in the shot, and have your organization's name, address, and telephone number as well as the date?

47. Do you have model releases from everyone in all your photos?

48. Have you checked to see if you need permits to shoot photos or hold special events in public places?

49. Have you sent out your art by first-class mail, messenger, or overnight courier and packed it in sturdy envelopes with stiff cardboard to protect it?

50. If the photos are for a feature story, do you have a clear understanding with the editor about exclusivity?

CHAPTER SEVEN

Preparing Materials for Broadcast

I n this chapter you will learn some of the special tricks for preparing material designed to be heard rather than read: news releases for broadcasters in written form, video and audio news releases recorded on tape, public service announcements and short features for television, as well as community calendar listings. You will also find out how to put together visual materials to accompany your TV spots or to add impact to your special programs.

When you are writing material for print media, you do not have to worry about how it will sound. "Trade your two left feet for a matched set at the Fifth Street Dance School" will look fine on paper, but "matched set" is difficult to say, and the announcer may stumble. So you must test all copy you have written for broadcasters by reading it aloud. If it reads easily, fine. If you stumble, rewrite your piece to eliminate the problem words.

Try to use short sentences when writing spoken material. Long, involved syntax with dependent clauses will be difficult to follow when it's heard. Unless you're selling snakes, avoid too many "s" sounds because the microphones exaggerate them and make them hiss on the air. Be careful when you use the words he, she, and they. Will your listener know to whom these words refer, beyond any possibility of confusion?

If your copy contains homonyms (words that are spelled differently but sound alike), be sure the meanings are clear. You don't want your listeners to wonder whether you are referring to a dashing fellow in iron clothing on a white horse—or the period just after sunset.

When your broadcast publicity material deals with political or controversial issues, and you're providing it in videotaped form, you'll want to be aware of the following provisions of Section 317 of the Communications Act of 1934, as amended, 47 U.S.C.

> If a station broadcasts a program or part of a program concerning political or controversial issues, and the material was provided without charge to induce the stations to broadcast it, the station must announce that it has been furnished and by whom.

News Releases for Broadcasters

The most important thing about a broadcast news release is that it must be short. Many broadcasters like stories that are 60, 30, or even 20 seconds long, sprinkled with a few 90-second "in-depth" items. So don't send the same news release to broadcasters and newspapers. Write a different version of the story for broadcast media, and limit yourself to 90 seconds of reading time at the maximum. You can tell how long a release will be by reading it aloud and timing it.

You can either write a brief but pithy release, just as you would like to hear it read on the air, or you can provide the information in outline form and let the news director draft the actual words. In either case, each news item should be on a separate sheet of 8 1/2 x 11-inch plain, white paper. At the top, list your organization's name and address, the date, the name and telephone number of the contact person, and the reading time in seconds. If the release is for immediate use, it should say "for immediate release." If you are getting it to the station early, but you don't want it released until later on, you should write "for release at 6:00 P.M. on Monday, February 29," or, "for release after 12:00 noon on Friday, August 13."

Your release must be typed, double-spaced, and on one side of the page only. Be sure to leave wide margins both on the sides and at the top and bottom. This is space the assignment editor and news director need to write instructions and make changes. A 55-character line will leave plenty of room on the sides. If you limit yourself to 12–15 lines of copy per page, your top and bottom margins will be wide enough. Following are some guidelines for writing good news release copy for broadcast:

- Use the present tense whenever possible. News is happening now.

- Unless you have a reason to be specific, round out your figures. If the sixth-grade class at the local school donated 365 books to your library, you could say, "almost 400 books are being given to the library." But if the kids made a point of contributing one book for every day of the year, and that point is central to the story, give the exact number.

- If any names in your release are difficult to pronounce, spell them out in phonetics enclosed in parentheses directly after the names. For example, "Writer Ken McEldowney (mack- ihl-down-ee) says . . ." will make it clear to the announcer exactly how the name should be pronounced.

- Keep background material to a minimum. If you consider supplementary information necessary, add a separate background sheet.

- Test your release by reading it aloud. How long does it take to read? Is it conversational? Easy to understand? Interesting?

Written out completely, a good broadcast news release might look like the following:

Citizens for Rapid Transit
1980 Strauss Street
Plains City 99998
Contact: Anand Gupta, 999-0500

FOR IMMEDIATE RELEASE
Reading Time: 0:38
September 15, 1992

A rapid transit system in Plains City could save a million barrels of oil a year, cut air pollution by 45 percent, and decrease average commuting time by one-fifth, according to a study released today by Citizens for Rapid Transit, or CRT for short.

The study, conducted by Ellington and Sczobosc (show-boss) Engineering, suggests that a $13-billion light rail system could be built in three phases during the next 12 years.

"We'll be mailing a copy of the study's highlights to every household in the metro area," says Gretchen K. Panaanen, CRT's president. "The rapid transit bond issue will be on the ballot this fall, and we want everyone to have the information in this study before they vote."

###

Some news directors prefer an outlined release. "Don't write the story for me," says KGW-TV's Larry Badger. "I'm not going to use it the way you write it. But give me the information." KTVU-TV's Fred Zehnder expands on this point of view: "The best press release enables the assignment editor to get an idea of what you're all about in five or six sentences and then to look down and see the important information set off. If all that information is in the text of the release, the editor has to go through and underline it, and it takes more time."

The above news release, in outline form, might look like this:

Citizens for Rapid Transit
1980 Strauss Street
Plains City 99998
Contact: Anand Gupta, 999-0500

FOR IMMEDIATE RELEASE
September 15, 1992

A rapid transit system in Plains City could have economic benefits for the entire metro area, according to a study done by Ellington & Sczobosc (show-boss) Engineering. The study was released today by Citizens for Rapid Transit.

Savings:	A million barrels of oil a year.
	A reduction of air pollution by 45%.
	A decrease of commuting time by one-fifth.
Suggested System:	A light rail system.
	At a cost of $13 billion.
	Built in 3 phases during 12-year period.
More Information:	Complete study with details, statistics.
	Mailed to all Metro Area households before Fall election.
	Includes rapid transit bond issue.

###

Public Service Announcements

Public service announcements (PSAs) are one of the most common kinds of publicity. Since they are short, broadcasters run a lot of them, and they are easier to get than specials, interviews, features, or news coverage. Even though they are only 60, 30, 20, or 10 seconds long, don't underestimate them. You can say a lot in 20 seconds. And since your

PSA will almost certainly be repeated several times, your message will have multiple impact. For example, MG Productions, a video production house in New York found that one of their client's spots went to 400 TV stations and aired 13,470 times, according to the Company's President, Margie Goldsmith, in an article in *Public Relations Journal.*

The Federal Communications Commission (FCC) defines a PSA as "... any announcement ... for which no charge is made and which promotes programs, activities, or services of federal, state or local governments ... or the programs, activities or services of non-profit organizations ... *and other announcements regarded as serving community interests*" (emphasis added).

That may sound bland, but PSAs in the 1990's are often controversial. James Wexler, vice-president of West Glen, a New York video production and distribution house, explains that "Today, the issues are ... hard-hitting and cover a wide range of topics. AIDS and drug abuse dominate the scene, followed closely by the homeless, concern for the environment, and missing children. Indeed, PSAs very much reflect the changing face of American society. Who would have thought even two years ago that the word 'condom' would have been allowed on the air? Or that networks would actually consent to air a PSA about kids who watch too much TV? The fact is they *did* and 'Couch Potato,' distributed by West Glen for the American Academy of pediatrics, received a flurry of publicity about its content, and was one of the 'hottest' PSAs on the air."

What do you do if you are not part of the government and you're not a nonprofit organization? You have two choices:

- You can take the "service" approach and provide material that will benefit your audience. If your business or trade association presents information that can be regarded as serving community interests, you have a good chance your PSAs will be used.

- You can underwrite a PSA for a nonprofit organization, and have them include a sponsor's credit, so your organization's name is mentioned. Since this practice is becoming more common, many television stations don't object to it.

If you ask them in theory, public service directors will often tell you that they don't ever use PSAs produced by businesses and trade associations. But when a public service director sees an interesting PSA, chock-full of useful information about the safe use of lawn mowers, for example, she will probably be inclined to use it because it does serve community interests, even if it was produced for the Power Tool Association.

For example, Planned Communications Services, an audio/video production house in New York City produced and distributed a TV PSA for the Aluminum Association. Called "Recycle and Save," the spot ran on 244 stations covering 364 cities in forty-six states. Viewers were asked to call a toll-free number for the address of their nearest recycling center. Before the spot went on the air, there had been about 400 calls a month. During the peak month of response to the PSA, 9,500 people called! The total exposure for the spot was 164 hours. The same amount of commercial time would have cost a whopping four million dollars at 1980 prices.

Planned Communications has also done PSAs on safe winter driving for senior citizens (Colonial Penn Life Insurance); Halloween safety (National Confectioner's Association); recycling your tires (Tire Retread Information Bureau); and the safe storage of detergent in households with children (Soap & Detergent Association).

The second approach is to sponsor a PSA produced by a nonprofit organization. In addition to the good feeling that comes from helping a worthy cause, your corporation can benefit by being identified with social responsibility in the view of the public. That's why credit to the business backing the effort is so important on sponsored PSAs. It is also possible, with careful planning, to weave your product into the finished spot in such a way that it is part of the fabric, and seems to belong right there. If you're planning to do that, choose a production house with some experience in producing sponsored PSAs that include product mention. Ask to see some successful spots they've produced, and be sure to look at the usage reports, showing how many stations ran the spots. Find out how the production house knows that the product mentions weren't edited out of the spots. And, finally, ask to speak to references at several sponsoring companies.

Many stations prefer to use local spots, written or produced by organizations in their own towns or cities. But they'll also air national spots for either of two reasons:

- They know the national organization has a local chapter or affiliate in their area.
- The spot will serve the public interest of their community.

Large national organizations often have a lot of media production money, and their spots can be quite polished. But that doesn't mean that your organization's PSA, written at your kitchen table, doesn't have a chance.

There are a number of formats for PSAs. Some stations will accept any of them, and other broadcasters have definite preferences and rules. Always find out in advance what kinds of spots are accepted by the stations you will be approaching, as well as each station's exact technical requirements for taped PSAs. "Minor technical errors, like making a PSA a few seconds too long or too short, can cause unnecessary problems and even rejection of a PSA in which great effort and expense was invested," says Andrew McGowan, vice-president of Planned Communications Services.

Keep in mind that your PSA is competing with commercials for the viewers' attention and interest. A single commercial can cost a million dollars to produce and air on TV. That can be awesome competition, and you may find that you need production help with your spots.

If you're working with a nonprofit or community organization, your first step is to ask the stations in your area if they will help you produce PSAs in their studios. Although many stations offer PSA production help to nonprofit and community organizations and government agencies, studio time is tight, and only a few spots are produced each month. If the station does offer this service, ask how far in advance you will have to make arrangements.

If you can't find help at the stations, try approaching advertising agencies in your area. Many advertising people are willing to help nonprofit organizations produce PSAs. But keep in mind that even if they offer their services, the donation is usually limited to creative work only. Production costs may still be sizable, and *you* will have to pay for them. Ask at the start of any discussions with volunteer advertising personnel just what size they expect the production budget to be.

If you decide to have your PSAs produced commercially, check the list of PSA production houses in Chapter 12. Or, ask the program directors at local radio and TV stations for their recommendations. If a local production studio is mentioned by several program directors, it's a good bet that studio does a nice job.

Technical Requirements for Radio PSAs

The least expensive kind of PSA is "live" copy, in which you write out your material and the announcer or disc jockey reads it live, on the air. The advantage of live copy is that it is cheap and can be produced quickly. While businesses and trade associations typically use pre-recorded PSAs, many nonprofit groups rely on live PSAs. If yours are clear, focused, and imaginative, they'll serve you well. But remember, when you submit your PSA as live copy, there is always the chance that the public service director or even the announcer will edit or change it—for better or for worse.

If you are lucky enough to have a production budget, you can submit your radio PSAs on tape or records. But don't reach for your hundred-dollar discount store cassette recorder. Taped and recorded spots must be professionally produced. You may not be able to tell the difference, but to the trained ears of radio people your amateur production will sound terrible. If you cannot afford to hire a sound studio, ask the broadcasting department at your local college if they can help you.

"Copies for stations should be on quarter-inch tape at 7 1/2 inches per second on five- or seven-inch tape reels, although some stations will accept cassettes or records. Tape is cheaper than records in small quantities. But over two hundred copies, records become less expensive," says Andrew McGowan.

Once you have decided to have your PSAs professionally produced, take advantage of every opportunity to create memorable, attention-arresting spots. There are some people who can remember the words and the music to advertisements from more than thirty years ago. Your PSA is really an advertisement, and you should try to make it as effective as the best ads.

Use sound effects, music, dialogue and drama, not simply a voice. Even if you have not dramatized your spot, consider using two voices. It will sound less monotonous, and your spot will be easier to understand and require slightly less of a pause between sentences, allowing you to get in a few extra words.

If you use any music or sound effects in your PSA, you must get permission from the copyright owner or buy material from a sound-effects house. Even a nonprofit organization could face a lawsuit if it uses copyrighted music or sound effects without permission.

When you submit a prerecorded radio PSA, send a script along with it. This makes the public service director's job much easier, and he will be more likely to use your spot. And whether you send "live" copy or tape, always include several different lengths. You may have a wonderful 30-second spot that the public service director simply adores, but she only has 10- and 20-second spots available. Send the four most common lengths: 10, 15, 20, and 30 seconds, and if you want to cover all the bases, you can also include a 60-second version.

Technical Requirements for Television PSAs

When you send "live" copy to TV stations, you should include visual material. Otherwise, while the announcer reads the material, the station may bore its viewers by showing a slide that reads "A public service announcement from WWWW." No matter how interesting the announcement is, that slide will brand you as dull.

Thirty-five millimeter color slides are the visual material for "live" copy television PSAs. But, before you spend money shooting and duplicating them, find out if the television stations you'll be approaching still use live copy for public service announcements. Some do—others don't. Live, script/slide PSAs will work for spots of 10, 20, and 30 seconds, but 60-second PSAs really require videotape to keep viewers interested.

If you find stations that will use live spots, write this rule down on your thumb: you usually need one slide for each five to ten seconds in your spot. That way the station can change images fairly rapidly, and your PSA will have the illusion of motion. And that illusion is essential if you want to keep a TV audience interested.

Many stations will not even consider using slides that are not mounted in glass. If the public service director tells you that her station will accept plastic or cardboard mounts, you can save some money, so it is worthwhile to ask.

When a 35-mm slide is televised, part of the image is cut off by the camera, and you lose about 10 percent of the height and 20 percent of the width. You might want to cut out several pieces of 5/8 × 23/32-inch paper. Place one of these pieces behind the slide and center it, and you can see that whatever part of the image is not over the paper will be lost in transmission.

Bear in mind that TV screens are horizontal, so your slides must be horizontal. Otherwise, that great shot of the mayor showing off one of the city's new police horses might end up as the headless horseman.

If you want to produce your own TV PSAs, your spots *must* be professionally produced with expert lighting, camera work, and editing. Few, if any, TV stations will use tape from home camcorders—unless you have *exclusive* footage of a major news event like a volcano eruption or an airplane crash.

When you create PSAs, you have to take three steps into account. Each step can and should be done in a different tape format:

- Shooting or producing the raw footage.
- Editing the footage into finished spots on a master tape.
- Distributing the spots to stations in several different formats to meet their needs.

There are several alternatives for shooting raw footage, according to Andrew McGowan:

■ Motion picture film gives the highest quality results. It's also the most expensive choice, so it's usually used only for big-budget PSAs. At some point during the editing, the image is transferred to one-inch videotape.

■ Shooting directly to reel-to-reel videotape cuts costs somewhat, but quality is not as good as shooting on film. Shooting done in a studio is usually directly onto one-inch tape. Location shots are most often done directly on BetaCam or M II videotape, the type that's frequently used by TV field crews. The image is often transferred to one-inch tape for editing.

■ Three-quarter-inch videocassettes can also be used for shooting. This is the least expensive alternative, and while the quality is acceptable, it's not as good as the first two methods. Transferring the image to one-inch tape for editing improves results.

"The spots should be edited *exactly* to standard length: 60, 30, 20, 15 and 10 seconds. And there should be no sound in the first and last half second, since this is how stations ease the transition between adjacent commercials," says Andrew McGowan. ". . . the name of the organization must appear somewhere in each spot, usually as a title at the end," he concludes.

Once you have your master tape, you need to produce copies, or "dubs" to send out to the television stations. McGowan advises, "Distribution format is a completely separate consideration from production format, because copies can be made from any one format to any other. In fact, the usual procedure is that a TV PSA is edited to a one-inch master from which copies are made in . . . the format preference of each receiving station or network."

As broadcasters update their equipment, their needs change, so you have to check continually with each station on your list. Very few stations accept film anymore, and most currently prefer three-quarter-inch videotape. But some television stations and cablecasters are still using one-inch and even two-inch videotape. By the mid-1990's, it's probable that many more stations will be using digital half-inch videotape, although few use it now, according to McGowan.

Some of the larger PSA production houses listed in Chapter 12 have continuously-updated databases that track station format preferences. If you use such a house to produce or distribute your PSAs, they'll take care of matching the correct format to each station.

Taped PSAs should always be accompanied by either a script or a story board. A story board is a sequence of pictures, in black and white or color, showing highlights of your spot. The audio portion is written under each picture. This helps the public service director get a concrete idea of just how good the PSA is, and it may convince him to preview your tape.

A typical script for a television public service announcement will look like the one below, which was produced by MRA Communicators, Inc. for the American Foundation for the Blind. Joel Saltzman was scriptwriter. For this sixty-second spot, there are two scripts, side by side, one for sight and the other for sound. CU means a closeup shot.

Video:	Audio:
Slow zoom-in on woman removing mixing bowl from kitchen cabinet.	(Sound under, ticking of timer)
Places it on counter with baking utensils, flour, eggs, sugar, etc.	In the next 60 seconds, this woman is going to bake a cake—without looking once.
Medium shot, moving mixing bowl to center of table.	How does she do it?
CU, dispensing shortening with shortening measure KC 108.	Watch closely, because something she does . . .
CU, adding pre-sifted flour to mixing bowl.	. . . is going to give her away.
Medium shot, reaching for milk container.	
CU, measuring 1 cup of milk, pouring it into mixing bowl.	
CU, stirs batter by hand.	
Zoom-in on breaking egg. CU, overhead view of separating egg with egg separator, KC 807.	
Medium shot, reaches for bottle of vanilla; zoom-in on feeling for label.	There's the clue. A label printed in braille.

Medium shot, pours out 1 teaspoon of vanilla.	She isn't looking at what she's doing because she can't; she's blind.
Medium shot, pours egg whites into large mixing bowl.	. . . But she can bake a cake—and cook anything else she wants.
CU, placing mixer into bowl and mixing.	She uses aids and appliances made available by the American Foundation for the Blind—things like:
CU, shortening measure in use.	This shortening measure.
CU, egg separator in use.	The egg separator.
CU, bottle of vanilla with braille label in hand.	Labels made in braille.
CU, CM 20 timer on table.	(Timer rings) . . . Even the timer.
Zoom-out from timer to woman removing cake from oven.	For a free catalog listing these and 200 other aids and appliances write:
CU, overhead view of cake with address information superimposed, letter-by-letter, as if being written by hand.	Aids for the Blind Box 111 New York, 10011

What length PSA should you send to television stations? There's no one correct length, according to Andrew McGowan. "As in radio, length preferences for PSAs vary among television outlets. Almost all use 30-second spots, but some may prefer 60's or one of the shorter lengths. Rather than trying to determine the 'ideal' length, consider this: most stations will air more than one length of the same message, so producing and distributing a couple of lengths is probably the ideal. And since each additional length usually can be produced and added to the distribution package for less than half the cost of the first spot . . ." it makes a great deal of sense to provide several lengths, says McGowan.

This is important if you're aiming for prime time in large metro areas, where the competition for air time can be brisk. "Ten-second spots are likely to get the most exposure in heavy viewing time periods, particularly in major cities . . . . Sixty-second spots will get 15 to 25 percent less airplay. . . . PSA directors specifically request that you don't submit a 15-second PSA alone; they prefer two for a 'split 30' . . ." according to an article by Margie Goldsmith in *Public Relations Journal.*

Special Requirements for Television Network PSAs

The television networks also run PSAs. They must, of course, be of national interest. And the competition for network air time is stiff. "When submitting a PSA for preview by the networks, it should be on 3/4-inch videocassette. When they accept a PSA, the networks will request multiple copies in the format they use for broadcast," says Andrew McGowan. The names and addresses of the network public service directors are in some of the media directories listed in Chapter 12. If you will be submitting preview PSAs to them, it would be wise to contact them ahead of time and ask for their specific requirements.

Format for Live Public Service Announcements

Since you have to establish your organization's credibility, particularly at first, it is wise to send your live PSAs on letterhead. Even though businesses can get PSAs, you may have to document your status as a nonprofit organization. In many larger cities, public service directors require a copy of your IRS tax-exempt-status letter. Organizations raising funds should give the permit number from the city, county, or state agency that certifies that they are legally entitled to collect money. You might send PSAs for months and never know that the reason they weren't being used is because you didn't provide this information. Ask two or three public service directors in your town whether they require documentation before they run PSAs.

". . . because stations are much less likely to air PSAs that ask for money than ones that give information, the most effective 'fund-raising' spot may be one that has only an oblique reference to contributions," according to Andrew McGowan.

If you are sending different lengths of the same PSA, each spot should be on a separate 8 1/2 × 11-inch sheet of paper, since this is the way stations handle them. Use one side of the sheet only, and do not staple them together because that makes them harder to handle.

At the top of the sheet, list the following:

- A contact person and telephone number.
- The date you expect the spot will arrive at the station.

- The reading time, followed by the words "public service spot."
- The word count.
- The words "use until," followed by the last date on which you would want your spot run.

It's important to include an expiration date on PSAs. The publicist at the Chelm Library didn't include a "use until" date on the public service spot telling job seekers about vocational books. So when listeners misunderstood the spot, and thought the library was actually offering jobs, the publicist had to call each station and ask them to stop using the spot, a time-consuming and embarrassing task. If he had included an expiration date, the problem would have taken care of itself.

A heading on a public service spot sent out on letterhead might look like the following:

```
Contact: Sam Berg, 999-5656
January 18, 1992
Use until: March 3, 1992
20-second public service spot
43 words
```

Public service spots should never say "news release" or "for immediate release." If you are sending them in ahead of the time you want them used, combine lines two and three of the heading so they read, for example, "use between January 18 and March 3, 1992."

Your live PSA copy should be double- or triple-spaced and typed in a narrow 35-character column because it is easier to read aloud than lines that are typed all across the page. Although PSAs are often typed in all capital letters, you should use upper and lower case because that, too, reads more easily.

Words to be emphasized should be underlined, but don't overdo it. All emphasis is, after all, no emphasis. And just as in a broadcast news release, difficult names should be spelled phonetically and placed in parentheses following each name.

There are two things to consider about the telephone number in your spot. Think about who will hear and see your spot. "If you put a spot on a New York TV station telling people to go to the Mayor's Office on the Aging, the spot is going to be seen in White Plains, Hackensack, and Garden City," says Andrew McGowan. Other cities and towns may not have a Mayor's Office on the Aging, so it's important to say which city the telephone number refers to. And give the area code as well. You might not even give your telephone number at all, if your organization is in the telephone book. Say, "You'll find us in the telephone directory under . . ." McGowan concludes.

Last of all, if you are sending out a script/slide PSA for TV, you'll need video and audio columns in your script. Each slide should be numbered on its mount. And in the video column of the script, indicate the number for each slide and a brief description written opposite the audio part of the narrative it illustrates.

Writing Public Service Announcements

When you write a PSA, remember who your audience is and what someone is doing while you speak. During a radio spot, there's a good chance your listener may be cooking dinner, talking with neighbors, or driving home through a horrendous traffic jam after a long day at work. You have to compete for your listener's attention, and you have to keep it once you've gotten it.

If your spot is for TV, consider that the picture comes half a second before the sound starts. "I think you need to start with the most arresting visual you can do, so that you are not saying, 'here comes another commercial,' " says John Rand of Reva Korda & Associates.

"There's a natural tendency to break," Rand continues. "Viewers have just seen a very exciting drama, and it's the end of the scene. The impulse is to talk, go to the bathroom, get a drink, or do something during that commercial break so that they can be back when the quarter starts, or the next scene opens, or the interviewer introduces the next guest. This is a natural time not to listen. People are not sitting there waiting for your PSA."

It will be easier to rivet the viewer's or listener's attention if you start by telling him why he should pay attention to you. Don't say, "You should listen to me because . . ." Think, instead, of how your message will benefit your listener. Start it with a strong statement of that benefit—a short sentence or two that appeals directly to the listener's self-interest. Then follow that with the good old "who, when, where, why, how and what." Conclude by telling the audience what you want them to do: call you, write to you, come to an event, or change their thinking on an issue.

"You've got to make sure that your most important point of interest is done right away," John Rand stresses. "So you might say, 'Your son may not go to college. That's right. If you don't help our library now, we may have to close. There will be no other place for him to get the books he needs.' But you wouldn't say, 'Don't forget the library. It's a really marvelous place. We have so many books. And, you know, we may have to shut down if we can't raise more money, and your son . . .' You should make sure the viewer is riveted before he can leave," says Rand.

Be sure you grab people's interest by finding a way to make *your* message fascinating. Never try to get attention by talking about something "more interesting" and then switching to your message; that implies your message is dull. Yes, borrowed interest is often used in advertising, but that's bad advertising, since you are not talking about *your* product or service.

For example, it's not effective to open your PSA by saying "Just as Nero, the Roman Emperor, played the violin while the city burned to the ground, so, too could you be letting things burn right now if you haven't developed a fire safety plan for your home." In that case, you've delayed the message. You've taken valuable time, and cluttered the scene instead.

"You've got to establish your identity right from the start," Rand continues. "And you've got to mean something to that person right off, so that he is involved. Your story should come from within your product, your institution, your business. It should come from your own strength."

"The viewer feels cheated when you start with something that has nothing to do with your message, and suddenly you start selling. What you're doing is putting your sell in the middle of some entertainment. It's already in the middle of some entertainment. So you've diluted your appeal with this borrowed interest, and you've taken the person's mind off your message," says Rand.

The PSA below uses borrowed interest:

> Before you buy a new household appliance, I'm sure you look at several makes and models. When it comes to buying life insurance, you should use every tool available to help in your selection. The Chelm County Insurance Agent's Association has a booklet to help you buy the right kind of insurance. For your free copy call 121-3700.

A typical radio listener will probably ask himself what life insurance has to do with appliances and ignore the rest of this announcement. If he does get past the confusion, he may miss part of the message while he puzzles it out. Even if he gets the whole message, the spot hasn't told him that there *are* different kinds of life insurance. Many listeners don't know this, and rather than talk about appliances, the spot should explain why all life insurance is not the same.

A common problem with PSAs is that they try to say too much. Choose one main point in a spot that is 30 seconds or shorter, and make sure that everything else supports, clarifies, and elaborates on that main thrust. In a 60-second PSA, you can sometimes manage to include two points, but they should be related.

The following spot includes too much information, And the listener would have a hard time figuring out what is important.

> The distinguished Chelm Dramatic Arts Ensemble and the Chelm A Capella Chorus will present alternating programs of drama and choral works which probe man's inhumanity to man among other philosophical issues. Featured in program number one will be, Richard Smith's two classics: *Miss Marie*, and *The Wonderful Washerwoman*, as well as the contemporary choral piece, *Interstate 98*, by Wiggins-Starbank. Program number two, a tantalizing selection of contemporary dramas, will include *The Night They Closed the Disco Down* by M. T. Head, *Lance's Promise* by Jean Spear, and the poignant *DDT and Old Denim* by Marsha Costello, as well as art songs by the little-known German Romantic composer, Werner Rosenkopff. Both programs will be performed on weekends, except Friday nights, from April 17 through May 12 at either the Downtowner Theater or the Highway Playhouse. For information, dial 131-4826. Or write Box 15662, Chelm Main Post Office.

Your PSA must contain solid information about your organization's services or cause. A spot announcement that says, "Don't forget your recreation center," is hardly interesting. "People feel they know a lot about you," says John Rand. "If you start off with a general story, either they will have heard it before, or it can apply to anyone else who has the same kind of service or institution. So you're not helping yourself. If people haven't helped you before, there's no new incentive to help you now, just because your name pops up. When your announcement is finished, you want them to say, 'boy, that recreation center (library, store, political group) gives me a lot more than I thought!' "

Tell people what you do, specifically. Mentioning your organization's name is just not enough. Your name is only important to you.

Verify all information. Be sure that you can back up the facts, figures, and statements in your PSA. "If you make statements, you should be able to substantiate them; otherwise they don't go on the air. It's truth in advertising, even though it's free," says WCBS-AM's Teresa DiTore.

End on a forceful note. "Keep the end of your spot focused and simple. If you have a lot of clutter at the end, you're taking away from the telegraphic impact. Be single-minded. Be strong. And make only one point. The last line should be a call to action. You should end as strongly as you began. You can't get your audience all excited in the first line and then leave them in a morass of generalities," is John Rand's view.

Editing Your PSAs

When you go over your copy, keep in mind that "There's no formula or trick," says John Rand. "It's just economy of the greatest order. When you have that short a message, especially when you're not of primary interest to the person you're trying to reach, every word must count. You must eliminate all unnecessary words. And never let up your pace. Make it short, make it staccato, keep it going. No long, drawn-out sentences that people will bog down in. Your writing should be almost telegraphic. And your words should have rhythm."

Writing PSAs is like writing poetry: you have to get your word's worth. Every word has to carry meaning. Go through your copy and cross out as many words as you can. You'll find you can make your copy stronger by eliminating most of the adjectives. And the word *that* can often be dropped. Be merciless with your blue pencil.

As you edit, try to vary your sentence structure and length. Says John Rand, "I think you can, in advertising, . . . [write] a sentence that starts with a preposition. I think you can have three words set off by periods: Wild. Wacky. Wonderful. That moves. It's quick. It's telegraphic. Those are not complete sentences. But I think they help you when you want people to hear you." Don't be afraid to edit more than once, or even more than twice. If you can let the copy sit overnight between those editing jobs, you'll have an easier time. Try to arrange your work schedule so there is always time for this important step.

Read your copy aloud and time it. Try not to say too much in one spot; it's hard to understand even a professional announcer when he has to speak out of both sides of his mouth to cram all the copy into the time slot.

Finally, look at your organization's name. "Especially in radio spots, when you have to state the name, sometimes more than once, a long name can be a problem," says Andrew McGowan. "I've seen names that take ten seconds to recite and leave no room for a message. Stations for the most part require that the full name of the sponsoring organization be in the spot. They won't take a shortened version unless the name can be simplified officially and legally. I've seen broadcasters reject spots that didn't have the full name of the organization." So, you might want to follow the example of the Extended Studies Program at California State University, Bakersfield. Their official alternate name is CSB Plus.

Some Effective PSAs

The following spot, prepared by Barbara Marshall and Kristyn Halbig, directors of public relations for the University of Wisconsin Extension, is a good example of a straightforward PSA. Notice that it immediately identifies its audience and tells them what the service benefit is.

> Musicians, look at what the UW-Extension Indianhead Center in Shell Lake has for you this summer.
> Trumpet and synthesizer symposiums will be offered at the Center August 4th through the 8th.
> The trumpet symposium will be taught by three outstanding musicians—Dominic Spera, Renold Schilke, and Ray Crisara. Chris Swanson, founder of the New York Improvisation Ensemble, will be teaching the synthesizer courses.
> College credits are available for these classes. For more information write: Darrell Aderman, Indianhead Center, Shell Lake, Wisconsin 54871.

Below is the audio part of "Couch Potato," the 20-second version of a spot distributed by West Glen for the American Academy of Pediatrics. It was released to 400 television stations nationally. The spot got excellent pickup by the big three networks, MTV, Nickelodeon, and more than 200 local stations for each of two versions. The intense discussion this spot generated in the media led to international airplay in Holland, Italy, Belgium and England, as well.

VIDEO	AUDIO
1. Boy and girl on couch watching television	MUSIC: Up and under
2. Boy turns into potato	CHORUS: "Couch Potato"
3. GRAPHIC: Too Much T.V.!!	DEEP VOICE: "Too much T.V."
4. Boy potato holds television	BOY: "Leave me alone, just let me groove on my tube!"
5. GRAPHIC: Don't just plop in front of the T.V.	HIGH VOICE: "Don't just plop in front of the T.V. 'cause you've got nothing else to do."

6. Girl potato on couch	GIRL: "Gotta have that . . . Mama can I buy that?"
7. GRAPHIC: Watch out for overeating.	HIGH VOICE: "Watch out for overeating."
8. Family of potatoes turn back into humans.	"Don't be a . . ."
GRAPHIC: From the American Academy of Pediatrics.	CHORUS: "Couch potato. Couch potato."
	CHORUS: Out

When the New York Diabetes Association wanted to explain that contributions are still needed because there is not yet a cure for diabetes, they decided to use a humorous approach. Although the tone of voice in the original is very important, you can get a good deal of the flavor from the following script for a 30-second prerecorded radio PSA. Written by Howard Weinstein, the spot won an award from the Community Agencies Public Relations Association (CAPRA) in New York.

> *Voice 1*: An apple a day keeps diabetes away.
> *Voice 2*: No, it doesn't.
> *Voice 1*: A peach a day?
> *Voice 2*: Nothing keeps diabetes away. There's no way to prevent it and no cure either. It can be very serious, but it can be controlled with proper care.
> *Voice 1*: A pomegranate?
> *Voice 2*: Doctors and scientists are working very hard to find out what will.
> *Voice 1*: A watermelon a day?
> *Voice 2*: You can't eat a whole watermelon.
> *Voice 1*: If it's a small one.
> *Voice 2*: Do something to help. Call the American Diabetes Association today.
> *Voice 1*: Avocados? Nectarines? Casaba melons? Cantaloupes?
> FADE OUT

The National Society to Prevent Blindness approached Planned Communications about doing a PSA asking parents to write for a free home eye test for their preschool children, and the two organizations came up with an unusual approach. Folk singer Tom Glazer wrote a song, which he performed in the following 60-second TV spot. This is the audio portion:

Tom Glazer sings:
Precious sight, precious sight,
Oh the lovely things I see,
The lovely things I see,
In my sight, in my precious sight.
Precious days, precious nights,
And a thousand precious sights,
A thousand precious sights,
That I see in my precious sight.
Glazer voice over:
Vision problems could limit a child's view of things forever.
Age three or four is the prime time for the first vision test. Ask
your Society to Prevent Blindness to send you a free home eye
test for preschoolers.
Tom Glazer sings:
And the precious faces that I love so well,
Much more than mere words can say,
Precious love, precious love,
Precious gifts from above, gifts from above,
That I see in my precious sight every day.
Superimposed title:
Address to write for the free home eye test.
By Tom Glazer, © 1980, Songs Music, Inc., Scarborough, NY
10510. Used by permission.

The Advertising Council, which has done public service advertising for Smokey the Bear for decades, supplied the following simple and effective script for a 30-second TV PSA. It appeals to people who are concerned about ecology or interested in the chains of events that cause ecological problems. The audio portion of the script reads this way:

A fish died. Because it couldn't breathe. Because its gills got clogged with silt. Because mud ran into the river. Because there was nothing to trap the rain. Because all the trees were gone. Because someone got careless with fire. So please be careful with fire. Because.

Video News Releases

Instead of sending your printed press release to television news directors, what if you shot some great video footage of people using your new instant wipe-on baldness remover—and added narration? Then you had it edited down to 90 seconds, and offered that, instead of a press release. Would it work? It sure would! You've just created something called a video news release, or VNR for short. In only a short time, it's become a very popular publicity tool for those organizations that can afford the price tag of $15,000 to $30,000.

A video news release is just like a television news story. It must be objective as well as sound and look like a news report. Since television news stories run between one minute and 90 seconds each, your video news release should fall within that time frame. Package it in a format that's ready for on-the-air use, but also allows stations to edit the material. And you can't focus on plugging your product or service—this has to be a *news* story.

Since VNRs look and sound like news stories, news directors have very strong feelings about them. Medialink, a satellite distribution service for VNRs, sponsored a national survey of television news directors in which three-quarters of the responding journalists said that video news releases should be "clearly identified" as public relations releases. "Identification must include the source of production, and who is the ultimate sponsor of the VNR," according to Medialink's president, Laurence Moskowitz. This is actually a legal requirement when the VNR involves political or controversial issues, according to Section 317 of the Communications Act of 1934.

Since a VNR is a news report, you have to make any mention of your product an integral part of your story. As James Wexler explains, "A good video news release should be structured so that your client's message is entwined with the newsworthy material, and can't be separated."

The bottom line is that with VNRs, as with any other publicity material, you have to think like a journalist. "If you're in the business of packaging news for public relations purposes, you try to produce it as if you were on assignment for the individual station," says Paul Gourvitz, President of Sheridan-Elson-Gourvitz, a video production house in New York.

There is a three-step formula that works well for VNRs—whether they're about products, services, or causes. In an article in *O'Dwyer's PR Services Report*, West Glen president Stan Zeitlin explains, "First, *establish a problem*, which then becomes your news peg. Second, *tell how you or your product can solve the problem*. Third, *summarize with a wrap-up of problem and solution without getting too commercial*." Although this is a workable approach, it's not cast in stone. Your creative team may develop a different angle that will serve you well.

But the subject of a VNR is only part of what makes it appealing to journalists. According to the Medialink survey of television news directors, 83 percent of them say that "... a suggested local angle increase[s] the likelihood ..." they will use a video news release. Andrew McGowan has two solid suggestions for localizing VNRs:

■ Suggest a news peg for local illustrations of the story. In one case, a world-class hospital approached Planned Communications to create "... a VNR to gain national coverage for the anniversary of their performing the country's first coronary bypass operation. Our plan included suggesting to stations that they use the VNR as a news peg to do a [second, local angle] story on how many such procedures are done by a hospital in their area [and that they] interview the longest surviving patient ..." in the vicinity.

■ Provide a list of local experts from your organization who can cap off the story with a local perspective. Planned Communications did a VNR for a national association of colleges that was "completed" by the station interviewing the president of a member institution in its area. "This combination should achieve more coverage than either the national office or the members could alone" McGowan points out.

Making Sure Your VNR Is Broadcast Quality

If you want broadcasters to run your video news release, it has to meet industry standards of *broadcast quality*. This term can be confusing, since it refers to both the technical format and the content.

From a technical point of view, broadcast quality refers to measurable standards. James Wexler explains that "You can actually measure the intensity of the signal on a tape. If the signal is too weak, you won't have broadcast quality. VHS [ordinary home videotape], for example, is not broadcast quality because the electronic data on the tape is not sufficient to create a picture that can be broadcast and received clearly." That's why your VNR must be produced and edited by professionals using broadcast quality equipment.

"Broadcast quality in video news releases also has to do with style," Wexler continues. "A broadcast quality VNR has the look and feel of a local news story." So, you wouldn't use fancy visual effects or music in a VNR, because that would make it look like an advertisement.

To capture and keep your viewers' attention, the video should be visually stimulating, with signs of real life right there in the background. Since VNRs shot in the studio often look dull and artificial, shooting at the location of the actual story gives a more interesting, "newsier" result.

"It's better to have something more interesting to fill the frame than just a bare studio," says Wexler. "When we're doing an interview, we'd rather have someone in an office or at their work location."

Technical Requirements for VNRs

To produce VNRs of broadcast quality, there are a number of things you must do.

First of all, bear in mind that all broadcast news stories are made up of basic building blocks called *sound bites*. A sound bite is a newsmaker speaking on camera, so you see him on the television screen. Sound bite building blocks are tied together with narration by an announcer. As Paul Gourvitz explains, "A typical news story begins with a reporter putting it in perspective. Then there are one, two or three sound bites, each with a different newsmaker's voice." The narrator smooths the transition from one sound bite to another, making logical connections between them and putting them in perspective. After the last sound bite, the reporter draws a brief conclusion, and closes with a *tag*—for example, "This is Soanne Soh reporting."

To be acceptable to news directors, your VNR should fit within a 60- to 90-second time frame. "However there is no set rule" for how long a VNR should be, explains James Wexler. "The story must tell itself." So your VNR may run for 66 seconds—or 87—as long as you keep it below 90 seconds long. (Sixty-four percent of the news directors responding to the Medialink survey felt that 90 seconds was a good length for a VNR.)

Make sure your raw sound bites will work within this framework, so your video editor can shape them into a VNR without cutting your newsmakers and spokespeople off in mid-sentence. That's why you don't want someone in your video news release talking for 30 seconds. "That's just too long," says James Wexler. "But they usually have to speak for longer than four seconds, just to make sense of what's being said. The best length for each sound bite is somewhere in between 10 and 20 seconds—and that's an artistic call." This need for very concise statements may mean you'll have to spend time training your spokespeople to talk in bursts of 10 to 20 seconds—well before the raw footage for your VNR is recorded.

The second technical requirement involves the sound tracks on the videotape. Broadcast quality tape has two tracks for sound. All the sound bites should be on one track, but the narration should be on the other. James Wexler explains that ". . . this lets a news director . . . air the story without your narration. Using the timed script you supplied

... the station's announcer can read the audio portion and make the story sound like the station's own." Since many news directors will want to supply their own narration, having separate sound tracks is a very important factor in getting your video news release aired.

For the same reason, Medialink's Laurence Moskowitz advises "Never superimpose your own written information on the actual video-tape," unless you also supply an alternate version of the finished story, as well. Many TV news departments want to supply their own titles using the typefaces that match their station's style, and they can't do that easily if all you've given them is a version that already has titles.

Moskowitz adds that you should also never have your narrator or reporter on-screen because "Stations do not want a reporter appearing in their newscast who is not on their staff." (60% of the stations Medialink surveyed would not use a VNR in which the sponsor's reporter appeared on-screen.)

Still another technical requirement for video news releases is the inclusion of additional raw material on the tape you provide to stations. This lets the news director produce his own story, with his own an-nouncer and his station's look, feel and point-of-view. This extra foot-age is called *B-roll*. In fact, 21 percent of the television newspeople responding to the Medialink survey were even willing to work with a B-roll alone—without any publicist-prepared story at all!

Of course, there's a contradiction here. Your organization spends thousands of dollars to produce a finished, videotaped news story from *your* viewpoint. Why should you let journalists edit it? That's a good question, and you should be prepared with an answer, because your organization's top executives may indeed raise it. The explanation is simple: you have no choice. This is not advertising, and, just as with a printed press release, you have to *earn* coverage. You have to accept the possibility that journalists may not see eye to eye with you—and that editors will edit. But, if your VNR has a good news peg and you have nothing to hide, it's likely that those editors preparing their own stories from your raw material will give you favorable coverage.

Paul Gourvitz sums it up, "That's the beauty of B-roll; it gives News Directors options. If they like what you sent them, but it isn't exactly the way they would do it, they can edit the story to suit themselves."

B-roll can include several different types of material, and you can even plan several types of very useful shots, especially for your B-roll, that will help a news director create a better finished story. James Wexler describes one example. ". . . let's say you're doing a story on a hospital. You might give them a few extra shots of the medical procedure taking place, so if for some reason they want a longer story than your edited piece, they have the raw material."

Paul Gourvitz explains another case. "In an edited story about a nuclear plant, which you're trying to keep to 90 seconds, you might have a wide shot of the nuclear plant. And then you'd go inside and show one or two interior scenes. But in B-roll you might give them a zoom-in, a zoom-out, a static shot of the exterior, and a few more inside shots. That way they can pick what they want. What you're doing is trying to provide variety for them."

One of the problems with videotape editing is something called a *jump cut*. This is a sudden, jerky movement of a person—or a head or hands—when a piece of the tape is removed during editing. Video editors use what's called a *cutaway* to avoid jump cuts. When you plan your VNR, ask the video production house what types of material they recommend for *cover footage* to make it possible for the news director to do cutaways.

If your video news release is shot on location, you will also want to include the standard types of shots news directors rely on. An *establishing shot* is used at the start of a story. It's a wide angle view, which puts the location into perspective and helps the viewer get an orientation. You should also include *zoom in, zoom out,* and *static* shots for both outside and inside locations. Zoom in shots start in the distance and get closer, so you move from the broad view to the more specific, with the details emerging as you go. They are more likely to be used at the beginning of a story, or when the camera moves to a new scene. Zoom out shots are the opposite; they start close in and move out, and are most likely used at the close of a story. Static shots keep the same perspective. The people in them can move but the camera perspective stays the same.

Finally, you should provide news directors with an index for your VNR. This should be in two forms: a printed copy that goes with the support materials, and a copy that's on-screen right at the start of the tape. Your index should tell the news director whether the tape includes titled and untitled versions of the finished story, describe additional sound bites, and list any cover footage, establishing shots, zoom-ins, and zoom-outs, as well as extra exterior and interior shots. Be sure your video production house includes exact tape locations for everything listed in the index.

Producing a VNR

Producing a broadcast quality VNR, even an ultra-brief one, involves an astounding number of steps. Tempting as it may be to take shortcuts, particularly if you're working with a tight budget, you can't leave any of them out. But if you understand how the production process works, you *can* cut costs with careful planning.

Shrewd strategizing can make it possible to produce several VNRs from one shoot at a far lower cost than if they were produced individually. For example, you could create VNRs with different news pegs: one version could be hard news; but two others might be evergreen. You might produce one in English, and another in Spanish. Or, you could produce longer mini-features, running up to ten minutes, from footage taken at the same shoot. But, you probably won't be able to do this unless you plan ahead to get the footage you need for each video version.

The first step in producing a video news release is to develop a concept. This is a rough outline that describes the news peg, the goal for your piece, who will speak, what points they will make, where the tape will be shot, whether you'll be able to cut costs by using any "stock" footage from a film library, what props you'll need, and what types of shots are necessary both for the finished story and for the B-roll. Think of a concept as a starting point, not a blueprint. Your concept will change as you and the production house start work and discover what is possible, what could be done if you had unlimited funds, and what can't be done, even if you do have all the gold in Fort Knox.

The next step is usually handled by the production house. They have to look at each location indicated in your concept, and check to find or anticipate any problems that could make a shoot impossible. A good location scout will ask and answer questions like these:

- What kind of lighting is called for?
- Are there deep shadows at any time of the day?
- Is there a possible crowd control or security problem?
- What props will be needed to make studio scenes look real and interesting?
- Are the locations available when you need them?
- Are permits needed?
- What are the user fees, if any?

Once you and your creative team have developed a concept and secured the locations, you can build the concept into the script, including tight descriptions of each shot. The narrator's dialogue in the script should be complete and polished; however, lines for the newsmakers will depend on each person's style. Some speakers need to be provided with the exact words they'll use on camera. Others do much better with a loose outline. You'll have to find out their preferences.

Be prepared for several meetings with your production house just for this phase of the project. It takes time to do it well, and if your creative team tries to do it without you, you probably won't be satisfied with the results.

Once the script is written, all locations have been arranged for, the props have been bought, rented, or borrowed, and the production house has secured camera and lighting crews, you're ready to shoot. Bear in mind that you'll only be shooting the sound bites. The narration will be recorded later, in a sound studio, and added onto the tape.

You should be at the shooting. And don't be surprised if it takes hours and hours to get enough footage for a 90-second finished story plus B-roll. A professional producer will insist on shooting many "takes" for each scene, to make sure that one of them will be perfect. But the time you spend at the shoot will be well worth it. As Margie Goldsmith of MG Productions explains in an article in *Public Relations Business,* "Whenever I shoot, I insist that a company representative be present so the client can have final approval along the way."

Once the tape is shot and *in the can*, you and your producer should view it, before the editing session. Your task is to choose which *take*, or version, of each scene is the best one. As Margie Goldsmith explains in an article in *O'Dwyer's PR Services Report,* editing studios charge by the hour. "It requires a great deal of time to roll back and forth looking for the perfect take . . . and you are paying for every minute of the search," if you do it at the editing studio rather than ahead of time.

When the editing is done, and you have approved the final result, the production house makes two master tapes: one for safekeeping, and one to use for duplicating. Then their station relations staff takes over, and works with you to develop supporting materials like backgrounder sheets, names of local contacts for interviews, facts about your story from each local area, and anything else you can think of that will help sell your story. Of course, they will include a pitch letter that sells your VNR and a timed script in the support package.

Finally, you have to decide how you'll distribute your VNR. Unless you want the expense of sending cassettes and support packages to every television station that reaches your target audience, you have two basic choices:

- ■ Have the production house's station relations staff send out an announcement offering the VNR, including all the supporting materials *and* a prepaid reply card the news director can fill out if she wants the cassette. If the production house has a toll-free number, include that, as well. When a station asks for the cassette, it's mailed out, with a *second* package of supporting materials, in case the news director has mis-placed the first packet. You can also have the station rela-tions staff call stations that don't respond—but you may want to limit the telephone follow-ups to the most impor-tant stations on your list.

■   You can have the station relations staff make the contacts as above, but offer to send the VNR and B-roll by satellite. If the video production house doesn't have satellite facilities, they can work with the dedicated satellite transmission ser-vice (see Medialink, which is listed in Chapter 12). Compare costs carefully before you decide if you want to offer sta-tions this option, and be sure to balance the increased cost of satellite transmission against the savings of eliminating multiple cassettes.

Satellite transmission of VNRs is still new enough so that it's really hard to say if news directors prefer it or not. One survey (conducted by a satellite transmission facility) shows that they do—overwhelmingly. Another study (conducted by a distributor of videocassettes) concludes that they don't—overwhelmingly. If you're a member of a professional organization for publicists, you might want to compare notes with colleagues who have had experience with each method of transmitting video news releases.

Questions to Ask a Video Production House

Be very careful when you choose a production house for your video news release. That choice can mean the difference between a newsworthy video and a pile of expensive cassettes accumulating dust on the shelf.

According to an editorial in the December 1989, issue of *Public Relations Journal*, ". . . a growing number of distributors/producers themselves are concerned about suppliers who deal in poor quality VNRs lacking viable news or feature angles . . . . And many feel that there should be a code of ethics for the VNR industry."

If you ask a video production house the following questions *before* you sign a contract with them, you'll have a better sense of whether they can do an excellent job:

■   How many seasoned television news people are on their staff, and what are their qualifications? It's much more likely you'll get broadcast quality stories from experienced journalists. With the spate of cutbacks of television news

staff in recent years, many highly qualified journalists are
now working for video production houses.

■ Is all their equipment broadcast quality?

■ Can they guarantee that they will meet media deadlines?
This is especially important if you plan to use video news releases to announce or respond to breaking news, where you
may have to produce an entire VNR, from script to placement, in one day.

■ Do they have a full-time station relations staff that places
VNRs and other publicity material with broadcasters? It
takes a lot of work and know-how to place video news releases effectively with television stations, so you should be
working with experts. If you have found a really cracker-
jack production house that doesn't have this capability, you
should arrange for one of the larger video news release distributors to place the story for you.

■ How often do they update their media contact database? Is
it computerized? What types of specialized reporters does it
include? Can they sort lists of stations geographically and by
audience rating? Does their database include information
about each station's technical needs?

■ What, exactly, is included in their contract? What is extra?
Can they guarantee they'll shoot this VNR in one day? Will
there be overtime? Under what conditions? How much will
it cost?

■ Who have they worked for? Can they supply references?
Can you see other video news releases they've done? What
kind of airplay did their sample VNRs get, and do they have
documentation to prove it?

Radio Wrap-Arounds

There is a radio equivalent to the video news release, called a wrap-
around, radio actuality, or audio news release. They're not as popular
as VNRs, and not all radio stations seem eager to run them. But they're
relatively inexpensive and quick to produce, and some radio stations,
particularly in smaller cities and towns, will be interested in running a
timely wrap-around. Your wrap-around should run for 90 seconds or

less, and be professionally recorded on audiotape. Any competent sound studio can record a radio wrap-around for you.

Wrap-arounds start with an announcer introducing the story. Next comes the voice of a newsmaker, in a sound bite that lasts between 10 and 20 seconds. If your wrap-around uses more than one sound bite, the announcer provides a transition between each of them. At the end of the wrap-around, the announcer sums up the story, and adds a tag line ("this is Soanne Soh reporting"). The result sounds just like the typical radio news story.

Broadcast Feature Programs

Video news releases and radio wrap-arounds are not the only pre-recorded publicity material you can successfully place with broadcasters. You can provide prerecorded programs that run for as long as an hour or as short as two minutes. Producing them is similar to creating video news releases and radio wrap-arounds.

"The secret," according to Andrew McGowan of Planned Communications, "is finding a formula for content and format that satisfies your objectives, broadcasters' programming needs, and audience interests. It's easier than you may think: stations are often quite willing to 'barter' airtime for good programming they can get without charge."

McGowan strongly suggests that you offer feature programs on an exclusive basis to one—and only one— broadcaster in each market-place. "What usually characterizes this kind of project, is that the commitment is to a continuing series, most often in one-season (13 week) units, that each station airs on a constant schedule." He gives two examples of successful broadcast feature programs developed by Planned Communications:

■ "Trends in Living," a weekly half-hour television show sponsored by the National Association of Realtors, presented studio interviews and stories filmed on location. Topics covered included urban renewal in Baltimore, high property values near national parklands, and home equity loans. It ran for 13 weeks on 75 stations.

■ "A Minute for Health," a radio feature, has been sponsored by pharmaceutical, insurance and other health care companies. The show covers subjects of concern to the sponsors and names the company in closing credits. It has been given airtime worth an estimated value of $4.6 million by 1,077 radio stations.

James Wexler suggests a somewhat different, library approach, to distributing television feature programs. "Television library programs are made available to broadcast stations and cable systems throughout the country without charge," Wexler explains. Of course, this involves promotional mailings, but once they know about your titles, program directors request the cassettes for preview. If they like what they see, they can decide to use this free loan material in open time slots or as regularly scheduled shows. Once the programs have been aired, the videocassettes are returned to you.

Returned tapes must be inspected for damage and loss of broadcast quality before they are sent out again. How can that happen? Keep in mind that the images and sound on videotape are captured in magnetic fields stored in the tape's coating. If the coating is damaged during playback, or the tape is exposed to magnetic fields during shipping and handling, the picture and sound can lose quality—or even disappear in spots. Wexler figures it takes about 50 cassettes per title to make the basis of a library generating 600 showings per year for each program.

Broadcast television stations prefer 5- to 10-minute long feature programs; whereas cable systems are more interested in 28-minute and 54-minute features that fill half-hour and hour-long slots, but leave time for commercials, according to Wexler. "The most usable subjects for free programs are health, sports, entertainment, travel and recreation . . . . Opening and closing credits are permitted as well as limited sponsor or product exposure during the program," he concludes.

Since producing features can be expensive, it's a good idea to survey program directors at a sample of your target stations. Get their input after you create a rough concept, but before you start scripting. You'll find out quickly if they're interested, and whether some changes to your concept could mean your feature will get more airplay.

Community Calendar Listings

Community calendar listings are similar to PSAs except they are used for promoting events, rather than ideas, causes and services. They usually air for 10 or 15 seconds, although some stations have different formats. In smaller towns and cities, public service directors will need them a week or two ahead of time. In a large metropolis, lead time may be as long as eight weeks.

The following is a 10-second community calendar listing:

> Learn how to check your home for signs of termites in a free workshop sponsored by Plains City Real Estate Board at a location near you. For information call 990-8888.

Television Specials

Some television stations are merely conduits for programs produced elsewhere and fed to them by the networks or independent producers. Others produce their own programs in their studios. If the station does its own programming, you can ask it to produce a special program about your product, service, cause, or industry. You just have to convince it that you have material that is interesting to its viewers. Pitch to it much the same way you'd pitch a feature story to an editor at a magazine, shifting the emphasis to the visual aspects of your material.

You will increase the impact of a special program if you provide the station with good visual material. TV people don't like "talking head" situations where there are no interesting images to relieve the monotony of endless speaking. The National Association of Broadcasters (NAB) recommends that you check with the producer of the show well in advance of the production date, to make sure that your material is the right size, shape, and format for the station and that the technicians will have equipment ready to handle it.

"Simple, uncluttered art work and photographs televise best," says the NAB. "Care must be taken to assure good contrast. Otherwise graphics may be lost against the background. Printing should be in bold, heavy lines, with a minimum of words." Black against white is fine; however, pink against yellow will probably look like mud on the screen because of the lack of contrast. And, ". . . dull finishes are more satisfactory than glossies that reflect light."

If you're not sure how many words can fit on a TV visual, watch for an advertisement where they flash a telephone number on the screen. Does it fill the screen from side to side? Is it a simple ten-digit number with an area code? Can you see why each line must be limited to 12 letters, numbers or spaces, and that three or four lines are the limit for each visual?

Television stations want professional looking visual material from you. No station is going to jeopardize its technical reputation or risk losing its audience by using sloppy slides, tapes, or visuals. "We are inundated with so many promos for nonprofit organizations that we can be selective. Whether it's for a prime-time program or a PSA, the better it looks, the more chance of getting it on the air." says KSTP-TV's Linnea Crowe. Again, it is always wise to check technical requirements with the producer or public service director well in advance. This gives your material the best odds for garnering air time.

Always ask the producer or director whether your visual material can be returned to you. It almost always can be, but usually arrangements must be made ahead of time. Just to be on the safe side, *keep* the original slides, charts, photos, and videotapes. Send duplicates to the station.

When you work with cablecasters, ask if there is studio space and time available to record your programs on videotape. You may be pleasantly surprised. According to the *New York Times*, fledgling producers have increasingly been given access to professional training and facilities by cable operators. If cablecasters do not have studios, but will let you provide programs on videotape for transmission over the public access channel, find out the technical requirements before you start the reels rolling. Most cablecasters use three-quarter-inch videotape, but some require one-half-inch tape.

What do you do if you need help producing videotapes? Nonprofit or community organizations have some options. First ask the broadcaster or cablecaster if he has any suggestions. You might also contact the communications or broadcast department at your local college. They may welcome the chance to give their students practical experience, and you'll get your program videotaped at little or no cost. You may even find that the college has unusually creative, capable students, and your program may be of professional caliber. If you're not sure whom to talk with, call the public relations department. They should be glad to help you, especially if you offer to give the college credit for its contribution to your videotape.

If your organization is a business, you should find a video production house or an advertising agency with television experience to conceptualize, script and tape the program for you. Sure that's expensive up front, but you want results. And the results will almost always be far better with a professionally-produced television program.

Checklist—Preparing Materials for Broadcast

1. Have you read your material out loud and cut out anything that's difficult to say?
2. Are your sentences short?
3. Have you avoided too many "s" sounds?
4. Is it clear what the words "she," "he," and "they" refer back to?
5. If you have homonyms that sound alike but have different meanings, are those meanings clear from the context?
6. Is each broadcast news release on a separate piece of 8 1/2 × 11-inch paper?
7. Does your news release heading include your organization's name and address, the date, the name and telephone number of a contact person, and the reading time in seconds?
8. Is your release typed, double-spaced, on one side of the sheet only? Is it no longer than 90 seconds maximum?
9. Have you used the present tense and rounded out the numbers?
10. Have you spelled out in phonetics any names that are difficult to pronounce?
11. Have you found out which news directors prefer releases in outline form?
12. Have you asked if the station has policies about PSAs? Do you know what format and length they prefer and if they use tapes, "live" copy, or both?
13. Have you thought about how your business or trade association can present information in PSAs that serves community interests and meets your goals?
14. Have you considered underwriting PSAs for a nonprofit organization that could help you meet your goals?
15. Can you come up with a creative way to work your product mention into the heart of a sponsored PSA?
16. Have you given the public service director a choice of two or three lengths for your PSA?

17. If you're producing prerecorded PSAs, are they exactly 10, 15, 20, 30 or 60 seconds long?

18. Have you made sure there is no sound in the first and last half-second?

19. Have you asked your local stations if they will help you produce your PSAs?

20. Have you checked with public service directors to find out the station's technical requirements for PSAs?

21. If you are producing prerecorded PSAs, do you have rights to use the music and sound effects?

22. Have you sent a script or a story board with the spot?

23. Have you considered sending out a script and prepaid request card, rather than massive numbers of prerecorded PSAs?

24. Have you checked with the producer to see whether she'll shoot on film, videotape, or videocassette?

25. Who will distribute your taped PSAs, and how will the distributor know which format each station prefers?

26. Do they have an up-to-date station information database?

27. Do you know which stations use live copy for PSAs?

28. Do you know what their requirements are for visual material?

29. Have you timed your live copy scripts to fit common time slots?

30. Have you included visual material with your live copy for TV PSAs?

31. Do you have one slide for each five to ten seconds, and are the slides all horizontal?

32. Do you know whether your target stations insist on glass-mounted slides, or if they'll accept cardboard or plastic mounts?

33. Have you checked which parts of the images in your slides will be cut off around the edges?

34. If you are sending out a script/slide PSA, does the script describe each slide?

35. Have you numbered the slides and keyed them to the script?

36. If you're involved in a nonprofit organization, have you found out if public service directors in your area require

copies of fund-raising permits and your IRS tax-status letter?

37. Have you thought about increasing station acceptance of your PSAs by not mentioning fund-raising directly?

38. Does your PSA heading include a contact person and telephone number including the area code, the date, an expiration date, the reading time, and the number of words?

39. Did you list the *w*'s and the *h* before you started writing your PSA spot?

40. Is your spot double- or triple-spaced and typed in upper- and lowercase with 35-character lines and wide margins?

41. Have you kept in mind that your audience will probably be doing something else besides just listening and watching?

42. How will you grab their interest immediately?

43. Have you limited your PSA to one main point?

44. Have you avoided borrowed interest in your PSA?

45. Have you closed by asking people to take an action?

46. Can you back up the facts, figures, and claims in your PSA?

47. Is your organization's name too long? Should you come up with an official alternative?

48. Have you let your PSA sit overnight before you edited it?

49. Have you cut out extra words, particularly adjectives?

50. Have you planned your video shoot so you can get as much use from the taped material as possible?

51. Is your video news release as objective as a news story?

52. Does it look and sound like a news report?

53. Is it 90 seconds or shorter?

54. Can you shorten it even more by putting some of the material into a backgrounder?

55. Have you identified your organization as the source of the news?

56. Have you entwined mention of your product or service with the news peg?

57. Have you established a problem, solved it with your product or service, and drawn a conclusion?

58. Have you provided suggestions for localizing your VNR?

59. Can you shoot all or part of your VNR on location?

60. If all or part of your VNR must be shot in a studio, can you use props and stage settings to make it look like it's shot on location?

61. Have you trained your spokespeople to talk in 10- to 20-second units?

62. Has your production house kept the sound bites and narration on separate tracks?

63. Have you included one version of the edited story without any titles on it?

64. Have you made sure your narrator never appears on screen?

65. Have you planned your B-roll before you shoot?

66. Does your B-roll include extra sound bites, establishing, static, zoom-in and zoom-out shots, as well as cover footage?

67. Have you included an index at the start of the tape and enclosed a printed copy with the support materials?

68. Have you developed a detailed concept and a script before you start shooting?

69. Do you know whether your spokespeople need tight scripts or prefer loose guidelines?

70. Have you rented or bought any props you'll need?

71. Have you scouted for locations?

72. Has your producer looked at lighting and crowd control considerations for each location?

73. Do you have permits and reservations for locations where they're needed?

74. Is there any "stock" footage you can use to cut your shooting costs?

75. Will you and any other executives from your organization who need to give approval, be present at the shoot?

76. Have you arranged to view the raw footage to choose the best takes before the editing session?

77. Will you be at the editing session so you can give your approval at each stage, and help cut costs by speeding up the process?

78. Has your production house made both a dubbing master for duplicating copies, and a second master for safekeeping?

79. Does the support package sent out to news directors include a timed script, background material, and a pitch letter?

80. Have you decided whether you want to distribute your VNR by mailing cassettes or by satellite? Have you compared costs for these two distribution methods?

81. Have you asked each video production house you're considering how many seasoned television people are on their staff?

82. Is the production house's equipment all of broadcast quality?

83. Can they guarantee they'll meet media deadlines, particularly with breaking news?

84. Do they have a full-time station relations staff? If they don't, will they be comfortable working with one of the larger video houses that also distributes VNRs and does have this staff?

85. How often do they update their media contact database?

86. What types of information does the database include?

87. What, exactly, is included in their contract? Under what conditions will there be extra or overtime charges?

88. Have you considered creating radio and television feature programs?

89. Do you understand the difference between PSAs and community calendar listings?

90. Have you asked about the technical requirements for visual aids for TV special programs?

91. Did you find out if your visual materials can be returned to you? Do you have duplicates just in case?

92. Do your visuals have good, sharp contrast? Are they bold and uncluttered?

93. Have you limited typeset visuals to 4 lines of 12 characters each?

94. Do your visuals have a dull, nonreflecting finish?

95. Does your local cablecaster have studios you can use? Technical help? Editing equipment? Are there fees involved?

CHAPTER EIGHT

Getting on the Air

O nce you have mastered the art of writing for broadcast and preparing good visuals for different types of TV formats, you will need to understand how to approach broadcasters most effectively.

Americans listen to an average of three hours of radio every day. And 98 percent of the homes in this country have at least one television set. There are 11,403 radio and television stations licensed by the Federal Communications Commission (FCC), as well as several hundred low-power TV stations, almost 10,000 cablecasters, and dozens of cable networks. Add that up and you get a huge potential audience for your organization's publicity. All you have to do is produce interesting, newsworthy, informative material and know how to persuade journalists to air it.

Whether you are approaching your local radio or television station, cablecasters, or the networks, you need to consider what kinds of air time are generally available and which format will work best for you.

In the previous chapter you learned how to prepare material for the PSA format, as well as for community calendar listings, newscasts, and short features. This chapter will discuss how to reach the right people with your material. It will also explain how to obtain other types of air time involving live appearances.

The following types of airtime are available to publicists:

Public service announcements (PSAs). PSAs are the easiest kind of air time to get. Your approach here should be through the station's public service director. Specific hints for placing PSAs will be discussed later in the chapter.

Community calendar listings. These are handled in much the same way as public service announcements. They're generally available only to nonprofit and community organizations, but businesses can sometimes be listed if the event is free and serves the public interest. Unless you're contacting a very large station with a staff person assigned to handling community calendar announcements, you should send your listings to the public service director.

News broadcasts. Most radio and television stations have news programs, and broadcast news is becoming more influential. "In 1986," according to Medialink's Laurence Moskowitz, "a nationwide Roper poll found that more than 50 percent of the public got *all* of their news from television." Station executives have found that while producing news reports is relatively low-cost, they increase listener/viewer ratings. "In some markets," according to *O'Dwyer's PR Services Report*, "local stations are now generating two and a half hours of news daily, in addition to carrying the network evening news. In many U.S. TV markets today, these local shows account for 40 to 50 percent or more of stations' profits . . ."

To place your publicity material on news programs, contact the news director or the assignment director at larger stations. And if the station has morning talk shows that include news segments, find out who handles those. It may be someone on the talk show staff, rather than the station's news director. To supply publicity material to news directors, you can send written material, audiotapes or videocassettes— or use the telephone to make "live" reports or transmit taped radio wrap-arounds.

Short features running from one to 10 minutes. These may be of interest to public service directors and program directors, as well as news departments at stations with longer newscasts. But be careful: if you send the same pitch to two or more journalists at the same station, and more than one is interested, you have an embarrassing problem. They can't all cover the story, so you'll have to take it away from one (or more) of them. That's not very healthy for your working relationships. Approach one person at a time, and if he isn't interested, try another. You can also try to get a station to produce a short feature itself, or offer to supply a finished program on audio- or videotape.

Special programs. These are entire shows devoted to your organization, are longer than features, and can run for 15, 30 or 60 minutes. Your material may fit into a series with a regular time slot and host, or the station may create a single program especially for your organization or cause. KGW-TV in Portland, Oregon, for example, has produced specials on preventative health care, myths about rape victims, and heating with wood stoves.

Special programs may range from two- or three-minute mini-programs repeated several times during the week, to full-fledged hour-long, in-depth documentaries. Bear in mind that even half an hour is a lot of time to fill, and an hour can stretch from here to eternity. If you have never been on the air before, start small. Ask to be on one of the shorter programs, or see if you can share a special program with one or two other organizations.

Always try to limit the length of special programs so that you end before the audience is satisfied. Then they'll be more interested in seeing the activity in person, getting more information, or listening to you next time you're on the air.

Your pitch for a special program should be made to the station's program director.

Talk and interview shows. These are a great way to get your message to the world, since talk shows are always looking for interesting guests. It is much easier to arrange an appearance on a talk or interview show, whether live, by telephone, or by satellite, than it is to set up a special program or a short feature. Like specials, talk shows are effective when you want to present a long, detailed message.

Arrange your appearance by calling the talent bookers for the shows that interest you. (A number of the media directories discussed in Chapter 12 include listings of talent bookers.) Your television appearance can be in person, on videotape or via satellite tour, or in person or by telephone for radio talk shows. Find out which methods are acceptable to each show's talent booker—and then figure out the best approach for you.

Free-speech messages or guest editorials. Here individuals or groups can offer opinions on major public controversies. You will probably record the message at the station in your own voice. Most stations that run editorials encourage organizations with opposing viewpoints to record replies. These formats are useful to alert your community to a problem or to take a stand in an ongoing debate. You should contact the station's editorial director to make your request.

Compiling Broadcast Data

One of your first tasks as a publicist is to put together a list of broadcasters and cablecasters who serve your area. Your list should include the following:

- Names of public service directors.
- Names of news directors.
- Names and formats of locally originated programs.
- Deadlines and lead times for these programs.
- Lead times for PSAs and community calendar items.
- Each station's format requirements for PSAs.

Making this list will be a pretty easy job in rural areas and small towns, but if you live in a large city, it can be complicated. Remember that stations in other cities and even other states may serve your area, too. Check to see if the TV listings in your local paper include any helpful information, and supplement this by looking at *TV Guide* and the *Yellow Pages*. The media directories listed in Chapter 12 will help you round out the information for your local area, or plan a national campaign. Most large libraries have at least one of these directories.

An association of public service directors in your city may publish a guidebook with a lot of the information you need. These radio and television access guides are becoming more common as the National Association of Broadcasters encourages its members to produce them. Call the public service director at the largest station serving your area and ask her if there is a media access guide for your town. She should also be able to send you a list of locally originated programs produced by her station. Ask if the station offers tours of its studios, and if it does, take one at the first opportunity. It will help you understand how broadcast journalists work.

If your organization is a nonprofit one, you might also call the local United Way office to see if they sell a local media list. It will be well worth the price if they do.

You will have to update your list continually. Media people move from job to job at an astounding speed, and even radio stations have been known to change their formats and their call letters, or to disappear from the airwaves entirely. In cable TV, growth is so rapid and changes so frequent that you'll need a second set of toes, since you'll always be on them. A channel that was empty yesterday may be filled tomorrow with 24-hour satellite-beamed newscasts—or locally originated programs.

Selecting Suitable Stations

A publicist who wants to place material on a station he doesn't listen to or watch should become familiar with that station first. How do you become familiar with stations across the country when you're working on nationally-oriented publicity? There are two ways. One is to familiarize yourself with the program descriptions in some of the more complete media directories. The other technique is more involved. Hire a clipping bureau to provide you with transcripts, audio- or videotapes of programs that you absolutely *must* appear on. When you're pitching your idea to a news or program director on the other coast, he should be impressed, indeed, if you're familiar with the content and format of some recent programs on his station. (The larger clipping bureaus listed in Chapter 12 offer this service.)

If you work for a small nonprofit or community organization that doesn't have such a large budget, try to get volunteers from chapters in your target cities to tape the programs you're targeting.

You have to decide whether you want to approach your audience via TV or radio. Your choice will depend on the particular message and the type of audience you want to reach. There are important differences between radio and television audiences. For instance, morning and evening "drive time," when people are commuting to and from work, is when most folks listen to the radio. After dinner, Americans switch their allegiance to TV, and radio's audience gets much smaller. Keep in mind that broadcast TV reaches a broad audience, but radio stations and cablecasters are often more selective. By choosing a particular radio station or cablecaster, you can aim your publicity at teenagers, young adults, people over age forty, Blacks, people with a Hispanic background, opinion makers, and other defined groups.

You will improve your audience targeting results even further if you can get some of the demographic material that many stations prepare for potential advertisers. For example, it might tell you how many women listeners work outside the home, the average age of the audience, and how much the typical listener earns. Although you won't usually be able to specify the time of day your "live" copy will be used, you can select talk shows to target based on demographic information and the differences between audiences at various times of day. Ask the public service director if she can supply you with any demographic material for her station. If she cannot, ask if there is somebody in the station's advertising department who can. Make your request as specific as possible.

Let's say you want to reach retired people with a PSA about your anti-crime program that provides escorts for older Americans who have to walk alone at night. Even if the station does not have a neat packet of demographic information, they will probably be able to tell you what portion of their audience is over age sixty-five. And you may be surprised when you find out which stations older people tune into. Or suppose your company has just launched a line of products for new mothers. Although none of the stations in your target area may be able to tell you how many of their listeners are women with newborns, you will be able to eliminate stations with audiences that are too young or old.

Some stations try to reach a broad audience, but even they may be willing to use some PSAs that appeal to a segment of their listeners. "Because we air at least 230 spots per week, some of these spots are geared to specific communities," says WCBS-AM's Teresa DiTore. "We focus on smaller communities because I think people out there like to hear their communities mentioned. But we need a nice mix of things that appeal to everybody and things that appeal to one particular segment."

Working with Public Service Directors

Public service directors are usually more willing than reporters, editors, and news directors to talk with new publicists about the station's needs and preferences, and about where a particular organization fits in. Says Mary Jane O'Neill of the New York Association for the Blind, "It's important to know the public service directors on radio and television. The better you know them, and the better they know the organization you're promoting, the more apt you are to get your material aired."

When you approach public service directors, bear in mind that they are extraordinarily busy; they work in a pressured world surrounded by nonstop deadlines. A typical public service director might also double as the station's editorial director and speech writer, as well as hostess and producer of a couple of talk shows. She may also assist with the overall direction of the public affairs department, all without any clerical assistance whatsoever. Each day she receives piles of mail and dozens of telephone calls. Therefore, when you call a public service director. be brief and to the point. Always ask if it is a good time to talk; if it isn't, offer to call back at a better time. Never just drop in and expect a public service director to have time to chat with you.

The public service director, as the name implies, is your prime contact for public service material, particularly for PSAs and community calendar listings. But she doesn't run the news department. So, don't send your news releases to the public service director and assume that she will ease your way into the newsroom. She probably won't, because she doesn't have the time.

Determining a Station's PSA Policies

First of all, ask the public service director if the station has any special policies regarding PSAs. In addition to basic information about format, length, and lead time required, find out if the station prefers a particular angle or approach. Although many broadcasters will use taped copy and will read "live" copy as it is written, some stations handle PSAs differently. "We use fact sheets that the individual announcers play around with so they sound different each time they're read," says Ken Barlow, public service director for KOFM Radio in Oklahoma City.

"Our station is 'personality' oriented, and our . . . [announcers] have more influence on people in this area than . . . [the celebrities] they send out on tape. I rarely use the script that is sent in, preferring to adapt it to fit the individual personality's style," explains Harry O'Toole, public service director for KDKA-AM in Pittsburgh.

In some areas, stations will use PSAs for one-time events. In other cities, PSAs are reserved for ongoing programs and information efforts, while single events are covered in a community events calendar. At KGW-TV in Portland, Oregon, for example, PSAs usually run for three months. The length of PSA usage may even vary from station to station in your hometown, so when you talk with public service directors, ask about their policy for single events.

Be sure to find out how much lead time the station needs for PSAs. West Glen's James Wexler explains that "Public service directors usually need one or two weeks to screen a spot and another one to two weeks to schedule it. For example, a spot intended for airing the beginning of August should be in the mail by mid-June to allow time for shipping and previewing."

There is one area which almost all broadcasters have declared off limits in PSAs—at least for now. Your PSA cannot deal with material or people on the ballot in an upcoming election, because stations want to avoid being swamped with requests for equal time. In fact, you can't use a well-known political figure as the announcer in your spot if he's going to be on the ballot, even if he doesn't mention his candidacy or politics. Planned Communications' Andrew McGowan tells about an organization which discovered this the hard way.

"They made some spots using a basketball player as a spokesman. When they were getting ready to submit the spots to the TV station, the basketball player decided he was going to run for the U.S. Senate. And the spots couldn't be used because rival candidates would have the right to demand equal time," says McGowan. The money lost on the production costs for their TV spots was considerable; a hard lesson, indeed.

If your organization is going to use a spokesperson, check and double-check to make sure he or she doesn't have secret political ambitions which could knock you out of the water. Although the law covering the Federal Communications Commission's Equal Time doctrine has been called into question by a recent court decision, many broadcasters will take a wait-and-see stance, and will not air PSAs starring political candidates until the FCC issues a new ruling or the legislation is rewritten. Meanwhile, it's best to be cautious.

In addition to political candidates, "You should also beware of using TV, radio, and movie personalities in your spots. They could be linked, permanently or temporarily, with a particular TV or radio station. If that's the case, the other broadcasters will not use your spots," says Ravelle Brickman.

Mailing PSAs

Mail delivery of PSAs is not as effective as working directly with public service directors, but the results are still worthwhile. There will be times when you will not be able to use the personal approach to public service directors because you will be sending out too many spots or mailing them to stations in other cities and states.

When you mail PSAs, be sure to include a brief cover letter. Explain why the event or service or campaign is important, how it meets the needs of people in the station's area, and when it is taking place. Mention the type of audience you're seeking and the time during which you would like the spots to air.

A cover letter to a public service director might look like the following:

Dear Public Service Director:

Many people are getting married later in life these days, and women are becoming mothers in their late thirties and early forties. Although most older women have no problems with pregnancy, there is an increased risk their babies will have Down's syndrome. This disease, which causes mental retardation and other problems in the infant, can be detected by using a quick diagnostic test on pregnant women over the age of 35.

When the expectant mother knows the results of the test, she can make an informed decision about whether to continue the pregnancy. During the next six months, a grant from the Louise Jones Foundation will make it possible for the Plains City Women's Health Center to offer this test, at no cost, to any pregnant woman in her first trimester who is over age 35. There is no residency requirement.

Enclosed are 20, 30 and 60-second PSAs explaining this service. We would very much appreciate your running these spots until December 31. It would also be helpful to us if you could use the enclosed stamped and addressed reply card to let us know when and how often the spots are used.

We think we've covered the bases in this letter, the PSAs themselves, and the enclosed background sheets, but if you have questions, please call us. Many thanks for your help.

If you intend to use professionally prerecorded spots, you may not have a budget large enough to send cassettes to every station on your list. Instead, screen broadcasters to make sure they're interested before you send them the tape. Screening takes a lot of work, according to an article by Margie Goldsmith in *Public Relations Journal*. For a small national campaign, "The follow-up will probably need full-time attention: preferably two full-time people per spot, to telephone public service directors. You will average between three and eight telephone calls per station, and it will take one person two to three weeks, full-time, to contact 200 stations."

While calling each station is the best way to interest public service directors in your spot, you may not have the time and staff to do it. In that case, you'll probably want to use the following approach outlined by Andrew McGowan:

> For a large national campaign, we often send a query letter first to a large number of radio stations—on occasion virtually all the stations in the country. A cover letter 'sells' the campaign, and [we include] one or two script sheets to be used as 'live copy' right away. The station is invited to order the recorded spots by returning a postage-paid card. This approach is very cost efficient; we don't send out four or five times as many . . . [cassettes] as are going to be used. We get a script to every station, and we pick up a couple of hundred of them who will use the script, but would not order the . . . [cassette]. The total response runs between ten and twenty percent.

Placing PSAs to Best Advantage

When deciding where to send your PSAs, keep in mind the differences between commercial and educational stations, and between local and national coverage.

PSAs are run on virtually every commercial radio and TV station, according to the National Association of Broadcasters. James Wexler explains that his firm's research shows PSAs are actually needed to fill these open slots because most stations simply can't sell all the commercial time they have scheduled.

Although a lot of unsold commercial time will be available during off-peak listening hours, PSAs are aired around the clock, including prime time. During January, February and the summer months, when there are fewer paid commercials running, there is more time for PSAs than during the rest of the year.

Since public radio and TV stations don't run advertising, they do not have unfilled advertising slots, and as a result, some of them don't run as many PSAs as the commercial stations.

Local PSAs often have an advantage over nationally oriented spots. Broadcasters know that their audience is interested in community events, problems, issues, and information, so running local PSAs is good for the station's ratings. If you can localize a national PSA campaign, you'll almost certainly increase your total airtime. Andrew McGowan explains how to do this:

"We have at times arranged for sponsorship by local affiliates . . . [of the national organization sponsoring the PSA], tagged the spots with their names and word-processed cover letters on their stationery to each public service director by name. Or we asked stations to add the local tag (space was left for it on the spots) from a list of affiliates we supplied."

Broadcasters in the smaller cities and towns desperately need PSAs, so this is where many national organizations will want to place their emphasis. "We get smaller stations writing to us all the time asking if we can send them spots," says McGowan. "They don't sell as much commercial time, and they have more time available, but the number of organizations looking for them is smaller."

On the other hand, broadcasters in large cities are swamped with requests for PSAs, and even though the average commercial station runs more than two hundred spots each week, many more are rejected. Jim Dressier, public service director at KEZX-FM in Seattle, estimates that he uses half of the three hundred spots he gets each week. Some stations are only able to use one-fifth or one-tenth of the spots publicists send them. So if your organization is trying to run PSAs in large cities, you are competing for airtime.

For a national PSA campaign, you should plan on sending your spots to at least 200 stations to have an impact, according to Margie Goldsmith of MG Productions. If you send out fewer PSAs, your efforts will be spread too thin.

Monitoring PSA Coverage

There are several ways to find out if and when your PSAs were used. One way is to listen to or watch the station, but you may not be tuned in when your spot graces the airwaves. And this won't work when you're handling a national PSA campaign.

If your PSA is a good one, of interest to the audience, you may notice that your telephone lines are jammed and sacks of mail crowd your office. In fact, offering free information, particularly if you include a toll-free number in your spot, is a very handy way to track PSA usage. But not all PSAs, even some very fine ones, are designed to produce tidal waves of telephone calls and mammoth mail deliveries. Since there is no direct response to the spots, it is a challenge to track their usage.

Some of the larger stations will automatically let you know when and how often your spot was used. "I choose the PSAs, and they are entered in our records." says KNBR's Gimmy Park-Li. "I make certain they are used during different times of the day. Since we recognize that many nonprofit organizations can benefit by reporting them as in-kind contributions, we send them a letter telling them how many were run and what their approximate market value is."

Smaller broadcasters don't have the staff and computer facilities to keep track of PSAs, so don't expect every public service director to drop you a note telling you when your spots were used. There are several other ways you can try to find out exactly who used your spot:

- The least expensive means to track PSA usage is to include a stamped, self-addressed postcard with each spot. Type the name of the spot and the call letters of the station on the card, so all the public service director has to do is check off a box or two. Most public service directors will take the time to fill out such a card and mail it to you. And if you have a word processor, creating personalized postcards is a snap.

- Have one of the larger video production houses distribute the spot for you. They have the staff to follow up on your campaign by telephone and mail, and their report can tell you the number of stations using the spot, how many times it aired, the estimated audience size, and the approximate dollar value of the time donated by broadcasters.

- For television spots, Nielsen Research is developing an almost foolproof tracking method, which should be perfected and approved by the Federal Communications Commission soon— if it hasn't been already. Your spot is encoded with data which can't be seen or heard, but special monitors can read it directly from the airwaves. If Nielsen is monitoring that channel, and you've subscribed to this service, you'll know for sure that your spot has been used. For more information, see the listing under clipping bureaus in Chapter 12.

Working with Newscasters

Many radio station news departments have one full-time person, and a part-time assistant, if they're lucky. Some stations have no full-time news staff at all. As a rule of thumb, the larger the city and the station, the larger the news staff, and in metropolitan areas where the population is more than one million, the usual radio news staff includes several full-timers.

Try to imagine what it is like to run a news operation all by yourself—while handling other duties as well—and you'll begin to understand what many radio newscasters are up against and why they need material that fits their format without rewriting.

Since news staffers move continually from job to job, you will have to keep your contact list updated and your ear to the ground. If you hear rumblings that your favorite newsperson is about to move on, be ready to greet his replacement, quickly let the new person know who you are, and tell him how you can help him. Offer to fill him in on the local scene, since he may have just arrived from out of town.

Remember that many radio news directors are interested only in local news. They use network and wire service material to cover the national scene.

Television news shows are usually longer than their radio counterparts, and the average TV news staff is bigger. The larger the city, the larger the news staff, with some stations in major metropolitan areas employing dozens of people in their newsrooms.

In some large cities, broadcasters want all the news in writing, and to them you should submit standard broadcast news releases as described in the previous chapter. But there are many places where you can call the newsroom and read a statement over the telephone that will be taped for broadcast. (This is more common for radio, less usual for TV.) News directors will be more receptive to phoned-in news if they are familiar with your organization, than if they don't know you. However, the telephone approach may be fruitful anyway, if you have an interesting story, sound coherent and reliable, and if they can check the facts.

If you call after hours or on weekends, when the station's switchboard is closed, you will need the number for the direct line to the assignment editor. (Some of the media directories listed under Chapter 12 include these direct telephone numbers, but you can probably get them yourself simply by asking.)

Unless you have developed a working relationship with a particular reporter, calls and written material for broadcast news shows should be directed to the news assignment editor. At some larger stations, where reporters have specialty areas, contact the consumer affairs, business, or environmental reporter rather than the assignment editor.

Whenever you call a broadcast newsroom, assume that you are being taped. "We let them know we're taping. And we don't tape unless we're going to use it on the air," says Ralph Graczak, news director for KRAE-AM in Cheyenne, Wyoming. Still, there may be newspeople who won't bother to tell you that the reels are already rolling.

You can help get the tape recorder started by sounding professional and authoritative. Introduce yourself, state the essence of your story in three-dozen words or less, and then ask if the journalist wants to run a voice-level test. This test, based on a sample sentence or two of your speech, gives the journalist time to adjust his sound equipment to your voice, so you won't sound too soft and fuzzy or loud and harsh on the air.

It is a good idea to write out your story before you call it in. Even a practiced speaker can become tongue-tied or repeat material when ad-libbing on the telephone. Try to state the essence of your story in 20 seconds or less. Practice it out loud, using rising and falling inflections in your voice, so it sounds as though you are speaking instead of reading.

When you have finished reading your statement, be prepared for the editor or reporter to ask you questions. Try to anticipate these questions before you make the call, and write out your answers. If you notice that the reporter asks the same questions more than once, he is probably trying to get a briefer, more interesting, more quotable statement from you. If you can come right to the point, you increase the chances that your story will include your own words on the air and that your statements won't be heavily edited.

You can even prepare a taped, radio wrap-around ahead of time, call radio stations with your pitch, and feed it to interested news directors immediately. Although radio wrap-arounds can be used for many purposes, Andrew McGowan says they're especially helpful when for example, your organization is sponsoring a conference at which newsworthy statements will be made, but obtaining national broadcast coverage at the conference, itself, would be difficult. In that case, advises McGowan, "You arrange for key speakers to be interviewed . . . early in the conference or a few days before. Their statements are recorded, edited, and, with an announcer's intro and bridges, turned into one or more complete radio stories about one minute in length. Then newsrooms at radio networks and individual stations are called and offered the story, which can be fed to their recorders in the same telephone connection." McGowan finds that such stories cost about $2,500 to produce and place with newsrooms covering 2,000 to 3,000 or more stations.

In addition to symposia and conferences, McGowan suggests that radio wrap-arounds are useful for:

- ■ new product announcements.
- ■ survey or study results.
- ■ tie-ins with holidays or events.
- ■ statements on controversial issues.

When you approach a TV news director or reporter, tell her if the story has visual possibilities. If your Lions' Club picnic will feature a brightly colored hot-air balloon, be sure to mention it when you call. Visual potential is powerful bait for TV news staffers.

Whether you are calling radio or TV newsrooms, do not approach them near deadline time. For TV, avoid the hour just before a news show. If the radio station you're calling has an hourly news program, the best time to talk with the news director is immediately after the show.

Even though radio and TV are "instant" forms of communication, broadcasters do need lead time. This is especially true with TV news. "Get the damn thing here early enough!" says KGW-TV's Larry Badger. "That's the number one priority. Even if you have to say 'hold for release tomorrow.' But get it here so we can read it, and we can decide whether it's newsworthy, if we want to send a video crew to cover it on location, and how we're going to cover the story."

Pitching Video News Releases

When you pitch a video news release (VNR) to a television news director, always consider how journalists feel about this news vehicle. "VNRs are a sensitive topic at stations," according to *O'Dwyer's PR Services Report.* "They will usually admit to only the most guarded use of footage from outside suppliers and in some cases actually deny such usage even though they have done so." Yet 73 percent of the television news directors responding to the Medialink survey use as many as 10 VNRs per month, while only 14 percent reported they never use them.

Why would news directors say they *never* use VNRs, when they actually air them? Because news production budgets are being cut as broadcasters seek to fatten their bottom lines. But news shows are increasingly important profit generators, so they are being expanded. This means news directors are caught between the proverbial rock and a hard place. Journalists want to maintain their independence and write their own stories, but they don't always have the resources to do so.

Instead of reminding them of this dilemma, present your VNR in a way that makes it so newsworthy that journalists can't resist it. James Wexler points to four factors to stress when presenting your VNR to journalists:

- The information is of interest and importance to their local viewers.
- The desired footage exists only on the tape you [are] send[ing].
- The material can't be easily produced locally.
- [It has] . . . a *real* news peg.

While the last point may sound obvious, it isn't. West Glen's survey of News Directors and Assignment Editors shows that 75 percent of them feel that "Most VNRs do not contain a good news angle . . ."

What kind of airplay can you expect for your VNR? Well that depends on your news peg, the topic, and even the newsmakers on your tape (well known celebrities and politicians will increase the usage). You're also competing with other breaking news events—which can't be predicted ahead of time.

It seems that each person in the VNR field has a different estimate of how many viewers can be reached with a video release:

- " 'If you can reach an audience of three to four million viewers—that's Nielsen or Arbitron viewers, not some pipe dream of viewers, but numbers of people who actually watch local news and talk shows—you've done a good job,' says one major supplier," in *Public Relations Journal.*

- Based on her experience, Margie Goldsmith says, "On a two hundred station release, we anticipate at least 80 telecasts with an estimated reach of from 2,500,000 to 3,500,000 viewers."

- According to the Nielsen Research survey conducted for Medialink, ". . . the average VNR is seen by more than one million viewers in 20 markets, with a large number reaching a far larger audience."

But getting really accurate usage figures for video news releases is always a challenge, according to *Public Relations Journal*. ". . . for the many suppliers who strive to produce accurate usage reports, definitive monitoring remains a major problem, largely because getting and verifying the information from stations is so difficult."

When it is fully operational, Nielsen Research's tracking system, which encodes your VNR with data read by special monitors, will help you get more accurate VNR usage figures. (For more information see the listing under clipping bureaus in Chapter 12.) But if you're relying on usage figures supplied by a VNR distributor, be sure you understand exactly how they are calculated.

You should also consider that not all stations will use your entire VNR. "If a station uses 30 seconds of your story . . . re-edits your story or cuts its own story from the B-roll . . . that means they thought your story was worth their time. . . . That's quite a compliment," says James Wexler. They used as much material as they could in the available airtime.

According to the West Glen survey of News Directors, 64 percent of the responding journalists are inclined to edit their own story from

VNR footage and almost half would substitute their own reporter's voice for the voice in the prepared video news story.

Unless your video news release is about breaking news, you have to give news directors enough lead time to schedule your story. Forty-four percent of the news directors responding to the West Glen survey preferred a two week lead time; 20 percent needed three weeks.

Before the VNR is even produced, you can start by mailing news directors a "warm-up" pitch. Here's what to include:

- A backgrounder.
- A letter selling the story.
- Biographical sketches of spokespeople or newsmakers who will appear in the story.
- Localization ideas.
- Description of the B-roll contents.
- Printed copy of an advance story that can be read as "live" copy on the air.

Plan to make extra copies of this support material to send out, *again*, with the cassettes. Busy news directors may, with even the best intentions, misplace or throw out the supporting material. Make it easy for them by sending a duplicate set.

Let journalists know that you'll follow up, but also include a prepaid reply card and a toll-free number, if possible. If the VNR will be an evergreen, say so. If it won't, let them know how long it will stay fresh.

If you will be transmitting your VNR by satellite, there are two steps your distributor should follow before hand, according to Medialink's Laurence Moskowitz:

- Transmit an advisory note to news directors, preferably using a newswire service. "The advisory should contain the basics—the key elements of the story, background and description of the visuals, editorial and technical contacts, satellite coordinates and date and time of transmission . . ." says Moskowitz. It should also list ". . . the visual elements of the VNR, including . . . B-roll . . . graphics and how long the self-contained VNR runs. List the people featured in the VNR and why they are important."
- "A few hours before the satellite transmission, Medialink transmits the script . . . [by] newswire, along with a suggested anchor lead. The text of the VNR script is on the right hand side of the page, and the visual description on the left. This helps producers select elements from the

VNR as they watch it being recorded at the station from the satellite [feed]."

Approaching the Networks

You've just come home from your Rotary Club's planning meeting for Flag Day. After your nighttime cup of tea, you don your pajamas, turn off the light, and climb into bed. You toss. You turn. But no matter which way you arrange yourself, you can't get the thought out of your mind: "Can't we get network radio and TV coverage? After all, we're going to make the biggest American flag ever sewn, and we're going to hang it from the Marigold River Bridge. Sure, they did that in New York, but our flag is going to be twice as large as the one they hung from the Verrazano Narrows Bridge. Gee! If I only knew how to get to the networks."

It's not hard. Yes, there will be more competition than at your local stations. Your material will have to be more interesting, newsworthy, and unusual. And it will have to be of interest to a national audience. But relax! Approaching the networks involves the same skills as approaching local stations.

There are times when an organization gets network coverage without even trying. If your material is covered by a network affiliate, or by the local Associated Press or United Press International broadcast bureau, you may find that the story has gone out over the wires before you can say, "Jack Robinson."

You can, of course, try to help the process along. Some of the media directories listed in Chapter 12 will supply the information you need. Once you have the name, address, and telephone number of the network public service director, news assignment editor, specialized reporter, or talent booker for a talk or interview show, write or call him and make your presentation.

Making Live Appearances

You've flipped through some media directories and discovered that there are dozens of talk and interview shows bouncing through the airwaves in your town. It looks as though your organization will fit right in, and you can't imagine why you didn't think of this before. You're so excited, you wish you had two telephones and you could talk out of both sides of your mouth in order to contact twice as many producers. Your finger is poised over the telephone, ready to start. Cut! Hold it! You've left out part of the script.

Before you approach radio and TV stations, you have to figure out exactly what your objective is for this interview or talk show appearance. What key points do you want to make? How can you make those points come alive for your listeners with examples, anecdotes, facts, and figures they'll never forget? Make lists of these ideas. You'll need them later.

The next task is to convince the producer, host, or talent booker that your speaker will be an asset to the show. If you want to be invited back, you can't fudge here. "We have publicists who call us on every occasion," reports By Napier, program director for WCCO-AM in Minneapolis. Based on experience, ". . . we trust some and not others because some publicists will always say, 'I have a great interview for you!' And that person is not a good interviewee!"

So, before you try to place a spokesperson on talk shows, temper your enthusiasm, stand back, and ask yourself these questions:

- Are you, or the person you're trying to get on the air, really polished?
- Will you or she be able to hold the interest of the audience?
- Can some practice sessions help smooth the rough spots?

It's up to you to *make sure* that the spokesperson is really good and will be a credit to your organization. Publicists—even seasoned pros—can tell you horror stories about spokespeople who grabbed the limelight themselves and overshadowed the organization's message. Or "experienced" speakers who became tongue-tied and immobile in front of the cameras on live television shows.

If you're absolutely positive your spokesperson is first-rate, then you should write a tip sheet that summarizes the general topic to be discussed. Include five or six specific subtopics, a brief biographical sketch, and a backgrounder sheet on the issues, the topics, and your organization. Send that to the show's contact person, and let him know that you will call in a week or so to discuss the speaker with him.

Once you have made arrangements to provide an interviewee, you have made a solemn commitment. If you back out at the last minute, you'll wish your name was mud—because it will be far worse, at least at that particular radio or TV station. The American Red Cross's Harry

Cohn makes one suggestion to avoid last-minute problems. Sometimes a non-professional spokesperson can get so nervous about going on the air that he just can't face it. Plan to take the interviewee to the station yourself to prevent a last-minute no-show, Cohn advises.

The interviewee is not the only person who gets the last-minute jitters. Broadcasters get worried, too. "When we get close to the appearance day and start promoting the fact that a particular celebrity will be on our Boone & Erickson show, we get a little nervous that he may have missed the plane in Philadelphia. There's where we need a confirming telephone call, perhaps the day before," says By Napier. Even if your interviewee is not a celebrity, media people will appreciate that confirming telephone call.

Practicing for an Interview

The person to be interviewed should prepare for her appearance. She should practice answering questions, especially aggressive, rapid-fire questions.

She must make those lists of ideas, facts, figures, and anecdotes part of her thinking process, so she can discuss them easily and naturally, because memorized answers might sound as if she is reciting the material by rote.

If she has any hint of a monotone, make her practice raising and lowering the pitch of her voice. Get her to sing the material. Keep after her until your animation has rubbed off on her.

She can use notes on a radio show, but they should be no more than guideposts to jog the memory. These notes must never be on onionskin, or any other paper that rustles and rattles as the leaves are turned. That soft and quiet sound of turning pages will get amplified by the microphones so it resembles something like a thunderstorm. If your interviewee must use notes, have her write them on 3 × 5-inch index cards; they are easy to handle, quiet, and unobtrusive, and the small size of the card will prevent her from writing down too much material.

It can be helpful to your interviewee and her host if you provide a list of suggested topics and questions in advance. By Napier explains that talk show people appreciate publicists who provide background material and suggested questions. "There's no way our personalities have time to read as many books as we have authors on the air, even though they're very good at speed-reading." Whether your spokesperson will be discussing her new book, your organization's services, or the company's new product, be sure to help the interviewer understand your material. And don't be upset if he is not familiar with it. Interviewers are trained to ask the right questions, not to become instant experts. If he does the job right, you'll have a good interview, even if he doesn't know a whole lot about your topic.

If you want a product credit on the air, say so—in advance. If the show's producer doesn't agree, you want to know that up front. But if you can get agreement, the show's hostess or host will often help lead your spokesperson directly into the mention.

Your spokesperson should practice answering questions in ten- to twenty-second phrases. If a question calls for a longer answer, she should pause every twenty seconds. This will make it easier for the host or hostess to break in if it is necessary for a commercial interruption. She should also practice stopping the moment she is asked to because the engineers will not hold the commercial break just for her. Or anyone. She will not make a graceful exit if she insists on talking right to the last second.

When there's a microphone or TV camera staring her in the face, she'll probably have a tendency to speak much too fast. Fast talk will make her sound unsure, hurried, and nervous. Teach her to slow down and make deliberate pauses between sentences. Those breaks may seem like six-year silences to her, but they last for a mere fraction of a second, and they'll make her sound witty, wise, and very much in control.

Remember, also, that she is there to inform and entertain the listening or viewing audience. She should give her audience plenty of concrete information and not worry about giving away her expertise or too much of her book. Whether she is an author, consultant, teacher, or performer, she has to give her audience enough information so they'll know why they *have* to buy her book, engage her services, take her class, or see her show.

"If an interview really doesn't offer anything beyond plugging a book, if there's nothing entertaining or informative, we feel we're wasting our listeners' time. Although this may be the author's fault and not the publicist's, I think publicists should train authors better," says Napier.

What to Wear for TV

The clothing you choose for a television appearance can help you look stylish, cool and collected. But, if you wear the wrong outfit, it can undermine your credibility. That's because the TV camera exaggerates some colors and patterns and tones down others.

The National Association of Broadcasters (NAB) advises: "Wear medium tones of gray, brown, or blue in a style in which you feel most comfortable. Avoid distracting stripes, pronounced checks, or sharply contrasted patterns that compete for audience attention. Off-white or pastel shades for shirts and blouses are best. Avoid hats with wide brims since they cast sharp shadows on the face from overhead lights."

"Avoid highly polished gold and silver jewelry or large diamonds or rhinestones, since they reflect studio lights and tend to 'flare' and distort the picture. Pearls or dull-finished metal jewelry are preferable."

"If you wear glasses regularly, don't try to appear without them. Since your eyes are accustomed to glasses, they will react unnaturally if you do not wear them. The studio crew will arrange the light to avoid any glare or reflections." But, don't wear glasses that turn dark in sunlight: the bright television lights will make them darken, and you will look sinister.

"Women look their best in regular street makeup of natural tones. Eye shadow should be used sparingly. Makeup for men is necessary only for a shiny bald spot, a heavy beard, or exceptionally oily skin." Men with heavy beards should either ask for help from the makeup man or whip the problem with a shave just before going on the air. Finally, men with short hair should wait until a few days after a haircut before they go on TV.

Tips for the Actual Interview

When your spokesperson finally does get into a TV studio, she should ask the producer whether they'll be using hand signals. If so, she should find out which ones will be helpful for her to know. For both radio and TV interviews, she should take a moment to check out the type of microphone she will use. A tiny lapel clip-on presents no problem, but a large, old-fashioned mike that sits on a stand or is hidden in a table has a limited pick-up range. The interviewee should keep within that range, so there is no fading if she moves too far away.

Any jingling jewelry must be taken it off! And remember to tell her that *b*, *p*, and *s* sounds tend to pop, explode, and hiss over the air, and should be minimized as she speaks. Of course, she should always assume that all microphones are live, even after the interview has ended, until her host or hostess tells her otherwise.

The engineer may make a test recording of her voice and play it back for her. If she is like most folks, the sound of her own voice will embarrass her when she hears it played back. She is not the one to judge how she sounds. The engineer will add a touch of treble or a bit more bass if he thinks it will make her sound better. If her throat feels tight, she can relax by stretching or yawning—before she goes on the air, of course!

The National Association of Broadcasters has several more suggestions to make a person's TV appearance more effective:

- Avoid unnecessary movements and gestures. They distract from what you say and do. Quick hand or body movements also are difficult for the camera to follow. So move more slowly than you normally would.

- If you are being interviewed, look, listen, and speak to the person talking to you—unless you have something you wish to address directly to the television audience. In this case, look directly at the camera with the red light on.

- Resist the temptation to look at yourself on the TV monitor in the studio. It is distracting to the viewer. And to you, as well.

Satellite Media Tours

Not so long ago the only way for a spokesperson to appear on local television talk and news shows across the United States was to physically travel to the TV studios in each target city. While that method did allow for interviews with local print media and radio stations as well as personal appearances in each city, it was expensive for the organization, and time consuming and exhausting for the spokesperson.

Today, a satellite media tour allows the celebrity or spokesperson travel to a single television studio. The tour operator has prearranged as many as 25 interviews a day with talk show producers and news directors at television stations all over the country. The studio feeds a broadcast signal to a communications satellite, and one after another, the television stations use their satellite dishes to capture that signal. The stations can see and hear your guest, who will appear to be live, on camera, as far as their viewers are concerned. Your guest can hear the interviewer, even though she can't actually see him.

Satellite media tours open up all kinds of new possibilities for publicists. Here are just three examples:

- When January storms pelted Hawaii in 1988, the Visitor's Bureau wanted to tell tourists on the mainland that flooding had not hit the popular resort areas. On The Scene Productions, a Los Angeles satellite media tour operator, arranged a tour from the beach at Waikiki—within 36 hours after they were first called. The Visitor's Bureau feels that the satellite media tour helped prevent a drop in tourism.

- After a disastrous forest fire in Yellowstone National Park, the Wyoming Travel Commission wanted potential tourists to see that the Park was open again, and Old Faithful was still stunning. Medialink brought a portable satellite "uplink" truck into the park, and "the 'talent' and camera crew stood in front of the geyser . . . Stations were so pleased when they tuned in for their interviews, several timed their shots to Old Faithful's eruptions."

- Porter-Novelli Public Relations, a New York agency, did a satellite media tour to "bring" New York journalists to a press conference in London. Bob Seltzer explains that "An article that was favorable to one of our client's products was going to be in . . . a very prestigious British medical journal. We had an exclusive question and answer time for the American journalists. The Satellite Media Conference allowed us to get same-day coverage in the U.S., including a front-page story in the *New York Times*. With video satellite transmissions," Seltzer concludes, "you don't have to go there to reach there. Distance doesn't matter anymore."

Most television stations in the United States have satellite dishes to receive network programs. So it's no surprise that a survey of 167 television reporters by On The Scene Productions shows that nine out of ten television stations in large metro areas use satellite media tours as part of their news and talk show broadcasts. And 93 percent of the responding reporters felt that satellite media tours will be used more frequently in the future.

Although satellite media tours do offer immediacy, many television stations do not run them "live." A Medialink survey showed that more than 60 percent of news directors will tape the material for broadcast later on, while about one in eight journalists will run the interview live, as it is being transmitted.

Even though it takes some effort on the part of a station's staff to receive a satellite media tour, there's no guarantee that every station booking the interview will use it. Three out of four producers in the On The Scene Productions survey said that they have not used satellite media tour interviews for the following reasons:

- 39 percent thought the unused interviews were boring.
- 15 percent felt they were too commercial.

■   11 percent had technical problems with the tape that made it unusable.

■   8 percent said the interviews were bounced by more important, breaking news.

The bottom line is that when it comes to station usage, satellite media tours are no different from any other form of publicity material.

Arranging for a Satellite Media Tour

You will have to work with an outside satellite media tour operator, unless you work for a large corporation, with its own television studios, a *very* experienced technical crew, and a satellite "uplink." The arrangements are complicated and highly technical, so look for a highly experienced tour operator.

As Laurence Moskowitz explains, "A successful tour requires continuity. Switching smoothly from station to station during the interviews is crucial . . . . Unless you are fully experienced, once the tour is underway, stand clear . . . . The job of the coordinator is to make certain all goes smoothly—that your client does not overrun one station's window and thereby interfere with another station's window. A skilled coordinator can manage the windows effectively. If he sees that your talent is very engaged with one interview, he can alert the next station that the segment will be late," Moskowitz concludes.

Although a satellite media tour can be booked in a matter of hours in a crisis situation, you should plan routine tours at least six weeks ahead of time. You'll want to work closely with the tour operator to develop an overall concept, decide what material to include in your B-roll, book the talent, scout the locations, locate props and stage settings, and draw up the list of news and talk shows you'll pitch to. Keep in mind that satellite media tours should be offered to one station in each metro area on an *exclusive* basis.

Since one or two stations may cancel at the very last minute because of breaking news or technical problems, you should schedule an extra booking or two, advises Moskowitz.

Like any other publicity material, a strong local angle can make your tour more appealing to journalists. Fully 82 percent of the TV reporters and producers responding to the On The Scene Productions survey pointed to a local angle as a major criterion for using a tour. The same survey showed that certain topics are most interesting to producers and reporters.

Topic	Percentage of journalists interested
Celebrities	35
Topical Issues	30
Breaking News	30
Sports	21
Recording Artists	17
New Products	16
Medical/Health	14
Authors	12
Food	10
Business News	2

There are some similarities between video news releases and satellite media tours. According to the On The Scene Productions survey, eight out of ten journalists prefer tours shot on location, rather than in a studio, and they want to have B-roll material to use for editing their own story based on the tour interviews. The B-roll material is taped ahead of time. During the tour, "The taped material is usually 'fed,' or transmitted, prior to the interviews and again during an intermission," explains Laurence Moskowitz. He suggests that you have a press kit prepared for the news reporters or producers. "Include a brief biography of your spokesperson, a summary of the issues, a statement of the importance of the story or idea, and any news clippings that tell your story in a straightforward, desirable way." Suggest possibilities for local angles, and questions for the interviewer. This printed background material should be sent to the station ahead of time.

When you are a satellite media tour participant, get to the studio early enough so you have a chance to get settled and make sure you have everything you need to be comfortable during your interviews. Check to see that your earphone fits securely, and that you know what to do if it pops out of your ear. Bear in mind that this is how you will hear what your interviewers are saying to you. Ask for a dry run, while you talk, so you can handle instructions from the tour coordinator and questions from the interviewers naturally and easily.

Be certain there's a cue card or Teleprompter to remind you of the name of the interviewer and the city you're currently talking with. Otherwise, after several interviews, you may lose track. Ask the crew to let you briefly practice looking straight at the camera while you talk.

This will give the illusion that you are looking right at the interviewer—and help you get used to talking to someone you can't actually see.

Finally, ask your tour coordinator to introduce you to each interviewer before the actual interview starts so you can banter for a moment or two. That helps set up a warm and friendly interview, and gives you a chance to make sure that the interviewer is pronouncing your name correctly.

Promoting Special Programs

So you've taped that special program and it will be aired in three weeks. Can you go back to your office, put your feet up on the desk, lean back in your chair, and relax? No, you can't, at least not until you've spent some time publicizing your show. This is especially important with locally originated programs on cable TV, where you often have to create your own audience. Be certain that your organization's newsletter or promotional material will have information about your special. And think about whether there are people who do not ordinarily get your promotional material who should know about the show. Can you reach them with a special mailing?

It is a good idea to send copies of newsletters and promotional material with information about the show to the station's public service director or producer. This lets them know that your organization values the air time and takes itself seriously. You can also call the station's public relations director and ask if he plans to send out a news release about your special. If he is not planning to do so, ask him if it's OK for you to prepare one, and promise to send him a copy.

Your release should go to the television and radio editor at your local newspapers. Did you know that more people read the TV listings than any other part of the newspaper except the front page? Even people who buy the paper just for wrapping fish will look at that TV section.

Lee Winfrey, television writer for the *Philadelphia Inquirer* and president of the Television Critics Association, will accept a press release directly from an organization—if the station's publicist is not going to send one out. He likes at least a week's lead time. "Written material," he says, "is easier. It's also more reliable. And I might miss the phone call. The best packet includes material on when the show will air, what it's about, who is in it, who produced it, and an 8 × 10 black-and-white glossy or two." You should also send your news release to the editors of association, club, and specialized newsletters.

Finally, you might try to get the station to run 10-second spots, often called "bumpers," promoting your special program. Depending on the station's policies—and the amount of free airtime available—bumpers can run during the week before your special, or the day, hour, or even the few minutes ahead of showtime.

Thanking Broadcasters

By all means, write notes of thanks after your organization has received coverage on the air, but be careful how you word them. In the case of a newscast, be sure that you compliment the journalist for the good job she did when she covered your organization's story, and never imply that she did you a favor. It is probably best to send the thank-you note directly to the journalist, and not to her supervisor. According to KTVU-TV's Fred Zehnder, "Some publicists feel it's wise to write a letter to the general manager. That's a little intimidating to the news department. A letter of thanks usually indicates that you've given preferential treatment to somebody, and no news department wants to be accused of that."

Showing appreciation after a special program is also important, particularly if you want another show from that station in the future. Drop a brief thank-you note to the producer and the public service director. If you've been on an interview show, send a note to the host or hostess as well. Don't imply that a favor has been done; focus on what a first-rate job he did. Describe any public response or reaction to the show. If your telephone lines are jammed with callers and your letter carrier looks like a beast of burden bent over double under stacks of mailbags, be sure to mention that. Broadcasters, like everyone else, have the very human need to be praised for a job well done.

Approaching Cablecasters

Although cable TV has built an impressive audience, it is still a media that is growing and changing rapidly. While new systems can have more than one hundred channels, the typical cablecaster has 33, with nine empty ones, according to the National Cable Television Association. Any way you add that up, it spells opportunity for enterprising publicists. By 1990, there were over 9,000 cable TV systems, and 58 percent of the country was wired for cablecasting. Most cablecasters are equipped to receive network programming via satellite from dozens of cable-only networks. Twenty-five of those cable-only networks reach more than 18 million viewers each. Three of them—Entertainment & Sports Programming Network, Cable News Network, and Superstation TBS—boast more than 50 million subscribers apiece.

If you want to place publicity material on a cable TV system, your first question is whether they have locally originated programs. Some cablecasters are merely pipelines; they can only bring in other stations or packaged programs produced in other cities or supplied by the cable networks.

Those cablecasters who do originate their own programs can help you in two ways. First of all, and easiest, they may already have regular talk shows, newscasts, and public affairs programs that use material from publicists. Find out if this is the case, and ask who the contact people are.

Some cablecasters will not have ready-made programs available for you to step into, but they might have public access channels. Public access channels are set aside by the cablecaster so that local organizations and businesses such as yours can have access to TV time. These access channels are often required as part of the contract with the city or county. About one-third of the cable systems that have locally originated programs have public access channels.

Although this is usually a free service, there are some cablecasters who charge for the use of their public access channels. Always ask about this at the beginning of your conversation, so there are no surprises later. If there is a fee, it may seem large at first, but if you compare the cost per person you reach with your message, you may find that cablecasting is no more expensive than your organization's other promotions.

Depending on your area, cable may well be worth the effort and cost. In parts of New Jersey, for example, where there are no local broadcast TV news shows, people have turned to cable TV for news of local happenings, and cable has started to build a substantial audience. In other areas, cable programming is still third-rate, and it is not at all clear whether your time and money would be well spent.

You will have to do some research in your community to find out who watches cable TV and the access channels. While you may be able to get solid information on audience demographics for regular cable channels, there is little data on the viewership for public access channels. "But the consensus is that the audience is expanding," according to the *New York Times*. Where audience studies of access channels have been done by universities, they reveal ". . . a committed, desirable body of viewers, who boast high incomes, education levels and voting records and who watch access at least once per week . . . . the ragtag 'amateurs' are moving into the mainstream," the *Times* concludes.

The cablecaster can supply you with some audience data, and the TV writer at your daily newspaper may also have information he would be willing to share with you. You should also contact the Broadcasting or Journalism Departments at nearby colleges to see if they have conducted viewership research for channels in their communities. A major clue will be the kinds of advertisements your cable system carries. If large, established firms and national businesses are running ads, it is probably worth your while to try to get your message on cable.

Even if you decide that cable TV is not worth your time now, keep an eye on it. The situation might change in a few months or a year.

Checklist—Getting on the Air

1. Do you know who you should approach at radio, television and cable stations for the various types of airtime?
2. Are you familiar with the differences between the seven main types of air time?
3. Do you know your target stations' policies on the various airtime types?
4. Have you put together a media list?
5. Does it include names of journalists as well as titles?
6. Are you aware of the various deadlines and lead times at each station you're pitching to?
7. Do you know whether your target stations prefer live or prerecorded PSAs and news releases?
8. Do you update your information on station preferences and needs continually?
9. Do you have information on locally originated programs at your target stations?
10. If you work with a nonprofit organization, have you checked to see if there's an access guide for community organizations published in your city?
11. Have you checked to see if any of your target stations offer tours?

12. Have you become familiar with the programs on your "must appear on" list?

13. Have you asked about the availability of demographic material on station listeners?

14. Do you understand the difference between radio and television audiences, and when you should use each medium?

15. Do you want to reach a broad, general audience, or a specific, defined one?

16. How will that vary from one publicity campaign to another?

17. Have you learned about PSA policies at the most important stations on your list?

18. Do you know which stations will run PSAs for one-time events, and which will limit events to community calendar listings?

19. Are you trying to get to know public service directors rather than simply sending out PSAs?

20. If you do send PSAs by mail, have you included a cover letter that does a real selling job as well as a stamped, self-addressed reply card?

21. If you are sending out PSAs on a national or regional basis, can you get your local affiliates to submit them as localized material?

22. Can you include localized taglines or localization suggestions with your PSAs?

23. If you're sending out professionally prerecorded PSAs, have you considered pitching to broadcasters by mail first?

24. Are you planning to send spots to at least 200 stations for a national campaign?

25. Have you made sure no one in your PSA will be on the ballot in an upcoming election?

26. If you're considering using a celebrity in your PSA, have you made sure he's not identified with a particular station or network?

27. Have you timed the news stories on your local stations to see what length is preferred?

28. Do you have the telephone numbers for the direct lines to news assignment editors and news directors?

29. Do you know which stations have specialized reporters?

30. Do you always assume you'll be taped when you call a newsroom?

31. Do you write out your story before you call?

32. Are you prepared to answer questions?

33. Have you considered distributing taped radio stories by telephone?

34. Do you know when deadline times are so you can avoid disturbing journalists unless you have breaking news?

35. Have you made a list of visual possibilities before you pitch a television news story?

36. Have you made the pitch for your video news release so newsworthy that journalists can't resist it?

37. Does your pitch stress the importance of the material in your VNR to the station's audience?

38. Have you pointed out that your VNR is the exclusive source for this very desirable footage, and shown the news director exactly why it is so worthwhile?

39. Is your news peg highlighted in your pitch letter?

40. Have you discussed tracking your VNR's usage with your video production house or public relations agency?

41. Have you allowed at least a two week lead between delivery to broadcasters and airtime for VNRs that don't involve breaking news?

42. Have you thought about starting to pitch a VNR even before you produce it?

43. Have you built a feedback mechanism into your pre-production pitch so you can draw on journalists' opinions to produce a more newsworthy story?

44. Can you include an advance story with your pre-production pitch for journalists to read "live" on the air?

45. Does your VNR's support material include a pitch letter, background information on the story, brief bio sketches of the speakers, localization ideas, and a description of the B-roll contents?

46. Are you sending the support material with advance pitches *and* again with the cassettes?

47. If you're transmitting your VNR by satellite, will you or your distributor use a newswire service to send an advisory to stations?

48. Will you or your distributor send the timed script to stations by newswire before the VNR is transmitted by satellite?

49. Have you written down your objective for each talk show appearance *before* you pitch to the talent booker?

50. Have you sent the talent booker a brief tip sheet and followed up with a telephone call?

51. Are you *positive* your speaker will be interesting and dynamic?

52. Does your speaker's presentation have rough spots that can be polished with practice?

53. Have you figured out how your speaker can use anecdotes, examples, figures and facts to make the story come alive?

54. Have you made a list of key points you want your spokesperson to cover in an interview?

55. Can he handle aggressive, rapid-fire questions?

56. If the appearance is on radio, has he prepared brief notes in outline form if he feels he needs them?

57. Does he need "singing" exercises to help break a monotone?

58. If you want a product credit on the show, have you discussed this with the station in advance?

59. Has your interviewee practiced giving short responses and speaking slowly?

60. Have you given the talk show host a list of suggested questions and topics, as well as background material?

61. Is your spokesperson wearing medium tones and avoiding clothing with stripes and bold checks for a television appearance?

62. Is your speaker avoiding a white shirt or blouse in favor of ivory, ecru or pastel?

63. Is all her jewelry nonreflective?

64. Has she discussed hand signals with the studio crew?

65. Has she asked about the range of any fixed microphones and how she should position herself?

66. Have you taught her to assume all mikes are live?

67. Has she learned to tone down gestures and move more slowly than usual?

68. Has she practiced looking at the interviewer unless she wants to address the audience directly?

69. Have you found a highly experienced satellite media tour operator and checked her references?

70. Can you trust the operator enough so you'll feel comfortable standing clear during the tour?

71. Have you allotted *at least* six weeks lead time for tours that don't involve breaking news?

72. Will you develop an overall concept for your tour— ahead of time?

73. Can you stage it on location, rather than in a studio?

74. Have all locations been checked and reserved?

75. Have you planned your B-roll material?

76. Have you selected stations to offer your tour on an exclusive basis in each metro area?

77. Have you signed contracts with any outside spokespeople?

78. Have you rented, made or bought props and stage settings you'll need?

79. Have you thought about how to add local angles?

80. Have you sent background material to stations in advance?

81. If your tour doesn't deal with one of the popular topics, have you surveyed several journalists to make sure there will be interest?

82. Will the tour operator feed your B-roll material to stations during the tour?

83. Have you made arrangements to get to the studio early?

84. Has your spokesperson checked the fit of his earphone and tried it out before the tour begins?

85. Have you checked to make sure there is either a teleprompter or cue cards for each station on the tour?

86. Has your spokesperson practiced looking straight at the camera while talking?

87. Have you arranged for the tour coordinator to introduce your spokesperson to each interviewer before the actual interview starts?

88. Have you made arrangements to promote your special?

89. Have you sent copies of your promotional material on the show to the public service director and the station's publicist?

90. Are there key people in your audience you can reach with a special mailing about your show?

91. Have you asked the station if they're sending out a press release about your special?

92. If they're not, will you?

93. Have you suggested the station create and run bumpers for your special?

94. Have you written thank-you notes to newscasters, when appropriate, and to public service directors, producers, and hosts for special shows?

95. Are you sure you're thanking broadcasters for a job well done rather than implying they've done you a favor?

96. Have you made a list of locally-originated programs on your target cable TV systems?

97. Can you get cable TV time on a public access channel?

98. Is there a charge?

99. Are video production facilities and training available?

100. Can you get solid information on your targeted cablecasters' audiences?

CHAPTER NINE

When the Media Visit

P erhaps you've called a press conference. Or maybe the media are covering a special event at your plant, offices, or showroom. It might even be an emergency, such as a fire or strike, that brings the media to your doorstep. Whether you've invited them or they've invited themselves, *you* play a major role in determining the kind of coverage your business or organization will get. Procedures for planning and running smooth press conferences and special events are so similar that they are covered as a unit in this chapter, followed by tips for coping with sudden visits from the press in times of crisis.

Press Conferences and Special Events

The most common way to get the media to visit you is by holding a press conference. No, it's not a major meeting called only by politicians with pronouncements: ordinary mortals like you and I can arrange successful press conferences.

There is only one reason for calling a press conference rather than sending out a news release: the subject demands a question-and-answer format. If reporters want to meet and question your speaker, a press conference is in order.

Says Albert Feldman, public relations director of the New York Multiple Sclerosis Society, "It isn't how often you use a press conference, but why. A press conference should be called when there's a reason for two-way communication between the organization's spokesman and the media . . . . to permit a forum. If a press conference doesn't have that purpose, it will result in a loss of credibility to the sponsor. If everything can be made clear in a press release, then a press conference becomes superfluous. You do not use a press conference to achieve greater publicity."

Reporters and editors rely on press conferences to supply them with news they wouldn't get otherwise. On the other hand, so few press conferences produce useful news that many reporters and editors view them generally with suspicion. As Cindy Loose of the *Staten Island Register* puts it, "There are a lot of press conferences that are obviously just ploys to get publicity . . . . I think phony press conferences are a bad mistake. You're going to defeat your purpose. People are going to get mad at you, and the next time they see something from you, they're not going to pay any attention."

When the Chelm Institute for the Handicapped held a press conference to announce a new program to teach handicapped people the skills they need to work on assembly lines at electronics plants, they got a good crowd of reporters, but there was almost no coverage. R. E. Porter, business writer for the Plains City Morning Star, explains why:

"I couldn't understand why we were there. I got a press release about an innovative new program to train the handicapped in electronics assembly *skills. Even though the press conference announcement was not exactly clear, I drove all the way to Chelm because I thought there would be a good story."*

"When I got there, I wasn't sure what the program was about. When I left, I still didn't know. Aside from a few clichés and generalizations, they didn't tell us anything about the program. They could have told us about placements of handicapped workers on actual jobs, and there are probably some interesting things about how assembly line equipment is adapted for handicapped workers. But they didn't offer this information and they were vague when I asked them about these areas."

"Not only that, they seemed confused about whether they were presenting this new program or all of their programs."

"I only saw two or three people participating in the program, but I saw fifty people running it. And I didn't get to see the trainees working. None of them seemed handicapped, although their disabilities might not have been apparent. But that was never made clear."

"I couldn't tell if they were just inept, or if they had something to hide. I had suspicions of both. There were so many staff people there, it was like they were trying to overwhelm us, to keep us away from something."

When You Shouldn't Have a Press Conference

Before you set up a press conference, take a long, hard look at your plans and answer these questions:

- Is there a more effective way to handle this information?
- Do you really need a question-and-answer session with journalists?

If you answered no to the first question and yes to the second, your next step is to take a look at the press kit you have assembled for the conference. Honestly, can anything be added to this material? Does it cover all the bases from all angles? If it does, then send it out. You don't need a press conference! Nothing maddens reporters more than spending time at a press conference when they could have been given the same information in a press release or a press kit.

If your material is not hard news, consider approaching a few carefully selected reporters and developing stories directly with them instead of calling a press conference or inviting the press to an event.

The results can be better, particularly if you're introducing a complex new product journalists will want to examine closely.

This is particularly true in the computer industry, for example. A survey of 21 high tech editors cited in *Public Relations Journal*, concluded "Press conferences are regarded as rarely useful; press tours or mailed releases are preferred."

PC Magazine's Bill Howard explains why the journalists at his publication find press conferences only minimally useful. ". . . we very much prefer to see products before they are released, under a non-disclosure agreement. That's because we want to be able cover them when they're new, which means we have to write about them as much as three months before they're available. If we wait for a press conference to learn about new products, our readers won't know about them until they're old news."

There's still another reason press conferences don't cut the mustard, according to Howard. "We prefer one-on-one product demonstrations so we can cover the ground our readers want to know about. We're more technical than other magazines at the bits and bytes level."

You'll have to find out the preferences and needs of the journalists you work with. And if you determine that they don't like press conferences, don't worry! There's sure to be another, more effective way to work with them.

Where to Hold Your Press Conference or Event

If you work with a national or regional organization or a business, you have to decide which city is best for your press conference. You should consider the following factors when you choose a location:

■ Sometimes the subject demands an on-the-scene location. A press conference about uranium mining in Utah would, most likely, be held in that state. You could also hold a simultaneous, auxiliary conference in a more accessible location, perhaps using a satellite media tour to bring the out-of-the-way site to big-city journalists.

■ Some cities have specialized print and broadcast reporters who will be more likely than generalists to understand the subject of your conference and give you first-rate coverage. Washington, D.C. has reporters and commentators who specialize in stories relating to the Federal government. New York has more journalists who specialize in financial stories than any other American city. Press conferences concerning show business work best in Los Angeles and New York.

Journalists specializing in agriculture are concentrated in Chicago and Washington, D.C.

■ Cities where the local press usually gives you favorable coverage are better places for your press conference than areas where the media are neutral or hostile to your business or organization. Local reporters often set the tone for the conference and influence the attitudes of national reporters. On the other hand, make sure it doesn't look as if you're avoiding an obvious problem by running away from areas where you have troubles.

■ If you hope to get network TV and radio coverage, try to stage your press conference in a city with a network news staff. Don't choose a location just because it has network-affiliated stations, since the networks often don't use material from their affiliates except for disasters and major crimes. Check the media directories mentioned in Chapter 12 for lists of network news bureaus, or contact the network headquarters and ask.

Once you have chosen your city, you will have to find a good setting for your press conference. Determine whether most major media offices are in the same area of the city. If that is the case, (and it often is), you'll get better coverage if your conference is in that part of town.

Hotel and motel conference rooms are often used for press conferences, but private clubs and other centrally located meeting rooms are also possibilities. It is not a good idea to hold a press conference or special event in a building with restricted access. Reporters will not appreciate having to sign in and wait for security approval. If you must use such a facility, be sure you know in advance which reporters are coming. Give the list to the security guard and have a publicity staff member or publicity committee volunteer on duty with the guard to make sure that reporters are admitted instantaneously.

If you expect extensive radio and TV coverage, think about sound and lighting for your press conference. Some hotels have meeting rooms with complete built-in sound systems, which can make order out of chaos. Ask in advance. If you cannot find a meeting room with a sound system, take a quick look in the *Yellow Pages* to find and rent the sound equipment you need. Without a sound system, reporters converge on the speaker and poke microphones in his face. That can rattle even the best spokesperson, and interfere with his effectiveness.

Check to see if the room you rent has suitable lighting for TV cameras. This has two important advantages. First of all, *you* decide how to light the scene so your speaker and props look best. And second, television crews can travel lighter, arrive later, and spend little or no time setting up. Given the tight schedules in most newsrooms, this could be the deciding factor.

Check each potential press conference or special event site to see if it is accessible to TV crews. Are the passageways, doorways, and elevators large enough to accommodate bulky equipment? If the crews will bring their own lights, are there enough heavy duty circuits for them?

If the press conference is about a highly visual topic that TV reporters and newspaper photographers will want to shoot, consider holding it on location instead of in a conference room. Betty M. White, chief of the Public Affairs Office, U.S. Army Corps of Engineers, Omaha District, writing in *Public Relations Journal*, explains why. White called a press conference and party to announce a grant for a floodplain park, a new concept. Instead of the traditional practice of channeling a stream, the new park allowed for periodic flooding, a more natural way of handling the environment. No media people came to the press conference and party, which was held in a hotel. When White surveyed them afterward, she discovered that several of the TV stations had used the release, but they had gone to the location of the new park and filmed there. The moral of the story is that this conference should have been held on location.

KGW-TV's Larry Badger confirms this. "We'll do anything to avoid having to cover a news conference because they seldom make news. We want to show the end product of the announcement as opposed to the announcement. We want visual possibilities. There's just not that much of an impact if somebody says, 'I'm going to build a dam on the Snake River.' I want to go up to the Snake River and say, 'The dam is going to be built here. It will cost $20 billion. And it's going to flood this and this,' " Badger concludes.

If your press conference will be outdoors, be sure to plan for the following:

- Bad weather.
- Adequate lighting.
- Crowd control.
- Noise control.

Scheduling Media Events

Be aware of media deadlines. If you schedule your press conference between 9:00 A.M. and 11:00 A.M. on Tuesday, Wednesday, or Thursday, reporters from almost all the media will be able to attend and still have time to digest the material before their deadlines. Avoid holding press conferences when major national events and holidays will make it harder for you to get coverage. "I wouldn't want to hold a press conference on Election Day, during the primaries, or around Christmas," says Nancy Karen of United Way of Tri-State. "There's too much competition."

Invitations

Invitations for press conferences and special events are similar. They should always be typed with wide margins and limited to one page. Use a format that covers who, when, where, why, how, and what. Mention any photographic possibilities. If the conference or event is not in a well-known location, include travel directions.

Below are two examples of good invitations to press conferences and special events:

PRESS CONFERENCE   PRESS CONFERENCE   PRESS CONFERENCE

Plains City Bus Authority
1511 Industrial Avenue
Plains City
998-1144 (contact: Martha H. Einhorn)

Major Focus:
The recent 25 percent cutback in the Plains City Bus
Authority's budget has caused major maintenance problems.
Even though we have not increased wages and have cut back
service by 25 percent, we do not have enough funds to keep
up with inflation. This is causing major maintenance problems.
Almost half of the PCBA buses are out of service or in unsafe
condition.

Speakers:
PCBA chairwoman Marilyn Ilonescu will outline the problem and
answer questions. State Senator E. L. Press will announce the
revenue plan for PCBA he will present to the State Senate later
this month, which would authorize a bond issue and revenue

    – more –   – more –

---

sharing to end the funding crisis. PCBA is the only transit system in the state that has not received state or federal aid.

Where:

Conference Room, Plains City Bus Authority, 1511 Industrial Avenue, near Rider Road. Golden Road Exit, south 3 blocks, right on Rider Road to Industrial Avenue. Or the #12 Industrial Avenue Bus to Rider Road.

When:

Thursday, February 3, 1992 at 10:30 A.M.

Picture Opportunities:

- 337 buses, parked in formation, which are out of service because of mechanical problems.
- 122 buses with safety hazards, many of them highly photogenic.

###

MEDIA CONFERENCE   MEDIA CONFERENCE   MEDIA CONFERENCE

Plains City Solar Energy Company
6406 Industrial Avenue
Plains City
998-9800 (Contact: Harry M. Kwan)

Major Focus:

The first Sunwater Brand solar water heater will come off the assembly line at the new Plains City Solar Energy Company factory on Tuesday, April 3, 1992. This compact water heater is easy to install and costs less than $200. Governor J. Kousoulas will present the Plains State Energy Award to Martin Kagawa, designer of the heater.

Speakers:

Governor Kousoulas will present the award and discuss the contribution the Plains City Solar Energy Company will make to the state's economy.

Jane K. Manzelli, Plains State Energy Commissioner, will give figures and facts about the amount of energy that will be

– more –   – more –

saved by the solar heaters produced in this factory during the next year.

Mayor Michael Olaffsson will take a solar-powered shower.

Where:

Plains City Solar Energy Company
6406 Industrial Avenue
Plains City

Marigold Heights Road Exit, six blocks north to Industrial Avenue. Entrance to the plant is one block west on Industrial Avenue. Look for the huge yellow sun sign on the lawn.

When:

Tuesday, April 3, 11:00 A.M.

Photo Possibilities:

Mayor Olaffsson taking a solar-powered shower. (He will, of course, wear a bathing suit.)

The assembly line.

The presentation of the award by Governor Kousoulas.

The factory's sungarden, where gold and orange marigolds grow side by side with solar collectors.

-30-   -30-   -30-   -30-   -30-

The next example is a tip sheet inviting the press to a special event, prepared by publicist Joel Pomerantz for Rockaways' Playland, Inc.

TIP TO ASSIGNMENT DESK
Rockaways' Playland, Inc.
185 Beach 97th Street
Rockaway Beach, NY 11693
212-945-7000

Event:

1,000 handicapped, homeless, and underprivileged children from 20 hospitals, shelters, and health and welfare agencies in the metropolitan New York area will be treated to a funfilled afternoon at a Queens amusement park.

– more –   – more –

The youngsters, many in wheelchairs and on crutches, will come from Queens, Manhattan, Brooklyn, Staten Island, and Nassau.

When:

Thursday, August 7, starting at 1:00 P.M.

Where:

Rockaways' Playland Amusement Park Beach 98th Street, Rockaway Park, Queens

Background:

Annual "Fun in the Sun" outing is sponsored by Walter Kaner, *New York Daily News* columnist, who has entertained 64,000 children at his parties in the past 27 years.

Playland is donating free use of its rides; L.I. Lighting Co. is contributing refreshments.

Among groups participating: Cerebral Palsy of Queens and Nassau, Willowbrook State School, New York Foundling Home, Muscular Dystrophy Association, Queens Children's Shelter, Brooklyn Developmental Center.

Rain Date:

Tuesday, August 12, 1:00 P.M.

Contact:

Joel Pomerantz (212) 689-2288
Ann Leichner, Playland, (212) 945-7000

Whether you're contacting newspapers or broadcasters, send your invitation to the reporter who actually writes about your subject. Even though the invitation could be sent to the city editor at the newspaper or the news assignment editor at a radio or TV station, and forwarded to the right reporter, it would be better if you direct it to a specific journalist. The city editor and the news assignment editor are generalists, and they might miss something that a specialist would know is important. The larger the newspaper or broadcaster, the more important it is to get your invitation directly to the right reporter.

If your event or press conference will offer unusual photo possibilities, send a duplicate invitation to the photo assignment editor at a large daily paper. Be sure you let him—and the reporter—know who else the invitation has gone to.

Two very important people on your invitation list are the Daybook editor at United Press International and the Daily Budget editor at

Associated Press. They both compile lists of press conferences, conventions, meetings, product and political demonstrations, picket lines, and special events, which are sent out on the wires and arrive by Teletype in the newsrooms at broadcasters and newspapers. Not all press conferences will be listed by the Daybook and Daily Budget editors, but if yours is, your credibility is boosted substantially. A press conference seems more official when it is announced on the AP or UPI wires.

Reminder Calls

Once you have sent your press conference or special event invitation, you might think that reporters will appear without further prompting. Even with interesting, newsworthy events, that's not usually the case. Early on the morning of your event, call each reporter, editor, or news assignment director to remind them. The best time is probably between 8:00 and 9:00 A.M. The *Trenton Times'* Larry Kramer explains why:

"A paper's assignment desk is flooded daily. We may have looked at some future event and said, 'we're not going to have time to cover that.' And sure enough, that day is the quietest news day of the year. But we don't remember the story we threw away. Then somebody calls up and says, 'we're having a press conference on this and this,' and we say, 'whoops, that's not a bad one, let's do that.' "

However, some journalists do not like reminder calls. For example, David Morgan, news director for WOW-AM in Omaha, Nebraska, says that his office has a filing system to keep track of events. He feels it is his station's obligation to be there, without a reminder, if they've decided to cover the event.

If any of your media contacts express a strong wish not to be reminded, make a note of that and honor their preferences. But continue to remind everyone else.

Whatever you do, don't get carried away and call two, three, or four times, or have half a dozen people call to urge journalists to attend your event or conference. "That's a turnoff," says KTVU-TV's Fred Zehnder. "It creates such a negative attitude that the assignment editor (or reporter) isn't likely to cover an event even if it seems worthwhile. It smacks of real pressure tactics."

When you make those calls, be brief. Introduce yourself, tell the reporter or editor that you're having a press conference or special event, describe it in 15 words or less, and ask if she got the announcement. Be prepared for a negative answer; don't let it shake you up. You may have stumbled on an opportunity, since you can make the pitch one-on-one. Try to briefly convince her that your conference or event is newsworthy.

Before you ask her if she's coming, say, "Let me give you the time and location." You're trying to get her to write down the information because that helps involve her. If you feel that she really should have the information in the written invitation—or she asks for background material—offer to fax or messenger it to her.

If she has received the invitation, ask her if she's planning to cover the event or conference. She may tell you that she will not be there. Don't argue. Don't try to persuade her. Ask her if you can provide her with a release and background material after the conference is over. Find out when she'll need it. Then make sure she gets that material with time to spare, even if that means using messenger delivery, or fax, if she agrees to that.

Getting Your Act Together

Whenever you can, prepare visual aids for a press conference or event. Charts and graphs help reporters understand facts, figures, and comparisons more quickly. Pictures, props, slides, and videotapes make your presentation more interesting. And of course, the TV reporters will be delighted if your visual material can be televised; it makes their stories more interesting to viewers. That helps them. And since your message will be more effective, it helps you, too.

Make sure your speakers are brief and to the point. The purpose of your press conference is for reporters to question your speaker. A twenty-minute presentation is long, indeed, for a press conference. Some publicists limit their speakers to five-minute opening statements. You needn't cover every detail; if things are not clear, reporters will ask questions. And that is what you want.

Since questions and answers are the essence of any press conference, your speaker should practice answering every possible question, fair and foul, that may be thrown at her. If you have a diabolical, cynical friend, he will be most useful. Ask him to think up the nastiest, most underhanded questions. Have your speaker practice answering them until she can counter every question with a convincing, positive answer.

Your speaker should be able to make her central point in 10 to 20 seconds. If she can do that, she has a better chance of getting her statement on the air uncut and unedited. It may well be all the time she is allowed.

Radio and TV people might ask for brief interviews after the conference presentation. Be prepared to schedule them on the spot, and have an area set aside to conduct them.

Anticipating Problems

The last thing you want at a press conference is your competition or opposition. If the conference is on private property, you can exclude them. If you expect a demonstration or heckling and harassment from your opposition, take steps in advance to quickly and quietly contain it.

List all the things that could go wrong and figure out how you'll cope if they do. Murphy's law changes when you make contingency plans: If it can go wrong it will, unless you've spent a lot of time preparing for problems; then it probably won't.

On the Big Day

"Always attend the events, conferences, and broadcast interviews you have arranged," says public relations executive Ravelle Brickman. "You, the publicist, are the host or hostess. You make journalists feel welcome when they are visiting your organization, and you help people from your organization feel at ease when they visit the media. But most important of all, when you are on the scene with the media, you will get to meet journalists. And that can and should be the start of your working relationship with them."

Don't invite many people from your organization to your press conference. Since they will probably not know any of the journalists, they will tend to talk with each other. That behavior is natural, but it gives the appearance of aloofness. The people from your organization or business who do attend should greet journalists, make them comfortable, and answer their questions. With only a few people from your organization on hand, there will be less of a tendency to talk among yourselves.

As the reporters and editors arrive, give them each a press packet that includes the following:

- A basic one-page release.
- A longer three- or four-page version.
- A copy of the speaker's statement.
- Background information on your business, organization, product, industry or cause.
- A brief biography of the speaker.
- Copies of any relevant documents.

- Any other information you think will help a reporter write a good story.

- Small souvenir items, such as pennants, T-shirts, or imprinted balloons.

- Product samples, if they will help journalists write stories.

Keep in mind that many photographers get no briefing about the story they are covering. Take some time to fill them in, and offer them copies of the press release or backgrounder sheet, but unless they ask for advice, (which is not likely), don't try to tell them how to shoot their pictures.

Don't wait for latecomers. Start your press conference on time even if there is only one journalist there.

If you're demonstrating a product for journalists, practice ahead of time so everything will move right along without a hitch. Bill Howard explains that busy journalists want you to "Run through your demo quickly, and stay within the allotted time. Make sure you get to the point very quickly. Suppose the two principal editors are called out after 25 minutes for a deadline conference. And all you've shown them so far is your introductory flip chart. Well, you're out of luck!"

Record your press conference on audiotape—or videotape if you can afford it—using broadcast quality equipment. The tape will help you write the news release to send to those newspaper and TV reporters that didn't attend, and it can also be edited into video news releases and radio wrap-arounds for release directly to broadcasters. Moreover, you will have a record of the information and of your organization's positions on the issues for later use, perhaps with your board of directors, shareholders, volunteers, members, or staff.

"We might send copies of the tape to our chapters. Sometimes we offer them to National Public Radio for the program 'All Things Considered.' We tape if the information we're presenting at the press conference is of importance and deserves to be preserved," says Albert Feldman of the New York Multiple Sclerosis Society.

One final arrangement is often overlooked, particularly by organizations without full-time offices. Have someone on hand at the telephone number listed on your press conference or special event invitation, so that media people who cannot attend, can call for information, and get an immediate response. And make sure that you have thoroughly briefed that telephone person.

Following Up after Your Conference or Event

What if you give a press conference and nobody comes? Should you slink off to the wilderness, find a hole, and crawl in, never to emerge into the world of publicity again? You don't need to do anything that drastic. Believe it or not, all is not lost. Even if no one arrives or only a few journalists join you, if you act quickly and confidently, you may still get—or even increase—coverage.

The journalists who did not come *will* want to hear from you. "They may have been busy with other assignments, and even if they did not honor you with their appearance, they are entitled to [the] news . . . ." says Albert Feldman. "If you decline to give them news, the next time you run a press conference you can be sure those people will not show."

Put your pride on the shelf, confidence in your voice, and your brain in high gear. And don't refer to the number of people who attended your press conference or event; that is not important. What matters is that you have newsworthy material. Period.

Your first step is to call the number listed on your invitation. Ask your telephone monitor if there are any messages. (If there are, you'll begin to feel better immediately.) Make a list of journalists who called and asked for information. Add the names of reporters who said they would not cover your conference or event, but asked for follow-up information. That's your primary list.

Next, write a 20-second radio statement, or edit a radio wrap-around from the tape of the press conference. Call the radio stations that didn't attend. Contact those on your primary list first, then the others. Your pitch might be as follows:

> Hello. This is Harry Kwan of Plains City Solar Energy Company. I'm sorry you weren't able to be at our press conference this morning. I've got quite a statement from Governor Kousoulas. Do you want to run a tape now, or do you need a voice-level test first?

The reporter or news director may ask you to read the statement or play the tape twice. The first time you read it he will adjust his equipment to get the best recording level, and the second time he will record. If it is newsworthy, and they are not swamped with material that day, many radio stations will use your statement uncut. It's certainly worth trying.

Your next step is to write a brief one-page press release summarizing the announcement made at your press conference or describing your special event. This should be sent to the newspaper and TV reporters who didn't attend. If you have any visual material you can reproduce easily for the TV stations, it's worth including, as well. If you recorded your press conference or media event on videotape, and you have a video production house that can work *fast*, you could even edit a video news release from your footage, and distribute it to television stations.

You will have to work quickly in order to meet deadlines. This is especially true if you had some coverage and wish to expand it. Once the stations or papers that did attend have run your story, others are less likely to; it's already stale news. So, this is no time for writer's block or introspection. You should have prepared all your material, made your calls, and delivered your stories by 3:00 P.M., at the latest. After that, you're entitled to a leisurely lunch with cocktails.

Publicity at Trade Shows

Trade shows draw journalists by the dozens, and if it's a major show, you can bet that every important writer, editor and reporter in the industry will be there, looking for news. Help them find it, and you can get great publicity for your business or organization, whether you're exhibiting or not—but you have to plan ahead of time.

Start by contacting the trade show's management firm at least 6 weeks before showtime. They may have a list of journalists who have preregistered for the exhibition. Sometimes the list is only available to exhibitors, but even if you won't have a booth, it can't hurt to ask. If you can't get a list from the manager, call your key contacts at the major trade magazines in your industry to find out who will be covering the show.

Once you have a list, read through it and ask yourself what information you have—and news pegs you can develop—that will interest these journalists. Offer them interviews with any of your company's experts who will attend the show, and let journalists know if you will be exhibiting or introducing new products by sending them a tip sheet several weeks ahead of time.

You should also ask the exhibition's management these questions:

- Are there press rooms available at the show? What equipment will they have for journalists? If you know that the trade journalists you work with will need equipment that won't be provided to cover your story, you can arrange to have it on hand.

- Can exhibitors display their press kits in the press room? Can you send your kits ahead? Who will receive them? Will they take responsibility for the kits? These policies will vary from one show manager to another.

- Does the show management notify the press of new product announcements to be made at the show? How do they handle this? What lead time do they need? Will their announcement be more effective than you can be, or can you do it better on your own?

- Is there a daily show publication? Will it include stories on new product announcements to be made at the show? What is the lead time?

- Has the management reserved rooms at show headquarters for press conferences and interviews with journalists? What facilities are available? Is there a charge for using them? Will these rooms meet your needs or do you have to rent your own space at the exhibition headquarters for press conferences and journalist interviews?

Finally, don't be swayed by the popular perception that you must exhibit in order to get publicity at a trade show. Joel Strasser points to a case where one of his clients was *not* exhibiting at a major trade show. "We found that there are a good number of editors who are interested in talking with the company even if they don't exhibit, so we set up press interviews in a hospitality suite."

Unplanned Visits from Reporters

Hopefully you will never have a fire, strike, explosion, accident, or major crime that brings the press, full of questions, to your doorstep without an invitation. Emergencies are difficult for the publicist, and if you want to cope with them well, you must plan ahead. Even if you think it could never happen to your organization or business, remember, the

Titanic was supposed to be unsinkable. So *you* ought to think through how to handle emergency situations.

Anticipating Emergencies

You should develop a written emergency plan and give your staff, volunteers, or members copies of it. Be sure the plan includes a list of officers, executives, staff, or volunteers who must be notified in case of an emergency. And be certain that everyone knows that *you* must be called at once, immediately after the fire department or the police.

Says public relations executive Ravelle Brickman, "If somebody gets murdered in your facility or there's a fire or major accident at your premises, it will be all over the news. Unless you, the publicist, are at the scene of the emergency to give the media your organization's story, reporters will rely on the police version and rumors. You want to be sure you get your organization's version to the media while the story is hot. The next day may well be too late. So you must know media deadlines and get your story to the press in time."

Replying to Questions

Your emergency plan should limit the number of people who can talk with the media during a disaster. This is a time when too many cooks will really ruin the broth. Aside from you, the publicist, only one or two officers or executives should be designated to make statements to reporters. Other staff or volunteers should be told to refer journalists' questions to authorized spokespeople, and you should explain to the staff why it's so important that they don't talk with media people.

Even though you and others authorized to speak may be, for example, rushing around trying to find out exactly how many people were killed and injured in an explosion at your organization's headquarters, you must talk to reporters. Let's suppose a reporter tries to collar you and ask questions. Because you're frantic, you start to get angry. You want to tell him to go to hell, but you say "no comment" instead. That isn't a very good idea. "No comment" sounds as if you have something to hide, and it may mean that the reporter will turn to other, possibly less accurate, sources for information. And those sources may be biased.

If you don't have any information, tell them you don't know yet, but you'll let them know just as soon as you find out. Try to anticipate their questions, and start working on answers immediately. If rumors are having a field day, you should deflate them as soon as you can—with facts. And although you may not be able to tell the press everything you know about the emergency or disaster because of legal problems, do not lie to the press. It will only cause you more problems later.

Don't ever guess about what happened, the cause of an accident, or the size of losses. Say you don't know yet, or that losses appear to be large or small, but cover yourself by using that word *appear,* for you might be overlooking something. And, even though you should try to answer reporters' questions honestly, don't volunteer information they haven't asked for.

You might give the press a written statement, but first check it with your lawyer. In the confusion surrounding an emergency situation, such a statement often helps reporters write accurate stories. Of course, you can't leave it at that; you will still have to try to answer questions.

Checklist—When the Media Visit

1. Do you really need to call a press conference?
2. Does your subject demand a question-and-answer session?
3. Does your press kit cover all the angles, thereby making a question-and-answer press conference unnecessary?
4. Do you know whether the journalists you work with prefer press conferences, press releases, or one-on-one product demonstrations?
5. Does the subject of your media event demand a particular location?
6. Is there a city with the best media resources for your press conference?
7. Will there be reporters in that city who are familiar with your subject matter?
8. Is the local press friendly to your organization, business, cause or industry?
9. Does the city you're considering have network news bureaus?
10. Are there wire service bureaus in that town?
11. Which part of town is most convenient for reporters?
12. Will journalists have immediate access to the press conference site without cumbersome security procedures?

13. If you're expecting major television and radio coverage, have you looked at the sound and lighting systems in the room you're going to use for your press conference?

14. Does your invitation let television news directors know that your press conference room has adequate lighting for their cameras?

15. If you're expecting television coverage, have you worked out lighting arrangements, in advance, that will make you look your best?

16. Are the doorways and halls in the building wide enough for television equipment?

17. Are there enough heavy-duty circuits for TV lights?

18. Should you have your press conference on location, rather than at a hotel or in your office?

19. If your media event will be outdoors, have you planned for possible bad weather, crowd control, noise control, and adequate lighting?

20. Is your event or press conference scheduled at a time that meets the deadlines of most of the media?

21. Have you avoided major holidays and events?

22. Are your press conference and special event invitations neatly typed and limited to one page with wide margins?

23. Do they include the "who," "when," "where," "why," "how," and "what?"

24. Have you included a one-paragraph summary, the names of the speakers, a brief blurb on each of them, the location, time, and date, and travel directions if needed?

25. Have you listed the picture and video possibilities?

26. Have you included travel directions if the event is in a hard-to-find location?

27. Have you sent your invitations to the reporters who actually cover your subject?

28. Did the AP Daily Budget editor and the UPI Daybook editor get the invitations, too?

29. Do you know which reporters hate reminder calls?

30. Have you practiced your reminder call pitch so you can describe your press conference or event in 15 words or less?

31. Did you make reminder telephone calls to the reporters you invited between 8:00 and 9:00 A.M. on the morning of the event?

32. Have you made a list of reporters who said they couldn't come, but want follow-up materials?

33. Have you planned to use visual aids at your press conference?

34. Have you rehearsed your speaker?

35. Have you trained him to speak in 10- to 20-second sound bites?

36. Have you worked with him to pare his opening remarks down to 5 minutes or less?

37. Is your spokesperson ready to answer every possible question—fair and foul?

38. Will you attend the special events and press conferences you arrange?

39. Will you, or someone on your staff, personally greet all reporters as they arrive?

40. Have you limited the number of people attending from your organization?

41. Do you have a press packet for each reporter in a handy location at your event or press conference?

42. Does it include a basic release, a backgrounder or longer release, a copy of the speaker's statement, background information on your business, organization, industry, product or cause, and any relevant documents?

43. Have you thought about how you'll handle your competition or your opposition if they appear at your media event?

44. Have you listed all the things that can go wrong at your media event—and how you'll handle them if they do?

45. Is someone available during your media event to answer the telephone at the number listed on your invitation?

46. Have you taped your press conference?

47. Have you called the person staffing the telephone to find out if there are any messages?

48. Have you written a 20-second radio statement or edited a radio wrap-around from your audiotape to release to radio reporters who didn't attend?

49. Have you called them and offered the statement or wrap-around?

50. Have you written a one-page press release based on the announcement made at the conference or the special event?

51. Have you delivered this to the print and TV journalists who didn't attend—along with your press kit?

52. If you recorded your media event on videotape, have you offered video news releases to major television journalists who didn't attend?

53. Have you delivered them by messenger, satellite, or overnight courier, and included your press kit?

54. Have you contacted trade show managers at least 6 weeks ahead of showtime to find out which journalists have preregistered?

55. What news pegs can you offer to induce these journalists to interview you and your staff at the exhibition?

56. Can you provide experts from your organization for journalists to interview at the show?

57. Do you have a room suitable for the interviews available?

58. Have you sent journalists a tip sheet several weeks before show time to let them know what news you will have to offer?

59. Have you found out what arrangements the show has for receiving and exhibiting your press kits?

60. Have you found out how the show's management notifies reporters of new products to be introduced at the show?

61. Can you get coverage in the show's daily publication?

62. Does your organization have an emergency media plan?

63. Does everyone know which staff and executives to notify in an emergency?

64. Does the plan designate the people from your organization who can talk to the media in an emergency or disaster?

65. Do staff members know why it's so important not to talk to the media in a crisis?

CHAPTER TEN

Controversy!

O h boy! Did you put your foot in it! You mentioned, in passing, that your
company wants to dump harmless chemical wastes into the river. Perhaps an investigative reporter discovered that your solar energy information center used government funds for well-intentioned research that
just did not produce any results. Or, maybe you're trying to cope with
a blizzard of news stories about a design problem with one of your
products that has resulted in serious injuries and even deaths.

Whatever the case, your telephone is ringing nonstop, and reporters are jumping through your doors and windows, pointing microphones in your face, and asking questions. Oh! the questions. You don't
know how to answer them. It's like a bad dream. Whatever you say, you
get deeper and deeper into a sticky morass.

Should you run for cover and blanket yourself with a patchwork
of "no comments" the moment you smell controversy? According to

public relations executive Richard Weiner, that's what has happened in the past. "Public relations people tended to be timid or cowardly with regard to taking a position on controversial issues. Public relations people traditionally said, 'Don't make waves, you can't get the last word in, try to be evasive, and don't be interviewed.' "

But it doesn't work. John and Jane Q. Public aren't dumb, and they know when an organization involved in a controversy is being evasive. Reporters aren't dumb either. If they don't feel you're leveling with them in a controversial situation, they'll go to other sources. And those other sources just may be your opposition, or your competition.

Handling Controversy

To handle controversy coolly, you need to distinguish between healthy controversy and really detrimental publicity. Then you should learn how to make advance preparations for coping with bad publicity, when to act and when to remain silent, how to reply to attacks when such action is called for, and how to handle difficult questions from the media.

The Positive Side of Controversy

Controversy is not necessarily bad. A good, healthy controversy can, under some circumstances, give you the chance to reach large numbers of people with your organization's point of view. And while under other circumstances it can be serious, indeed, it's almost never the end of the world.

Irving Rimer, vice-president for public information for the American Cancer Society, puts it this way: "Controversy can be one of the best things in the world for an organization. If you take a look at the big stories in cancer, they're primarily issue oriented. Cigarette smoking: front-page story. Should the federal government step up its war against cancer? Fraught with controversy."

"You will not fall apart," Rimer continues, "no matter how tough the opposition is, if you have done a good job over the years. You have to remember a basic truism: people get tired of conflict. They don't want it to last forever. And they will forget it."

Even if your organization is small and you don't feel very powerful, you might do better than you would expect if you find yourself involved in a controversy that gets media coverage. Says Richard Weiner, "Quite often the little guys include a lot of very intelligent people who by virtue of their intelligence and numbers, aside from the rightness of their cause, are quite able to succeed. On environmental and other public issues, the press and the media tend to side with the little guy." But, the big guy who responds with candor—and persuasive arguments—will get heard, too.

Being Prepared

One fine way to avoid many controversies and a lot of bad publicity is to make sure your organization or business is not busily hiding skeletons in the closet. But there are times when organizations with the cleanest closets in town and nothing at all to hide find themselves suddenly caught up in a maelstrom of controversy. And, yes, it could happen to *you!*

If you have any inkling that you will be involved in controversial issues, have facts and figures ready at all times. If your opposition or competition issues a statement and the press calls you for comment, you must be able to provide a clear, factual, persuasive statement with little or no warning. And if the press does not call you, you should call them as soon as you learn of your opponent's manifesto—to offer your response.

To be ready at all times, do the following:

- ■ Maintain a good file system with continually updated information drawn from opinion polls, trade and technical magazines, professional and trade associations, material from press clipping bureaus, and whatever other sources you can tap. This will help you respond to attacks with factual answers that can blow the offensive to smithereens.

- ■ Ask yourself all the leading, difficult, tricky questions the nastiest reporter could concoct. You could even have a panel of colleagues role play aggressive reporters. Then practice answering them in front of a tape recorder or video camera, so you can calmly analyze your answers afterwards.

- ■ It would be a very good idea to show the answers you develop to your lawyer, so he can help ensure they can't harm you from a legal point of view. If you're ever faced with difficult, hostile questions in an emergency situation, you'll be glad you did this exercise. Professional training in dealing with the media is listed under "classes and workshops" in Chapter 12.

- ■ Know how you can contact journalists quickly in an emergency, even after hours when main switchboards are closed.

At minimum, you'll need the telephone numbers for direct lines to newsrooms to reach reporters. But if your organization or business has frequent emergencies and crises, you may want to subscribe to one of the 24-hour newswire or broadcast fax services listed in Chapter 12.

■ You might also want to make contact with a satellite media tour operator equipped to respond to an emergency within hours. As *Public Relations Journal* points out, a satellite tour ". . . can turn around crisis communication problems in an afternoon, presenting . . . [your] point of view directly to 25 major markets."

■ You should know which journalists on your critical list subscribe to E-Mail, what their electronic addresses are, and how you can reach them through the electronic mail or database services you subscribe to.

■ You'll need to know what the press is saying about you— and your emergency situation—on a daily basis. Several clipping services can give you same-day, almost instantaneous updates on coverage of your product, issue or organization. (See Chapter 12.)

Journalists expect publicists to do such preparation, and well-prepared publicists are respected. Couple that with honesty, and a publicist can earn a reputation that's worth his weight in gold.

In addition, don't overlook the value of working out a common plan for counterattack within your field. You may find that other members of your trade or professional association are just as enmeshed in controversy as you are. In fact, trade associations are often formed because controversy has hit an industry.

"I think it's very important to find out who your allies are," says Irving Rimer, ". . . and not go in alone. Most issues are not focused on a single . . . [organization], but a broad interest . . . One of the first steps is to list all the people who have this similar interest. See if you can get together and work out a common cause. The very fact that there's a unity of interest makes your position with the media stronger. It also gives you the opportunity to seek out the best spokesman."

To Act or Not to Act

When it comes to controversial situations, you have to think strategically. You have to decide, says Rimer, whether you have ". . . a problem that will last for a period of time, that is going to have an impact, and you have to do something about it." If the problem will go away quickly on its own, you should probably ignore it. Ask yourself whether a reaction from your organization or business would only feed the fires of contention, or if it would make a real contribution to an honest debate.

Responding to Attacks

If the attack is coming from a newspaper or broadcaster, *The Publicist* advises the following:

"There are at least five things you can do when a publication or broadcaster says something untrue or distorted about . . . [you]. In escalating order, they are:"

1. Nothing.
2. Write a letter to the journalist who reported and/or wrote the story.
3. Write a letter to the editor of the medium, but not for publication.
4. Write a letter to the editor for publication.
5. Issue a reply, not only to the medium which published the statement, but to other media as well.

"In a surprising number of cases, number one is the best course . . . . Complaining about errors which are important to [you and your colleagues] but which seem trivial to the press and the public really accomplishes nothing aside from making you . . . feel better. Since you must repeat the misstatement at least partially in your reply, you may actually reinforce it . . . ."

"When you must reply, do so in writing rather than by telephone or in person. This enables you to marshall your arguments more calmly . . . . Concentrate upon your positive points, rather than a detailed rebuttal of the misstatements. The medium's audience probably will not remember the original story anyway. Never repeat the misstatement in detail . . . . Never attribute bad motives to the medium or question its integrity."

If you're attacked in a newspaper article, and you decide to respond, it's a fairly straightforward matter, according to Gil Cranberg, a professor at the University of Iowa. Writing in *Masthead*, he says, "Most newspapers routinely give the targets of attacks by the papers' own writers an opportunity to respond."

But, if the verbal assault is committed by a syndicated columnist, Cranberg points out, you might want to find out the names of *all* the papers that carry that columnist, so you can offer your response to each and every one of them.

If you are the subject of attack in a syndicated column, you should write a rebuttal and send it to the syndicate. Draw on as many facts as you can to make a calm and reasoned counter-argument. If you can include additional supporting data or documents to help you make your case, by all means, do so! Then contact the newspaper where you saw the attack, and find out the syndicate's address. Mail your response to the syndicate, asking that it be distributed to the editors at all newspapers that carried the column, and ask the syndicate to confirm that this was done. Include a copy of the column and the date it ran to help the syndicate identify it.

If this does not produce results, and you want to try again, find out the *columnist's* office address, which is usually different from the syndicate's. Write a letter to the columnist, explaining that you contacted the syndicate's office but have received no response. If you have access to the directory of syndicated columnists mentioned in Chapter 12, look up the columnist's address there. If not, contact the newspaper that published the column or the syndicate that distributed it.

If an attack is the work of discredited cranks who are keeping themselves well hidden, they will often become remarkably quiet if you let the media know who is at the storm center of this hurricane of words, and why they have been discredited.

In one interesting situation that took place somewhere in the real world about midway between Chelm and Plains City, a neighborhood recreation center found itself the target of letters to the editor and talk show call-ins complaining about the immoral goings-on at the teen drop-in center. The letters and calls, it turned out, were coming from the family of one person, a former maintenance man with an alcoholism problem who had been dismissed when a number of teenagers and several adults complained that they saw him drinking on the job. When his role was brought to light, not only did the letters and calls stop, but the neighborhood paper wrote an editorial supporting the recreation center's activities and ran a feature story about the drop-in center.

Handling Controversies under Negotiation

When you have had a meeting with your opposition and have come to an agreement over a controversy, issue a press release immediately. If you wait, your opponents could release material you don't agree with. Even though you thought you and they saw eye to eye at the meeting, that may not have been the case. If they get to the media first, you'll be on the defensive, not a good place to be in a controversy. Even if you are under attack, always be positive. Try to make it look as though you are the one who has taken the bull by the horns.

"The reply is never as effective as the attack," says Irving Rimer. "It doesn't get the same prominence, and it doesn't have the media's support."

Answering Difficult Questions

Admitting your problems to the press? Acknowledging to a reporter that there's another point of view beside your own? You say that sounds like suicide? Well, it isn't. You should not volunteer information about problems your organization or business is having, but when a reporter asks you difficult questions, she probably already has some information. In that case, the more human and helpful you are, the more understanding and receptive she's likely to be. Or to put it another way, *you* are in command of the situation if you reveal the bad news yourself, rather than waiting for a journalist to unearth it.

"I don't think it's a terrible thing to show some aspect of the organization that isn't as good as you'd like it to be. That, to me, establishes more credibility than anything else," says Cindy Loose of the *Staten Island Register.*

Tom Callaghan of the *Birmingham News* adds, "We'd like you to be straightforward about your shortcomings. If we ask you if it's true that people say this about you, or if we ask you about the negative points about your program, don't try to cover them up or evade them. Be willing to talk about those arguments and say 'yes, but,' or 'we see their side, but we have to do this . . . .' "

There are, however some occasions when, for legal reasons, you cannot answer a question. Or you simply don't know the answer yet. Just as in the case of a disaster, tell journalists that you can't comment for legal reasons, and then take a moment to let them know what those reasons are. Or tell them you don't know the answer yet, but you'll let them know as soon as you do. Be sure to let them know exactly what you're doing to find out that answer.

You may be pulled in two directions in a situation like this. Newton N. Minow, a lawyer who teaches media relations at Northwestern University's Kellog School of Management, explains why in an article in the *New York Times.* "Generally, lawyers tell executives to shut up while public relations people tell them to communicate . . . We want to teach students to balance the conflicting advice." It can be quite a balancing act, indeed, especially in a crisis situation. That's why you should discuss this issue thoroughly with your organization's top executives and board of directors, and decide on clear guidelines before they are needed.

In your discussion, be sure to point to the ongoing damage to public opinion—and perhaps profitability, as well—caused by the poor handling of controversies and emergencies by some of America's largest corporations. For example, the CEO of a major petroleum company appeared unconcerned when a huge oil spill fouled some of the most environmentally sensitive areas on earth. The head of an international chemical manufacturer couldn't seem to grasp the seriousness of a major industrial disaster. The petroleum producer and the chemical company sustained major damage to their public images because the media is quick to pick up disaster stories where the organization's spokesperson is not candid and concerned, or he denies that anything is wrong when the evidence clearly shows it is.

Even when legal considerations prevent you from speaking, never cut off a reporter with "no comment." Even if you are called at home after midnight, "no comment" is one of the worst of all possible responses. Cindy Loose explains, "It's always wrong because it's going to appear in the paper that you said 'no comment.' And anytime you say that, it's like pleading the Fifth Amendment. Even if you feel that a reporter is out to get you, if you say something, at least he can present some part of your picture. If you say nothing, you're certainly not going to get a fair shake. I'll always go to another source if the story is important enough. And that source is probably going to be one that is antagonistic to the organization."

Remember that a reporter's job is *not* to take what a publicist says at face value. She must question and probe what you tell her, even in noncontroversial situations. Her job is to analyze the news. And she knows that your allegiance is to your organization first and foremost, which is as it should be. She expects you to do your job, and you should expect the same from her.

It is possible to evade questions in order to present positive material first, and then to answer the troublesome points later. Let's say that a neighborhood recreation center was taken over by a new director three months ago, and it has come to light that there is a severe drug problem there. A reporter talks with the new director, and every time she mentions the drug problem, he answers by describing another good program his centers runs.

Loose's response to that situation is, "I want people to answer my questions. So it would be very irritating to me. If he inundates me with good stuff, I'm susceptible like anybody else, and I might pick up a point or two. But I want my questions answered, and I'll feel very irritated if I think I'm being evaded."

If, after evading questions for a while, the director says, "Yes, we have a drug problem. There's been one here for years. Since I've taken over I've done this and this to deal with it. We are quite concerned about it and we especially want community input to help solve it," Loose says her response would be positive.

"He'd probably get a better story out of it than if he just kept evading my questions. If I'm really interested in the drug problem, I'm going to talk to kids who have been in his program. I'm going to talk to people who are complaining about his program. I'm going to get all the worst possible information. The question is whether he's going to give me information easily and I'm going to be satisfied with that, so I'm not going to look for his worst critics who will do him much more damage than if he just admitted the problem to begin with."

If you don't know the answer to a reporter's question, admit it. Joyce Michels of the *Billings Gazette* gives the following advice: Say you don't know, but you'll find out. Ask when the reporter needs the information, and be sure you let her know by the deadline. Even if you can't come up with an answer, don't leave her hanging. Describe the steps you took to try to get the answer, and why you can't come up with it. She'll think more highly of you if you level with her.

If you are asked a question about a trade secret, be straightforward with the reporter. Explain that the material is confidential and you don't want your competitors to know about it, so you can't answer her question. She'll understand: after all, journalism is competitive, too.

If a question has legal overtones, refer the reporter to your lawyer. There may be times, particularly in controversies involving possible legal claims, when you cannot admit your organization's shortcomings. Never say anything that could be used to help establish liability in a lawsuit. If you tell a reporter that you can't answer the question because it involves potential litigation, she should accept that if she's a pro, especially if you let her know that she can contact your lawyer for a statement.

If controversy pounces on you out of the blue, try for a little breathing space so you can collect your wits and words. Listen to the reporter. Take notes. Say nothing. Ask when she needs to know. Ask for her telephone number and name. Promise to call back with an answer. You now have time to put on your thinking cap, create a careful statement, and anticipate any other questions the reporter may have up her sleeve, but, make certain you call back well before her deadline.

This discussion has assumed that reporters are asking honest, straightforward questions. Unfortunately, there are irresponsible, and even dishonest, reporters who will grab a controversy and try to sensationalize it. "Keep in mind," says public relations executive Nan Hohenstein, "that the media often want to present both extremes, not both sides. Ideally, it's best to answer the question, but too often the questions are not structured to accommodate your answer, or to give a comprehensive or insightful answer. They are structured to elicit a sixty-second answer, a yes or no, a paint yourself in the corner answer. Because most people can't think as fast as electronic impulses, it's permissible to give *your* answer, even if it doesn't quite match the question."

How Some Actual Controversies Were Handled

Cindy Loose of the *Staten Island Register* describes how one college president may have undermined his own position. "[I] called a private college that was having a little trouble with contract negotiations with the union. They fired a lot of people. The college claimed they were fired because it had financial problems, when it's pretty clear they were let go because negotiations were coming soon, and the college wanted to keep the union down."

"I called the union people. They were very cooperative. They had a story they wanted to give me. Then I called the president of the college, and I asked him a simple question: 'are you in a state of financial emergency?' Now that's a tough question because if he says yes it looks bad for the college, but if he says no, he's screwing with his union negotiations."

"He got very angry. Instead of answering me, he just said, 'I won't answer any questions relating to that.' So I asked about something indirectly related. He hung up on me."

"Now when I write that story, the only information I have to go on is whole sheaves of material from the union. But I've got absolutely nothing from the college, only 'no comment.' How do you think that story is going to come out?"

"And I'm willing to bet that after the story appears, the president of the college is going to complain. He's going to say 'you didn't tell my side.' My response to him is that I didn't have his side. How can I tell his side if I don't know what it is?"

The following anecdote illustrates how Irving Rimer took charge of a potentially negative situation and preserved the reputation of his institution. "In West Virginia," says Irving Rimer, "one of the leading papers was doing a story on the salaries paid to top executives in nonprofit agencies. They wanted the salaries of the executives in the American Cancer Society, and there was a problem getting the information at the state level. Finally the newspaper demanded them directly from us, so I said 'let's tell them. But let's also tell them what these people do and give them some news ideas along with the information.' "

"I called the reporter and said, 'I'm going to give you these salaries, but let me tell you what these people do. Dr. Bauscher, our senior vice-president of research, makes so much. He's the man behind the whole interferon story you've been writing about.' "

"The reporter said, 'Oh, that's the one I did last week.' "

" 'Yes,' I said, 'he's the brains behind it; he's the organizer behind it. And our chief executive makes so much per year. He is responsible for an organization that uses two million volunteers and has 2,500 local chapters. He's also responsible for what happens to the $146 million we raised last year.' And that's exactly what happened in the story. Instead of just giving him the salaries, I gave him the story behind the salaries."

"I think the principle is that if you raise money from the public, you are responsible to the public. If a responsible member of the press is asking for facts, then you should oblige. With understanding and interpretation, you can turn the story around."

In some cases it may not be worthwhile or wise to respond to an attack. Irving Rimer describes one such case. "In the past year, the American Cancer Society was confronted with ten consecutive programs on WNEW-TV in New York, moderated by Gabe Pressman. Night after night he attacked the Society, the National Cancer Institute, and the whole philosophy behind the cancer control program. Now we had agreed to participate in these programs with our best representatives, but Mr. Pressman's skill and editing overwhelmed them."

"Volunteers and staff members get most upset by this kind of criticism. It makes them uncomfortable. Representing their interest, we had a meeting with station management in which we were very critical of what took place. We asked that they correct the situation."

"They told us we could have a half-hour program, but we would be interviewed by Mr. Pressman, and he would have an opportunity to state his views. We thought that would be a useless exercise. As the station manager said to us, 'you know we've done a lot of good programs about cancer.' Which is true. So that wasn't worth pursuing beyond providing assurances to our own people."

In the following situation, a corporate executive managed to turn unfounded rumors into positive publicity for his company. Cordis Dow Corporation manufactures artificial kidneys. In 1978, their clipping service started sending them notices urging public-spirited citizens to save computer price codes, pop can tops, or even tea-bag tags, which could be exchanged for free dialysis time for needy kidney disease victims.

There was only one problem. When Robert E. Biel, manager of corporate communications for Cordis Dow, tried to find out where and how the tags, tops, and codes could be redeemed, he came to a series of dead ends. The Kidney Foundation had never heard of the campaign, hospitals had no information, and even the experts were puzzled. But the rumors persisted, and stories continued to surface in newspapers from Nashville to Newport.

"I started a one-man campaign to try to stamp out the rumor," says Biel. Cordis Dow tackled the problem through a "blitz" of the news media hoping to stop the unintentional hoax. The company felt that if people were willing to spend time trying to help kidney disease patients, their efforts should not be fruitless.

Since a successful kidney transplant is the best way to treat kidney failure, Cordis Dow's publicity material explained how people can arrange to donate their kidneys after death. Cordis Dow loses a customer when a kidney patient gets a transplant because the patient no longer needs artificial kidneys, so this was a truly public-spirited program.

In May 1978, the president of Cordis Dow sent a letter to the editor of the seventy largest newspapers in the country. A day or two later, Biel heard that AP was going to put the story on the wire.

Biel contacted the AP reporter working on the story and supplied him with more information. He also sent a mailgram to the editors who had been sent letters, alerting them to the forthcoming wire service story. Of course, he communicated with the Kidney Foundation, and they sent reinforcing letters to the seventy editors.

The story got extensive coverage in newspapers from coast to coast. Before Biel's blitz, Cordis Dow was receiving three to five news-clips a month about kidney dialysis collections. After the story ran, that dropped off to one clipping every two or three months. The whole campaign cost less than five hundred dollars.

Although each of these situations is different, there is one common denominator. If you tackle a controversial situation with an imaginative, carefully conceived plan that allows you to take the initiative and deal with journalists truthfully, you have an excellent chance to turn a potentially disastrous situation into positive publicity for your organization.

Checklist—Handling Controversy

1. Are you prepared with facts and figures so you can respond to an attack quickly?
2. Have you written down lists of leading, difficult, tricky and nasty questions reporters could ask you in a controversial situation?
3. Have you come up with answers to them?
4. Did you discuss these answers with your lawyer?
5. Have you taped your spokesperson answering these questions, and helped him make his delivery as believable as possible?
6. Do you know the numbers for direct telephone lines to newsrooms, so you can reach them after hours, when switchboards are closed?
7. Have you considered using a 24-hour fax or newswire service or electronic mail to handle emergency communications with the media?
8. Do you know which reporters on your media list subscribe to electronic mail, and what their electronic addresses are?
9. Do you have a way to track what the press says about you on a daily basis in a crisis situation?
10. Have you considered finding a satellite media tour operator who can put together a tour in a few hours in an emergency situation?
11. Do you know who your allies are?
12. Have you considered working with others in your industry or field on a common plan for counter-attacking your critics?
13. Will the controversy go away on its own?
14. Should you ignore it?
15. Will a response only serve to fuel the fires or reinforce wrong information?

16. Will your counter-attack make a real contribution to an honest debate?

17. Is your response based on compelling facts and persuasive logic?

18. Can you bolster it with documents or other supporting evidence?

19. Even if you have been attacked, can you make it look like *you're* the initiator of the debate?

20. Have you avoided restating misconceptions and wrong information?

21. Have you asked the publication or broadcaster for an opportunity to respond to an attack?

22. If the attack came from a syndicated columnist, have you contacted the syndicate and asked for an opportunity to rebut it?

23. If that didn't work, did you contact the columnist at his office address?

24. Can you discredit the attacker by exposing his hidden motives?

25. If you've negotiated an agreement with your opposition, have you made sure that *you* can issue a release announcing the agreement before they do?

26. Have you figured out how to discuss your organization's shortcomings in the most positive light possible?

27. Have you discussed with your lawyer the circumstances in which you absolutely cannot talk about a problem with the press?

28. Have you asked him how he would advise handling that type of situation without alienating the media?

29. Is your lawyer willing and able to handle media questions on these matters?

30. Does your lawyer understand why being candid with the media can pay dividends that can't be measured in dollars?

31. Have you discussed this issue with your organization's executives and board of directors and developed crystal-clear guidelines for spokespeople?

32. Have you removed the term "no comment" from your vocabulary?

33. Do you understand why a reporter *must* question what you say, especially in a controversial situation?

34. If a reporter is adversarial, can you answer her questions with *your* answers in order to paint a positive picture— and then deal with the problem candidly?

35. Can you admit that you don't know the answer to a reporter's question—and then offer to find out for her?

36. Are you confident enough to tell a reporter you can't discuss trade secrets?

37. When a reporter asking controversial questions calls you out of the blue, can you gain time by listening rather than responding, and offering to call him back later?

CHAPTER ELEVEN

Complaints and Solutions

You've sent out 87 press releases, 12 feature article summaries, and a dozen public service spots. But nothing has happened. Not a column inch in the paper, not a call from a reporter, not a single word on the air. What do you do now?

Whatever you do, don't despair! If you view this as a challenge, you have a fighting chance of turning the situation around. On the other hand, if you let anger overwhelm you, and vow to get even, or take on the media, you're sure to lose. "Declaring war on the press, tempting as it may sometimes be, is a game you can't win," says Stratford P. Sherman writing in *Fortune* magazine.

The first part of that challenge is to look long and hard at yourself, your organization, or your business and ask yourself these questions:

- How can you make your publicity material more interesting? Can you add facts and figures? Anecdotes? A local angle?

- Is your competition getting coverage? If so, what are their news pegs? Can you develop similar news pegs for your material?

- If none of your competition is getting "ink" or airtime, can you join with them in trying to get coverage for a forgotten industry or cause? This could break the ice and make it easier to get coverage later.

- Are there breaking news stories or newsworthy trends you can tie in to?

- Have you followed all the recommendations in this book? Yes, that's time-consuming, and no, it isn't easy. But, if you want the media to cover your story, you have to be willing to pay your dues.

If you are not getting the coverage you would like, or if it is not as complete or accurate as it should be, you really have to solve the problem yourself. Recent court decisions have weakened the Federal Communication Commission's (FCC) power to help you deal with broadcasters—and there wasn't a whole lot that could be done even before that. Moreover, the government never has regulated newspapers or magazines, so the bottom line is this: If you want to be a publicist, you have to rely on persuasion—and excellent publicity material. Combined with some of the techniques in this chapter, persuasiveness and excellence will open doors that are otherwise impervious to all the angry firepower you can muster.

Some tips for handling problems with the media follow. First of all, no matter how angry you are, remember that the person you are talking with is also human. Approach him with an attack, and he will react defensively. He will try to justify what he's done to explain why he can't help you. And once he has said he won't be able to work with you, it's hard for him to reverse himself because he'll lose face. On the other hand, if you approach a reporter or public service director with a request for help, you've set up a situation where he can become a problem solver. Many people like that role, since it provides a boost to their self-esteem. And helpers are not as likely to feel defensive.

Make sure that your protests are well thought out and presented in a constructive way. You'll need to go back to that reporter, editor, or public service director for future stories and spots. "You have to recognize that there's always a tomorrow, and you shouldn't burn your bridges ahead of you," says Robert Cummings of the *Maine Sunday Telegram.*

Using National Publicity as a Tool

Sometimes your organization, association, or business just can't generate much interest in the local media. But a thousand miles away, you become the out-of-town expert, and national media give you lots of play. If that happens, great! Keep copies of any newspaper clippings, and show these to your local editors and broadcasters to help convince them that you are, indeed, newsworthy. And if you're lucky, the word about your out-of-town media coverage will travel to your hometown by wire service!

As public relations executive Richard Weiner points out, "In some cases you're not able to get publicity in your local area, and then you get an article in *Time*, and the local media seek you out. Publicity begets publicity."

How to Handle Inaccurate Coverage

"Reporting, because it's done by people, is not always objective," says Tom Callaghan of the *Birmingham News*. Good reporters recognize this fact of life. As S. Griffin Singer, city editor of the *San Antonio Light* explains, "Sometimes we need our knuckles rapped. Maybe we've dropped the ball, or made mistakes. If we've got a problem, we need to know about it. And it's the same with the material the publicist turns in. If he has misled us, or there was a mistake in information . . . I would complain."

So, you see, it's a two-way street. Before you call the newsroom to complain that they've blown the story on your new microminiature widget, your Rotary Club's anti-crime program, or the impact of your state's new legislation on the gadget industry, switch roles for a minute. Think about how you'd react if the newsroom were calling to chew *you* out for botching *your* press release.

When you feel that the media have given you inaccurate coverage, you have to determine if the problem involves an *error* of fact or an *interpretation* of the facts that differs from yours.

Errors of fact are easier to deal with. Present the correct factual information with as much documentation as you can muster—and try to persuade the journalist involved to do a correction.

A journalist with a different point of view from yours, however, presents a challenge. You can make your task easier by explaining up front that there is a difference of opinion involved and that you'd like a chance to present yours to him and, ultimately, to his audience. Explain your point of view briefly, and back it up with as many facts as possible. Present reasons why his listeners, viewers or readers will want to be aware of your viewpoint. Be careful not to attack the reporter personally—in fact, the more you refer to his interpretation and contrast yours with it, the more legitimate you sound. Finally, ask the reporter if he can help you get coverage for your side of the story.

When your story has been poorly covered, or the information is inaccurate, see if you can develop a new angle and add new material before you call the reporter. That will save his ego; he can run a "new" second story with the correct information, without having to admit he made an error. The *Boise Statesman*'s Randy McCarthy feels that can be a decisive factor: "There's not really much I can do to rectify it after we've already done it. If we have an angle to camouflage the mistake, and we could get back into the story on a second shot, I'll try to do that."

Some reporters will be willing to rectify mistakes in print or on the air—even without a new angle. KGW-TV's Larry Badger has a ". . . general rule that the reporter who did the particular story with the problem corrects it on the air."

Many reporters will respond to a caller who presents another point of view that has not gotten ink or airtime. If, for example, KRAE-AM's Ralph Graczak gets a call from someone who says, "You didn't cover our side of the story," he turns on the tape recorder and asks the caller to tell his side, right then and there. So, if you call a broadcaster, it would be wise to prepare a brief twenty- or thirty-second statement. Then you'll be ready if he offers to roll the tape.

If you can't work out a solution with the reporter involved, you should probably let the matter drop, unless the story is going to have a major, serious, and continuing impact on your business or organization. In that case, you might want to see if you can arrange a meeting with the managing editor, the editorial board, or the news assignment editor. Explain to them that you'd like an opportunity to present your organization's side of the story. Let them know that you want to work with them to avoid any future problems. Some stations and newspapers will be receptive, some won't.

Help from the Federal Communications Commission

Although the courts may weaken Federal Communications Commission regulation of broadcasting further, as of June, 1990, FCC regulations offered limited help with the three following problems:

- You have been attacked on a broadcast.
- You are a political candidate denied equal access to broadcast time.
- You can *prove* that news coverage of your business, organization, or cause has been deliberately falsified.

But don't count on the FCC to solve your coverage problems for you, even if the courts leave their remaining powers intact. They move slowly. You, as a publicist, must move fast.

"Before complaining to the Commission, complain to the station," advises the FCC. "We encourage negotiations between candidates and stations . . . and have found that many disputes can be settled in that way . . . . When you do file a complaint with the Commission, send a copy to the station . . . at the same time . . . thus saving time in settling the complaint."

So once again, it's up to you to get what you want by persuasion and negotiation. Sure, you can cite FCC regulations to add weight to your argument, but the power of your presentation will come from your ability to convince broadcasters that you have a compelling argument— and that their listeners will want to know about it.

FCC Rules on Personal Attack

According to the FCC, "When a station broadcasts a personal attack or a political editorial endorsing or opposing a candidate for public office . . . it must provide a script or tape of the attack or editorial. In the case of a personal attack, a tape, script or accurate summary of the attack must be provided to the persons or group attacked."

The FCC requires a broadcaster to notify a person or organization that has been attacked, of the date, time, and name of the program within 24 hours. You must be offered a "reasonable" opportunity to personally respond to the attack on the air. And, if the original attack was made during prime time, you should insist that your reply time is not at midnight.

The only time the personal attack rule does not apply is if the comments were made during a newscast, news interview, or on-the-spot coverage of a news event. Nonetheless, you still might want to ask the station for a chance to reply.

The FCC's Policies on Fraudulent News Coverage

Under some circumstances, the FCC will act on complaints that news programming has been ". . . falsified, distorted, faked or staged." But it must have hard evidence that this was done deliberately by a station's management. And that evidence must come from somewhere *other than* the newscast, itself.

As one of the Commission's publications explains, "What is often alleged to be news suppression has usually been shown to be the exercise of editorial judgment. However, a serious public interest question would be raised if it appeared that a station licensee was deliberately excluding whole classes of subjects or events from its news coverage, based on private judgments or interests that conflict with the licensee's obligation to serve the public interest."

CHAPTER TWELVE

Sources and Services for Publicists

T he following directory will help you get some idea of the books, information, and services available to publicists. Many of the firms listed are in New York, the nation's public relations capital. You should check your city's *Yellow Pages* for local firms to widen your choices.

No prices are given here. Contact each service for complete information, including current prices. Be sure you understand exactly what they will provide for your money— always ask for written estimates and descriptions of services. Whenever you can, compare the prices and promises of two or three services before you sign on the dotted line.

This is not a complete list. If your curiosity is whetted and you want to know more about publicity resources, there is more information in the *Professional's Guide to Public Relations Services,* by Richard Weiner, which describes and evaluates about one thousand public relations books, services, and products, from clipping services, to media directories and video production houses. The guide is distributed by H&M Publishers, 44 W. Market St., P.O. Box 311, Rhinebeck, NY 12572, 914-876-2081.

Services

Classes and Workshops

International Association of Business Communicators (IABC)
One Hallidie Plaza, Suite 600, San Francisco, CA 94102, 415-433-3400, 800-776-4222.

Offers communication workshops and classes on a national, international and local basis. Contact them for complete information, and be sure to ask about sessions sponsored by local and regional chapters in your area.

Persuasive Writing for Publicists
The Communication Workshop, 217 E. 85th St., Suite 442, New York, NY 10028, 718-575-8000.

A two-day class, customized for your organization's needs and given on-site anywhere in the U.S. and Canada. Teaches you and your staff how to choose the most persuasive style and tone for publicity materials, and how to structure and organize them for maximum impact. Taught by Gary Blake, author of six writing textbooks.

Persuasive Presentation Techniques
Communispond, Inc., 485 Lexington Avenue, New York, NY 10017, 212-687-8040; 676 St. Clair St., Chicago, IL 60611, 312-787-0484; 160 Sansome St., San Francisco, CA 94104, 415-392-6600.

Conducts a variety of public workshops that teach you how to present persuasively, eliminate nervousness, think clearly under pressure, and learn how to control adversarial discussions. You are videotaped as you speak so you can actually *see* yourself on stage as others see you. Available in major cities or at your organization's headquarters.

The Douglis Visual Workshops

212 S. Chester Road, Swarthmore, PA 19081, 215-544-7977.

Workshops about communicating with pictures, for newsletter and magazine editors, as well as publicists. The sessions include skills and techniques of photojournalism, principles of visual communication, how to avoid clichés, editing photos, and hands-on experience. These two-and-a-half-day sessions are given in 14 major cities.

NYU/Public Relations Society of America Program

New York University, School of Continuing Education, Business and Management Programs, 310 Madison Avenue, Suite 1710, New York, NY 10017, 212-682-1435.

This joint program, sponsored by New York University and the Public Relations Society of America, presents two- and three-day seminars on publicity and public relations in New York City and Washington, D.C. Customized programs are also available on-site, at your organization's headquarters.

Topics include *Basic Public Relations Writing, Writing and Placing Public Relations and Public Affairs Materials, Managing Crises, Preparing for Radio/TV Interviews,* and *Publicity as a Marketing/PR Tool.*

Computer Software

Cliptrak™

Cetex Corporation, 37 Thunderhead Road, Medford, NJ 08055, 609-953-1406.

Cliptrak™ is a software package that lets you enter data about your publicity clippings and generate reports and graphs to help you analyze their impact.

Media Relations/Crisis Management (Public Relations Body of Knowledge Abstracts)

Public Relations Society of America, 33 Irving Place, New York, NY 10003, 212-995-2230.

A comprehensive collection of abstracts from books, journals, and articles on both media relations and crisis management, conveniently categorized for quick reference. Available in printed form or on diskettes for Apple and IBM computers.

NewsTrack™

The Right Brain, Inc., 420 N. Fifth Street, #970, Minneapolis, MN 55401, 612-334-5620.

Lets you enter information about your media contacts, assign them to categories, and produce sorted lists by the categories you need. You could, for example, print out a list of entertainment editors in Ohio. A contact log helps you keeps track of discussions with media contacts by adding your notes to their files, and a "to-do" list reminds you of upcoming tasks and deadlines.

NewsTrack™ lets you turn information about your clippings and airplay into helpful reports. The software also keeps track of the time you spend on various projects for billing or accounting purposes.

Public Relations Manager™

Cetex Corporation, 37 Thunderhead Road, Medford, NJ 08055, 609-953-1406.

This media directory software comes with up to 80,000 media contacts already entered for you, including the contacts listed in *Metro California Media, New York Publicity Outlets,* the *Oxbridge Directory of Newsletters,* and many others. The databases you purchase can include newspapers, radio, TV, cable, magazines, newspapers, trade journals, newsletters and internal corporate publications. You can also enter your own media contacts or have Cetex do it for you.

Public Relations Manager™ lets you sort by categories you specify and answer questions like "What are the newspapers in Target County with circulations of 50,000 or more?" or, "What national magazines with circulations greater than 20,000 cover gardening and horticulture?" Update service available.

PR Works™

Desktop Innovations, Inc., 742 Gilman Street, Berkeley, CA 94710, 800-669-6757, 415-525-9688.

This publicity management software stores information about your media contacts and editorial calendars in its database, reminds you of upcoming deadlines, organizes your tasks into priority lists, and automatically keeps track of your time. Available for the Macintosh. Call or write for information about the *PR Works* demo disk.

Targeter

Media Distribution Services, Inc. (MDS), 307 W. 36th Street, New York, NY 10018, 212-247-4800.

They'll install their media contact list of 150,000 editors and other key contacts in your personal computer, and update it daily by electronic mail. You'll be able to print out media lists, run mailing labels, and look up media contacts 24 hours a day. Also available in a networked version, so more than one person in your organization can tie his or her computer into the database.

Databases & Libraries

Burrelle's Information Services

75 E. Northfield Avenue, Livingston, NJ 07039, 201-992-6600, 800-631-1160.

They will search six of the major computerized databases for you and retrieve articles mentioning the key words you specify. The databases, which include NEXIS, Dow Jones, DIALOG, Data Times, VU/TEXT and Info Globe, give full-text access to backfiles of 65 newspapers, 150 trade and consumer magazines, 4 major wire services, and 200 specialized databases.

You can use this service to track competitors, research a market, and find background information for publicity material, to mention a few.

CompuServe Information Service

5000 Arlington Centre Blvd., P.O. Box 20212, Columbus, OH 43220, 800-848-8199.

Their special interest group for public relations professionals (called PRSIG in database lingo) lets you access data libraries of interest to publicists, post questions on a bulletin board for other publicists, and take part in on-line group discussions with leaders in the public relations field. On-line news services include the Associated Press Wires, Business Wire, Executive News Clipping Service, United Press International and *The Washington Post.*

DIALOG Information Services, Inc.

3460 Hillview Avenue, Palo Alto, CA 94304, 415-858-3785, 800-334-2564.

One of the largest database services, DIALOG includes more than 350 individual databases, the complete text for over 800 journals and newspapers, and up-to-the-minute news from more than a dozen wire services.

Because there is so much information available, using DIALOG takes some preparation and practice. They offer orientation seminars, 24-hour customer support by telephone, as well as video, computer disk and printed support materials to help you become an efficient information retriever.

GEnie
GE Information Services, 401 N. Washington St., Rockville, MD 20850, 800-638-9636.

You can access business and financial news through the Dow Jones News/Retrieval System or use the Quiknews electronic clipping service, which routes stories about topics you specify to your GEnie electronic mailbox. You can then read them at your convenience, and print out any stories you choose.

NEXIS® Advertising and Public Relations Library
Mead Data Central, 9443 Springboro Pike, P.O. Box 933, Dayton, OH 45401, 800-544-7390.

More than 200 full-text sources, including major trade publications in the advertising, public relations, manufacturing, and retailing industries, plus access to dozens of other databases as well. Lets you find out what's been said about your product, service or cause, identify and follow industry trends, track the competition, and develop a profile of your actual and potential customers.

Public Relations Information Center
Public Relations Society of America, 33 Irving Place, New York, NY 10003, 212-995-0148.

Probably the largest collection of publicity and public relations resources in the United States, with files on more than 1,000 topics, as well as books, periodicals and directories. The Information Center, which charges for its services, is available to both members and nonmembers. They can mail you information from their files within 24 hours, and they offer NEXIS® searches, too.

VU/TEXT®
VU/TEXT Information Services, Inc., 325 Chestnut Street, Suite 1300, Philadelphia, PA 19106, 215-574-4408, 800-323-2940.

The largest U.S. newspaper databank, they offer the full text of more than 200 newspapers and regional business journals from as far back as

January, 1985. Examples include *The Washington Post, The Los Angeles Times, Atlanta Business Chronicle, St. Paul Pioneer Press Dispatch,* and *Time* magazine. They also have back files of dispatches sent out by such major newswires as the Associated Press. Articles can be read on-screen or printed out.

Mat Services

Mat services take your press release or feature story and pictures, print them in easily reproducible form (called "mats" or "reproduction proofs"), and send them out to newspapers. Busy editors at smaller papers often use the entire article with the art because it saves time. And since they can use the reproduction proofs directly, without typesetting, they save money, too. Many corporations, trade associations, and nonprofit organizations use this method to get the message to readers exactly as they wrote it.

When you contact a mat service, ask them for samples and find out whether their fee includes providing you with clippings.

Associated Release Service, Inc.

2 N. Riverside Plaza, Chicago, IL 60606, 312-726-8693.

They prepare and distribute your release in typeset form to 8,100 suburban and community daily and weekly newspapers. All or part of their list can be used. Clippings are provided as part of service. They also distribute and track radio and television releases.

Derus Media Service, Inc.

500 N. Dearborn Street, Suite 516, Chicago, IL 60610, 312-644-4360.

They write a feature story based on your material, and send out glossy reproduction proofs to more than 8,000 daily and weekly papers in the U.S. All or part of their list can be used. Derus can send out a regular column series topped by a standing headline, or a specially made crossword puzzle based on your firm's product or service or your organization's cause. They can also send proofs to Canadian papers and Spanish language material to Hispanic publications in the U.S. Clippings are provided as part of the service for U.S. papers.

Metro Associated Services, Inc.

33 W. 34th Street, New York, NY 10001, 212-947-5100.

Sends reproduction proofs of monthly feature sections, each one with a theme like Home Improvement, Mother's Day Gift Guide, and Food &

Cooking. Each section includes stories from a number of organizations. The proofs are sent to 7,000 daily and weekly papers.

North Americas Précis Syndicate, Inc.

201 E. 42nd Street, New York, NY 10017, 212-867-9000; 1025 Vermont Avenue NW, Washington, DC 20005, 202-347-5000; 333 N. Michigan Avenue, Chicago, IL 60601, 312-558-1200; 4209 Vantage Avenue, Studio City, CA 91604, 818-761-8400.

Your release or a release adapted from your material is sent to 1,000 suburban dailies and 2,800 weeklies, in ready-to-print form. Their staff writers include a home economist, former reporters and editors, and public relations and advertising professionals, all of whom specialize in preparing material suburban papers can use. NAPS promises at least 100 clips per release, and they provide them as part of the fee. They guarantee satisfaction, or they'll do another release at no cost.

Media Lists on Labels and Computer Diskettes

All-in-One Directory

Gebbie Press, P.O. Box 1000, New Paltz, NY 12561-0017, 914-255-7560.

21,000 listings for daily and weekly papers, radio and TV stations, consumer, business, and trade magazines, farm publications, the Black and Hispanic press, and more. Available on floppy disks for the IBM or Macintosh, or in printed, bound form.

Bacon's Media Lists

Bacon's Information, Inc., 332 S. Michigan Avenue, Chicago, IL 60604, 312-922-2400, 800-621-0561.

Custom-selected lists on labels, with names of editors, reporters, news directors, and public service directors. Available for magazines, newspapers, broadcasters, and wire services. The lists are based on a daily-updated computer file. Also available on floppy disks for the IBM.

Burrelle's Press Clipping Service

75 E. Northfield Road, Livingston, NJ 07039, 201-992-6600, 800-631-1160.

Media contacts at more than 40,000 newspapers, magazines, broadcast and cable stations, as well as wire services are available on printed labels or IBM-compatible floppy disks. The names are drawn from a computer database, updated daily. You can specify lists by circulation, editorial function, coverage area, and many other categories.

Power Media Selects

Broadcast Interview Source, 2233 Wisconsin Avenue, Suite 406, Washington, DC 20007-4104, 202-333-4904.

The most influential media contacts in the U.S., available on labels, Rolodex® cards and floppy disks.

Talk Show Selects

Broadcast Interview Source, 2233 Wisconsin Avenue, Suite 406, Washington, DC 20007-4104, 202-333-4904.

Radio and television talk show contacts available on labels, Rolodex® cards and floppy disks.

Newswires

These private wire services are connected to Teletype printers at major newspapers and broadcast stations. For a fee, they will transmit your copy over their wires, exactly as you wrote it, directly into newsrooms, in minutes. This can increase the impact of your material, and it can be critical where time is limited.

Newswires are particularly important for publicists who have to meet requirements for prompt disclosure in cases where news might impact their organizations' stock prices.

Most wire services have interconnecting arrangements, and can send your copy over other circuits. If you're going to use a private wire service, staff your telephones for two or three hours after the material is sent out on the wire, so you can answer any questions editors may have.

Business Wire

1185 Avenue of the Americas, New York, NY 10036, 212-575-8822, 800-221-2462; 44 Montgomery Street, Suite 2185, San Francisco, CA 94104, 415-986-4422, 800-227-0845.

Business Wire's national circuit includes 2,000 newsrooms across the country. Your release can be distributed to the entire circuit or on a state or regional basis. Business Wire has special circuits for sports and entertainment news. They can transmit news photos by wire, and transmit your release to international newswires for world-wide coverage. Their Analyst Wire reaches key players in the investment community.

Business Wire also has offices in Atlanta, Boston, Charlotte, Cleveland, Denver, Los Angeles, Miami, Nashville, Newport Beach, Philadelphia, Phoenix, San Diego, Silicon Valley, and Seattle. Call one of the toll-free numbers for more information.

PR Newswire

150 E. 58th Street, 31st Floor, New York, NY 10022, 212-832-9400, 800-832-5522.

Their circuits cover 1,500 print and broadcast newsrooms in the U.S. alone. They operate 24 hours a day every day, and offer local, national, and international circuits. Translations for international dispatches are included in the service. Releases transmitted by PR Newswire are automatically routed to major business databases like NewsNet, NEXIS, and DIALOG. PR Newswire has a number of specialized circuits:

- North American Disclosure service to reach the business press and financial community in the U.S. and Canada.
- EntertaiNet, geared exclusively for entertainment editors.
- Feature News Service for early morning delivery of your feature story to the appropriate editor in 1,000 U.S. newsrooms.
- Satellite photo transmission of black and white photos to newspaper editors.

Nonprofit-Oriented Public Relations Agencies

The Advertising Council

261 Madison Avenue, New York, NY 10016-2303, 212-922-1500.

One of the five largest single advertisers in the United States, in 1987–88 they obtained media time and space worth $1.2 billion for nonprofit organizations and government agencies. They have conducted campaigns for United Way since 1946, Forest Fire Prevention since 1942, and Child Abuse Prevention since 1976. Recently, they've added campaigns for AIDS Prevention, Recycling, and the Child Find Mediation Program.

"We freely counsel leaders in government and private philanthropy who come to us for help, whether or not a Council campaign eventually emerges."

They have four criteria for projects they undertake:

1. The project must be noncommercial, nondenominational, nonpartisan politically, and not designed to influence legislation.
2. The purpose of the project . . . [is] such that the advertising methodology can help achieve its objectives.
3. If the organization is a fund-raising one, the Council will take into consideration whether or not it currently meets the standards of public and private accreditation organizations.
4. The project is national in scope, or sufficiently national so that it is relevant to media audiences in communities throughout the nation.

Public Interest Public Relations, Inc. (PIPR)

225 W. 34th Street, Suite 1500, New York, NY 10122, 212-736-5050.

PIPR specializes in promoting the issues and ideas of not-for-profit organizations. The agency has helped hundreds of civic, minority, educational and cultural groups communicate better through creative public relations campaigns. PIPR has won many awards for creative publicity for nonprofit organizations.

Pressbooks

Package Publicity Services, Inc.

27 W. 24th St., Suite 402, New York, NY 10010, 212-255-2872.

Publishes pressbooks and related promotional material for more than 1,700 major Broadway plays. Use these collections of suggested press releases, background information on playwrights, and copies of reviews to give you ideas for your own community theater publicity campaign. For best results, contact them three months ahead.

Press Clipping Services

In addition to letting you know when and where your press releases, feature stories, and fillers have been used, clipping services can help you keep track of what's going on in your field or industry. You can even use them to find out what kinds of coverage your competition is getting. And, they can help you monitor proposed regulations and legislation that will affect your business or organization.

Because clipping services, like human beings, are not perfect, some publicists use two or three services to make sure they get most of the articles they're interested in. You may want to experiment to find the best way to meet your needs.

Most clipping services still actually read thousands of publications, and send you paper clippings. However some of the database services can scan electronic versions of newspapers and magazines, as well as dispatches from the wire services, and automatically "clip" any item that mentions the key words you specify. You get your "clippings" in electronic form and have your computer print them out for you, or you can have the database service do the printing for a fee.

If you are interested in this service, be aware that each database service includes different publications and wire services. You'll have to find out if they cover your key publications, and if that coverage is full-text or just the highlights.

When you choose a traditional clipping service, find out whether they offer limited service for just your city or state, if that's what you want. Some services operate on a regional or national basis and charge you accordingly, even if that coverage is too broad for you. Also check with your State Press Association, since a number of them offer inexpensive clipping services. If you don't know where to find your state's association, call the managing editor of the largest daily in your area. He's sure to know.

Some of the larger clipping bureaus also offer services which analyze your clippings for editorial slant, product or key word mentions, number of readers reached, and photos used.

Bacon's Information, Inc.
332 S. Michigan Avenue, Chicago, IL 60604, 312-922-2400, 800-621-0561.

Provides clippings from more than 5,000 trade, business and consumer magazines, and virtually every daily and weekly newspaper in the United States and Canada. They can also provide clippings on any subject you specify, from abrasives to Zen Buddhism—all at a rate they claim is 30 percent to 40 percent lower than other national clipping bureaus charge.

In addition, Bacon's reads 50,000 foreign publications using 2,500 readers in 43 offices worldwide. Their Clipping Analysis Service transforms your hard-to-manage press clippings into clear, concise reports that measure the effectiveness of your publicity campaigns.

Burrelle's Press Clipping Service
75 E. Northfield Road, Livingston, NJ 07039, 201-992-6600, 800-631-1160.

They read all 1,642 daily, 834 Sunday, and 8,313 weekly newspapers in the United States, including Spanish language publications, 4,645 trade journals, 1,658 consumer magazines, and the dispatches from 7 major newswires. Canadian and foreign coverage is available. They monitor all network TV and radio news and public affairs programming, plus local TV news and public affairs programs in major metro areas, with typed transcripts available.

Burrelle's NewsExpress service reads 43 major U.S. daily papers and delivers your clips to you by fax—before 9:00 A.M. the day they appear. In addition, they can supply analysis reports of your clippings based on a variety of factors. And, they can archive your clippings and publicity materials on optical disks for fast retrieval and space-saving storage.

Cliptrak™

Cetex Corporation, 37 Thunderhead Road, Medford, NJ 08055, 609-953-1406.

Cliptrak™ is a software package that lets you enter data about your publicity clippings and generate reports and graphs to help you analyze their impact. You can also have Cetex enter your clippings for you.

DIALOG Information Services, Inc.

3460 Hillview Avenue, Palo Alto, CA 94304, 415-858-3785, 800-334-2564.

One of the largest database services, DIALOG includes more than 350 individual databases, the complete text for over 800 journals and newspapers, and up-to-the-minute news from more than a dozen wire services. Using key words and phrases, you can instruct their DIALOG Alert[sm] Service to give you daily, weekly, or monthly updates on any topics you wish, and retrieve the information from your electronic mailbox.

GEnie

GE Information Services, 401 N. Washington St., Rockville, MD 20850, 800-638-9636.

Their Quiknews electronic clipping service routes stories about topics you specify from their news and wire services to your GEnie electronic mailbox. You can then read them at your convenience, and print out any stories you choose.

International Press Clipping Bureau, Inc.

5 Beekman Street, New York, NY 10038, 212-267-5450, 800-752-1378.

Offers clipping service for newspapers in one city or state only, or the entire nation. Reads every daily newspaper published in the U.S. (more than 1,600), 7,000 weeklies and monthlies, and thousands of trade and technical journals. Has a back search department for all New York City newspapers and can arrange back search coverage for any publication in the U.S., so you can get copies of clippings about a subject that interests you from the past 10 years.

Nielsen Sigma System
A. C. Nielsen Company, 1290 Avenue of the Americas, New York, NY 10036, 813-734-5473.

Nielsen Research is developing an almost foolproof tracking method for *television* public service spots, video news releases and other pre-recorded publicity material. The Sigma System should be perfected and approved by the Federal Communications Commission soon—if it hasn't been already. Your publicity material is encoded with data which can't be seen or heard, but special monitors can read it directly from the airwaves. If Nielsen is monitoring that channel, and you've subscribed to this service, you'll know for sure that your material has been used. Please note that although Nielsen's main office is in New York, the telephone number for Sigma Service, which is handled outside of head-quarters, is in Florida.

NEXIS® ECLIPSE™
Mead Data Central, 9443 Springboro Pike, P.O. Box 933, Dayton, OH 45401, 800-544-7390.

Using the NEXIS database, you can automatically search for a list of key words, and get a daily, weekly, or monthly report on the topic, product or company of your choice.

Luce Press Clipping Service
420 Lexington Avenue, New York, NY 10170, 212-889-6711, 800-528-8226.

Provides coverage of every daily and virtually every weekly newspaper in the U.S., plus the AP, UPI, Dow Jones and Reuters newswires, as well as more than 6,000 trade and consumer magazines.

Luce can provide transcripts or videotapes of all regularly sched-uled national network TV news shows, and many regularly scheduled local TV news and talk shows in major metro areas.

Their AM Newsbreak service delivers clippings to you by fax on the morning they appear in the nation's top news sources. And, their clipping analysis service can provide you with reports analyzing your media coverage on paper or computer disk.

NewsTrack™

The Right Brain, Inc., 420 N. Fifth Street, #970, Minneapolis, MN 55401, 612-334-5620.

NewsTrack™ lets you turn information about your clippings and airplay into helpful reports using information such as editorial slant, effective audience reach and type of coverage.

Press Release Distribution Services

If you are mailing releases and feature stories on a statewide, regional, or national basis, you may find it worthwhile to use one of these press release distribution services. In addition to the services below, a number of state press associations offer the same service at a reasonable rate. If you don't know where to find your state press association, call your local library and ask the reference librarian if he can find it for you.

Bacon's Information, Inc.

332 S. Michigan Avenue, Chicago, IL 60604, 312-922-2400, 800-621-0561.

They'll print your release or press kit, duplicate your photos, and use their database of 175,000 media contacts by name to develop a customized distribution list for each release. They handle the stuffing, sealing, stamping, addressing and sorting, too.

They can reach the Black and Hispanic press, every daily and weekly newspaper in the U.S., all broadcast stations, and 8,400 U.S. and Canadian magazines. International distribution is available. Bacon's can also set up and maintain your organization's list on their computer.

Business Wire NewsFax Service

1185 Avenue of the Americas, New York, NY 10036, 212-575-8822, 800-221-2462; 44 Montgomery Street, Suite 2185, San Francisco, CA 94104, 415-986-4422, 800-227-0845.

Complete fax distribution service to the investment community.

MCI Mail

1150 17th Street, N.W., Suite 800, Washington, DC 20036, 202-833-8484, 800-444-6245.

Using your personal computer and a modem, you can send electronic mail (including publicity materials) to any journalist who has an MCI Mailbox Number. This service also allows you to send publicity material to fax and telex machines worldwide. Available 24 hours a day—important in crisis communication situations. They can store your letterhead and signature for fax transmissions.

Media Distribution Services, Inc. (MDS)
307 W. 36th Street, New York, NY 10018, 212-247-4800.

You provide them with ready-to-print copy, and they print, address, stamp and mail your publicity material for you. Their computerized database, which contains more than 150,000 editors and other key media contacts by name, helps you reach as many as 40,000 print and broadcast media in the U.S. and Canada. You can use more than 2,500 editorial and geographic classifications to target your publicity mailing to just the right journalists.

Their database, updated daily, includes all daily, weekly and college newspapers, TV and radio stations, cable and broadcast networks, business and consumer magazines, wire services, syndicated columnists, and even major freelance writers.

Newport Associates, Ltd.
7400 East Orchard Rd., Suite 320, Englewood, CO 80111, 303-779-5515, 800-733-5515.

A high-capacity broadcast fax service, with no set-up fees. Offers letterhead, logo and signature storage, cover sheets addressed to specific names, and confirmation of receipt.

PR Newswire Facsimile Service
150 E. 58th Street, 31st Floor, New York, NY 10022, 212-832-9400, 800-832-5522.

Their Facsimile Service can deliver your news to hundreds of editors and financial analysts at the same time. They'll keep your distribution list updated and store your letterhead electronically. You can send them copy by fax or by computer to computer transmission, using a modem.

Professional Organizations

International Association of Business Communicators (IABC)
One Hallidie Plaza, Suite 600, San Francisco, CA 94102, 415-433-3400, 800-776-4222.

The worldwide network for communication professionals, with affiliates in more than 40 countries. With dozens of chapters across the

United States, IABC offers a chance to meet—and learn from—other communicators. Services to members include workshops and classes, as well as a subscription to the award-winning publication, *Communication World*. The organization includes internal communicators (who aim their work at their company's employees) as well as publicists.

Public Relations Society of America (PRSA)

33 Irving Place, New York, NY 10003, 212-995-2230.

An organization of public relations men and women in business, government, PR agencies, and large nonprofit organizations. PRSA emphasizes professional development. They publish a *Code of Professional Standards for the Practice of Public Relations*. The organization has more than 100 chapters throughout the U.S. Write for information about the chapter nearest you.

Public Relations Student Society of America

33 Irving Place, New York, NY 10003, 212-995-2230.

The student affiliate of the Public Relations Society of America has 166 chapters on college campuses across America. Internship programs for qualified members offer students a chance to get practical, on-the-job public relations and publicity experience.

Women in Communications

P.O. Box 17460, Arlington, VA 22216, 703-528-4200.

An organization of professional women in the communication field, including radio, television, newspapers, publishing, advertising, marketing, and public relations. Attending local meetings is a good way to meet journalists and other publicists. Although the organization is primarily for women, men should check to see what it offers them. Write for information about the chapter nearest you.

Public Service Spot Production and Distribution

Medialink

708 Third Avenue, New York, NY 10017, 212-682-8300, 800-843-0677; 541 N. Fairbanks Court, Chicago, IL 60611, 312-222-9850; National Press Building Suite 1134, Washington, DC 20045, 202-628-3800; 6430 Sunset Blvd., Los Angeles, CA 90028, 213-465-0111.

Their PSA Express transmits your spot by satellite to 650 television stations nationally. This service includes monitoring the usage of your PSA.

MG Productions, Inc.

216 E. 45th Street, New York, NY 10017-3374, 212-818-0627.

They handle public service spots from concept to script, production, and editing. They also handle distribution, on a local, regional or national basis. PSA scripts can be localized, and produced in English, Spanish, Japanese and Chinese versions. MG has won national and international awards for their film and video productions.

Planned Communication Services, Inc.

112 E. 46th Street, New York, NY 10017, 212-697-2765.

Planned Communication Services will write the script and do all the production, distribution, and tracking for radio and television public service spots. Their database helps them send the preferred format to each station, and they are able to choose broadcasters based on actual PSA usage. In addition, they distribute PSAs to the 150 largest cablecasters.

Sheridan-Elson-Gourvitz Communications

120 W. 37th Street, New York, NY 10018, 212-239-2000, Los Angeles Office, 213-878-6508.

Complete production and distribution facilities for public service spots using their script or yours. They handle both radio and TV spots. Write for sample storyboards and scripts.

West Glen

1430 Broadway, New York, NY 10018, 212-944-9055; 3800 N. Wilke Road, Arlington Heights, IL 60004, 312-259-4343; 1888 Century Park East, Suite 1900, Los Angeles, CA 90067, 213-284-3231; Metropolitan Square, 655 15th Street, N.W., Washington, DC 20005, 202-639-4071.

West Glen can write, produce, distribute and track television public service announcements with a guarantee of the number of telecasts your spot will receive. They also distribute PSAs produced by others, and offer consulting on script development.

Satellite Media Tours

Medialink

708 Third Avenue, New York, NY 10017, 212-682-8300, 800-843-0677; 541 N. Fairbanks Court, Chicago, IL 60611, 312-222-9850; National Press Building

Suite 1134, Washington, DC 20045, 202-628-3800; 6430 Sunset Blvd., Los Angeles, CA 90028, 213-465-0111.

Medialink is the nation's only transmission network just for satellite media tours, video news releases, and public service spots. They offer complete planning, consulting and delivery services for satellite media tours. Their nationwide newswire service, used to alert more than 600 network and local television newsrooms to satellite media tours available for booking in advance, is tied into the Associated Press wire.

On The Scene Productions

5900 Wilshire Blvd., Suite 1400, Los Angeles, CA 90036, 213-930-1030. New York: 212-983-0123, Chicago: 312-404-5722.

On The Scene Productions specializes in arranging, producing and distributing satellite media tours shot on location, often producing more dramatic results (and higher media interest) than tours done from a studio. They are able to schedule a tour within 48 hours in a crisis situation.

Although they can and do work with virtually any subject matter, the company has extensive experience in the publishing and entertainment industries.

Specialized Public Relations Agencies

Dorf & Stanton Technology Communications

111 Fifth Avenue, New York, NY 10093, 212-420-8100.

International high-tech publicity expertise for products sold to other businesses and direct to consumers. Able to work with highly complex technical material. They also have extensive experience with environmental concerns and the environmental products industry.

Hill and Knowlton Division of Scientific, Technical & Environmental Affairs

420 Lexington Avenue, New York, NY 10017, 212-697-5600.

Specializes in translating complex scientific information into materials easily understood by people who lack a technical background. Advises clients on potential and current publicity problems caused by product ingredients and manufacturing techniques. Also designs and implements publicity programs for high tech products.

Levin Public Relations Marketing, Inc.

30 Glenn St., 4th Floor, White Plains, NY 10603-3213, 914-993-0900.

> Specializes in high tech and financial products sold to businesses rather than consumers.

Porter/Novelli

1633 Broadway, New York, NY 10019, 212-315-8000.

> Extensive health care experience, including work for pharmaceutical companies, health care facilities, and public health organizations. They have special expertise in creating alliances between companies and nonprofit organizations or government agencies.

Surveys

Medialink

708 Third Avenue, New York, NY 10017, 212-682-8300, 800-843-0677; 541 N. Fairbanks Court, Chicago, IL 60611, 312-222-9850; National Press Building Suite 1134, Washington, DC 20045, 202-628-3800; 6430 Sunset Blvd., Los Angeles, CA 90028, 213-465-0111.

> Medialink has an exclusive agreement with Nielsen Media Research to provide a weekly rotating panel of 125 news directors and assignment editors in TV news departments nationwide. The panel evaluates VNR ideas for Medialink's clients, so you can get ". . . an indication of newsroom opinion of your proposed video news release . . . [or satellite media tour]. While not a guarantee of usage, it is a valuable tool in helping you focus your . . ." VNR or satellite tour, says Medialink's Laurence Moskowitz.

The Roper Organization

205 E. 42nd Street, New York, NY 10017, 212-599-0700.

> Offers Limobus, a "tack-on" service which includes your questions in their regular surveys of a nationally representative sample of 2,000 adults. Surveys are conducted every month. Since you're paying for just a small part of the survey, this can be a very cost-effective way to get your questions answered. They also design and implement full-scale custom studies.

Video News Release Production and Distribution

Medialink

708 Third Avenue, New York, NY 10017, 212-682-8300, 800-843-0677; 541 N. Fairbanks Court, Chicago, IL 60611, 312-222-9850; National Press Building Suite 1134, Washington, DC 20045, 202-628-3800; 6430 Sunset Blvd., Los Angeles, CA 90028, 213-465-0111.

Medialink is the nation's only dedicated transmission network exclusively for satellite media tours, video news releases, and public service spots. They offer complete planning, consulting and delivery services for video news releases, but they do not produce them. "We are the nation's professional *distributor* of VNRs, not the manufacturer."

Their nationwide newswire service, used solely to alert more than 600 network and local television newsrooms to video news releases available for booking in advance, is tied into the Associated Press wire.

MG Productions, Inc.

216 E. 45th Street, New York, NY 10017-3374, 212-818-0627.

A full-service scripting, production, editing and distribution house, MG's creative approach has won numerous awards. They distribute VNRs on cassettes or by satellite transmission. Distribution and usage reports are computerized.

On The Scene Productions

5900 Wilshire Blvd., Suite 1400, Los Angeles, CA 90036, 213-930-1030; New York: 212-983-0123, Chicago: 312-404-5722

From scouting the location through distributing your video news release on cassettes or by satellite, On The Scene Productions handles video news releases from start to finish. They specialize in shooting on location, (which can produce more compelling stories that get better airplay).

Planned Communication Services, Inc.

12 E. 46th Street, New York, NY 10017, 212-697-2765.

Planned Communication Services will write the script and do all the production, distribution, and tracking for video news releases and their radio counterpart, radio wrap-arounds.

Their database helps them send the preferred format to each station, and they are able to choose broadcasters based on actual video news release usage. In addition to broadcasters, Planned Communication can distribute your VNRs to the 150 largest cable systems. They can also produce, distribute and track longer feature programs.

Sheridan-Elson-Gourvitz Communications

20 W. 37th Street, New York, NY 10018, 212-239-2000; Los Angeles Office: 213-878-6508.

> Complete production and distribution facilities for video news releases, using their script or yours. They can deliver video crews for any project in the world on one day's notice. All crews and technical people have broadcast experience. VNRs can be delivered to stations on mailed cassettes or by satellite.

West Glen

1430 Broadway, New York, NY 10018, 212-944-9055; 3800 N. Wilke Road, Arlington Heights, IL 60004, 312-259-4343; 1888 Century Park East, Suite 1900, Los Angeles, CA 90067, 213-284-3231; Metropolitan Square, 655 15th Street, N.W., Washington, DC 20005, 202-639-4071.

> West Glen will counsel you on the story angle and scripting of your video news release, provide full-service production and editing for studio and on-location stories, and then book and track usage of your VNR. Their in-house database includes information on each station's subject and format preferences.
>
> West Glen uses both internal and outside monitoring sources to report on how your VNR was used by television stations, and, in many markets, they can provide videotaped "clippings." They also distribute PSAs produced by others, with consultation available on newsworthiness and editing.
>
> In addition, West Glen specializes in rereleasing evergreen video news releases (containing material that will not quickly become dated) to cablecasters, where they get an additional audience. West Glen can also create a library of your prerecorded 5- to 30-minute television features, and lend them to broadcasters on a regular basis.

Writing Coaches

Business Writing Hotline

The Communication Workshop, 217 E. 85th St., Suite 442, New York, NY 10028, 718-575-8000.

> A subscription service that allows you to get instant help by telephone with writing problems. They'll work with you on anything from organization and tone to punctuation and grammar.

They also have a Fast Fax Feedback Service. Send your entire news release, PSA or other publicity document by fax and receive a critique and suggestions within hours. Both services are available from 9 A.M. to 5 P.M. Eastern Standard Time on business days. You must subscribe to these services in advance.

Sources

Books and Tapes

The Art of Plain Talk and *The Art of Readable Writing*
Flesch, Rudolf, revised 1986, 1985. Macmillan & Company, 866 Third Avenue, New York, NY 10022, 212-702-2000, 800-257-5755.

Two very helpful books about how to write plain English and how to test your writing for readability. Every publicist should read—and reread—these gems!

Associated Press Stylebook
Associated Press, 50 Rockefeller Plaza, New York, NY 10020.

Organized in a dictionary format, an "A to Z" listing of guides to capitalization, abbreviation, punctuation, spelling, numerals, and usage. Use this stylebook, and your copy will be acceptable to all AP newspapers and broadcasters. Also includes information on photo captions, and a list of all AP bureaus. Available in larger book stores.

Bibliography of Public Relations Books and Periodicals
Public Relations Society of America Information Center, 33 Irving Place, New York, NY 10003, 212-995-0148.

A thorough annual listing prepared by what is probably the largest library of public relations materials in the United States.

Communicating with Pictures
Douglis, Philip N., 1979. Lawrence Ragan Communications, Inc., 407 S. Dearborn Street, Chicago, IL 60605, 312-922-8245.

Written especially for house publication editors, this book will be highly valuable to publicists who either take their own pictures or work with photographers to get publicity shots. Crammed with practical tips about using photography to communicate.

The Copywriter's Handbook
Bly, Robert W. (Holt, 1985). Bob Bly, 174 Holland Avenue, New Milford, NJ 07646, 201-599-2277.

How to write effective publicity and promotion copy by one of the nation's leading freelance copywriters. Includes information on how to write persuasively, how to make sure you're communicating, and dozens of tips and techniques to make the writing task easier and more productive. Particularly useful if you need to go beyond publicity writing to turning out copy for newsletters, direct mail, brochures and ads.

The Designated Driver Campaign, Status Report
March, 1990. The Harvard Alcohol Project, Harvard School of Public Health, Center for Health Communication, 677 Huntington Avenue, Boston, MA 02115, 617-432-1038.

A fascinating report on the Harvard Alcohol Project's successful campaign to place designated driver messages in the media using PSAs and dialog in television shows. Not available in bookstores—contact the project directly.

Do it Yourself Marketing Research
Breen, George E. and Blankenship, A. B., Third Edition, 1989. McGraw-Hill Book Company, 1221 Avenue of the Americas, New York, NY 10020, 212-512-2000.

Although oriented toward marketing research, this book covers the basics of conducting your own surveys. The techniques described will help you do the research you need for your publicity program.

Effective Crisis Planning (videotape)
Public Relations Society of America, Video Library, 33 Irving Place, New York, NY 10003, 212-995-2230.

A team of three experts discuss and explain the principles and techniques of preparing a crisis plan for an organization.

Effective Planning and Budgeting for Public Relations Programs (videotape)
Public Relations Society of America, Video Library, 33 Irving Place, New York, NY 10003, 212-995-2230.

Features tips and techniques to help you enhance your skills for planning budgets that stay on track.

The Excellent Writer's Posters

The Communication Workshop, 217 E. 85th St., Suite 442, New York, NY 10028, 718-575-8000.

This series of quick reference posters can help you avoid common problems with publicity writing. Some of the topics are listed below, but write to them for a complete list.

- Avoid Sexist Terms
- Punctuation at a Glance
- Grammar at a Glance
- Avoid Slippery Language
- How to Organize Persuasive Writing
- 15 Most Common Misspelled Words

The Executive's Guide to Handling a Press Interview

Martin, Dick, 1985. Pilot Books, 103 Cooper, Babylon, NY 11702, 212-685-0736.

Don't let the title fool you! This book is for *anyone* who has to learn more about handling press interviews, be they executives or volunteers. Full of practical hints about how to handle journalists in controversial situations.

Great News Photos and the Stories Behind Them

Faber, John, 1978. Dover Publications, 180 Varick Street, New York, NY 10014, 212-255-3755, 800-223-3130.

A collection of 140 famous news photos from 1855 to 1976—and the stories of how they were shot. It will help you understand what makes a good piece of publicity art.

Handbook for Public Relations Writing

Bivins, Tom, Second Edition, 1991. NTC Business Books, 4255 W. Touhy Avenue, Lincolnwood, IL 60646-1975, 708-679-5500, 800-323-4900.

Practical guidelines for producing publicity material and press kits, and information on desktop publishing applications for publicists. Includes case studies and assignments.

How to Promote Your Own Business

Blake, Gary and Bly, Robert W. (NAL, 1983). Bob Bly, 174 Holland Avenue, New Milford, NJ 07646, 201-599-2277.

A do-it-yourself guide to publicity, promotion and advertising written especially for small business owners and managers.

How to Write Plain English
Flesch, Rudolf, Revised 1981. Harper & Row, 10 E. 53rd Street, New York, NY 10022, 212-207-7000.

> A fine book that will help you write direct, powerful, influential publicity material. Belongs on every publicist's bookshelf.

Keeping Your Eye on Television
Brown, Les, 1979. Pilgrim Press, 36-01 43rd Avenue, Long Island City, NY 11101, 718-937-9515.

> New York Times television critic Les Brown believes that the viewing public can influence television. He offers specific suggestions for citizen action to improve TV programming and explains how FCC regulation works—and when it doesn't.

Media Relations/Crisis Management (Public Relations Body of Knowledge Abstracts)
Public Relations Society of America, 33 Irving Place, New York, NY 10003, 212-995-2230.

> A comprehensive collection of abstracts from books, journals, and articles on both media relations and crisis management, conveniently categorized for quick reference. Available in printed form or on diskettes for Apple and IBM computers.

NTC's Mass Media Dictionary
Ellmore, R. Terry, 1990. NTC Business Books, 4255 W. Touhy Avenue, Lincolnwood, IL 60646-1975, 708-679-5500, 800-323-4900.

> A comprehensive dictionary of more than 20,000 technical terms, from abaxial lens to zapping, used in television, radio, journalism, publishing, graphic arts, advertising and public relations. Related entries are cross-referenced. This dictionary can help you understand what the experts are really saying.

PR Crises
Public Relations News, 127 E. 80th Street, New York, NY 10021, 212-879-7090.

> A collection of 10 case studies from the pages of *PR News* about how skilled public relations people successfully handled major emergencies. Includes information on responding to false rumors, how to develop a crisis plan, how to reply to unfair media attacks, and more.

Product Publicity: Making it Work for Products and Services (audiocassette)
Public Relations Society of America, National Professional Development
Committee, 33 Irving Place, New York, NY 10003, 212-995-2230.

Six public relations professionals discuss the elements of planning a
product publicity campaign. Topics include product publicity for goods
and services; publicity requirements for different product types; and
how product publicity programs relate to engineering and product
development considerations as well as the marketing plan.

Professional's Guide to Publicity
Weiner, Richard, revised 1982. Public Relations Publishing Company, 1633
Broadway, New York, NY 10019, 212-315-8000.

A collection of hundreds of succinct tips, rules, bits of advice, and candid
opinions about publicity from one of the best-known people in the field.

Public Relations in the Marketing Mix
Goldman, Jordan, 1984. NTC Business Books, 4255 W. Touhy Avenue,
Lincolnwood, IL 60646-1975, 708-679-5500, 800-323-4900.

An in-depth discussion of how to determine what kinds of public
relations an organization needs, techniques for writing a public relations plan and presenting it to management, the considerations involved in selecting public relations vehicles, and how to deal with
problem situations.

Public Relations Law (videotape)
Public Relations Society of America, Video Library, 33 Irving Place, New
York, NY 10003, 212-995-2230.

Information about laws that affect publicity, including copyright, trade-
marks, confidentiality, financial reporting requirements for public corporations, and the right to privacy.

Reporting for the Print Media
Fedler, Fred, 4th Edition, 1988. Harcourt Brace Jovanovich, Inc., 1250 Sixth
Avenue, San Diego, CA 92101, 800-543-1918.

A detailed workbook for beginning journalists, with whole chapters on
style, leads, features, and the use of quotations, coupled with good,
comprehensive exercises. Useful for publicists who want to improve
their writing skills.

Webster's New World Dictionary of Media & Communications
Weiner, Richard, 1990. Prentice-Hall Trade Books, Division of Simon & Schuster, One Gulf & Western Plaza, New York, NY 10023, 800-562-0245.

Publicists must be familiar with technical terms from many industries—including broadcasting, printing, television and video—to understand what the experts are saying. This single source for definitions of terms like baby kicker, niffnoff, B-roll, duckfoot and gobo, includes more than 30,000 definitions from 27 fields related to publicity.

Writing for the Media
Pesmen, Sandra, revised 1988. NTC Business Books, 4255 W. Touhy Avenue, Lincolnwood, IL 60646-1975, 708-679-5500, 800-323-4900.

A guide to writing for the media that can help get your releases and feature articles published. Includes over 50 examples and exercises.

The Yearbook of Experts, Authorities and Spokespersons
Broadcast Interview Source, 2233 Wisconsin Avenue, Suite 406, Washington, DC 20007-4104, 202-333-4904.

Used by more than 5,000 journalists to find experts and spokespeople. If you want journalists to contact you when they're working on stories in your field, consider a paid listing here.

Newsletters and Magazines

It's a good idea to write for a sample copy or check one in your library before you subscribe.

Communication World
International Association of Business Communicators (IABC), One Hallidie Plaza, Suite 600, San Francisco, CA 94102, 415-433-3400, 800-776-4222.

This award-winning publication is full of highly useful information about publicity and communication techniques, as well as the latest developments in the field.

Contacts
35-20 Broadway, Astoria, NY 11106, 718-721-0508.

A weekly newsletter with information about specific editorial needs of newspaper, magazine, and broadcast editors. A good way to find out about special editorial projects far enough in advance so you can supply material. Oriented toward organizations and firms involved in national or major regional publicity.

Jack O'Dwyer's Newsletter
The J. R. O'Dwyer Company, Inc., 271 Madison Avenue, New York, NY 10016, 212-679-2471.

A weekly report with information on new publications, staff changes, placement tips and opportunities, innovative publicity campaigns and programs, legal aspects of publicity, and more.

Media News Keys
40-29 27th St., Long Island City, NY 11101, 718-937-3990.

Published 48 times a year, this four-page newsletter lists staff changes, new formats and technical requirements, and editorial needs at newspapers, magazines, and broadcast stations. Especially strong in the broadcast area.

Media Report to Women
Communication Research Associates, Inc., 10606 Mantz Road, Silver Spring, MD 20903-1228, 301-445-3230.

A bi-monthly newsletter that covers the increasingly important role women are playing in the media, public relations, and advertising. It also reports on how women are being presented by the media.

O'Dwyer's PR Services Report
The J. R. O'Dwyer Company, Inc., 271 Madison Avenue, New York, NY 10016, 212-679-2471.

A monthly magazine with the latest on how to hire and make the best use of publicity services, as well as new sources and techniques for publicists. Regular columns cover video news releases, legal issues, publicity photo placement, accounting for publicists, among other topics.

Public Relations News
127 E. 80th Street, New York, NY 10021, 212-879-7090.

A weekly newsletter including full case studies of successful public relations campaigns; interviews with journalists; news about public relations agencies, accounts and staff; and key issues in the public relations field. Recent articles included material on public attitudes toward business, the increasing scope of public relations, state capitals as news sources, and how to achieve high visibility on a low budget.

pr reporter

PR Publishing Co., Dudley House, P.O. Box 600, Exeter, NH 03833-0600, 603-778-0514.

This weekly newsletter covers the broader field of public relations, including public affairs, employee relations and investor relations. Recent articles of interest to publicists included information on the first European public relations directory, how to handle the media in a crisis, how the new trademark law affects publicity, and how public relations outperforms advertising and marketing.

Public Pulse

The Roper Organization, 205 E. 42nd Street, New York, NY 10017, 212-599-0700.

A monthly newsletter based on opinion poll data assembled by The Roper Organization. Since it gives you an analysis of what Americans are thinking, doing and buying, it can help you anticipate how the public will react to your publicity efforts.

Public Relations Journal

Public Relations Society of America, Inc., 33 Irving Place, New York, NY 10003, 212-995-2230.

A monthly magazine for public relations professionals containing useful information for publicists working on a regional, national or international scale. This is a good source for the latest information on the trends and issues affecting the practice of public relations. Regular columns include crisis management, ethics, technology updates and book reviews.

Media Directories

You can save your fingers from doing a lot of walking by buying a few good media directories. Each directory has its own strong points. If your publicity is regional or national in scope, you will need more than one of them.

All-in-One Directory

Gebbie Press, P.O. Box 1000, New Paltz, NY 12561-0017, 914-255-7560.

A compact directory with 21,000 listings for daily and weekly papers; radio and TV stations; consumer, business, and trade magazines; farm publications; the Black and Hispanic press; and more. Available in printed, bound form or on floppy disks for the IBM-PC or Macintosh.

Bacon's Publicity Checker

Bacon's Information, Inc., 332 S. Michigan Avenue, Chicago, IL 60604, 312-922-2400, 800-621-0561.

Listings for more than 8,400 business, trade, farm, professional, and industrial magazines in the U.S. and Canada, and all daily and weekly newspapers published in the U.S. Gives editorial contact names with address, telephone, and circulation. For magazines, the *Checker* tells you if the editors accept bylined articles and whether the publication wants material on new products, general news, personnel changes, events, or new books. Also includes information on contacting syndicated columnists. Updated quarterly.

Burrelle's Media Directories

75 E. Northfield Avenue, Livingston, NJ 07039, 201-992-6600, 800-631-1160.

Publishers of more than one half-dozen directories including Black and Hispanic media, as well as local media contacts in Chicago, New England, New Jersey, New York, Pennsylvania, and the Washington, DC metro area. Includes newspapers, magazines, college publications, broadcast and cable stations, and wire services. Information for each media outlet includes contact names, deadlines and editorial focus.

Cable Contacts

BPI Communications, Inc., 1515 Broadway, 37th Floor, New York, NY 10036, 212-536-5266, 800-876-8506.

Listings for more than 575 local cable systems, national and regional cable networks, and pay channels. Includes monthly updates.

College and Military Contacts

BPI Communications, Inc., 1515 Broadway, 37th Floor, New York, NY 10036, 212-536-5266, 800-876-8506.

Lists contacts and audience information for 850 alumni publications, 1,000 student publications and 500 military publications in the U.S.

College Media Directory
Oxbridge Communications, Inc., 150 Fifth Avenue, Suite 636, New York, NY 10011, 212-741-0231.

> Listings for 6,833 student newspapers, magazines and yearbooks in the United States.

Directory of Women's Media
National Council for Research on Women, Sara Delano Roosevelt Memorial House, 47-49 E. 65th Street, New York, NY 10021, 212-570-5001.

> Listings for more than 700 periodicals and 100 women's presses and publishers, as well as other types of women's media.

Editor & Publisher Yearbook
Editor & Publisher, 11 W. 19th Street, New York, NY 10011, 212-675-4380.

> A wealth of newspaper facts and figures, organized in seven sections. Listings for daily, national, weekly, Black, religious, foreign language and college newspapers in the U.S. The foreign section covers newspapers in Canada, Europe, the Caribbean, Central America, Mexico, South America, Africa, the Middle East, Asia, the Far East, Australia, New Zealand and the Pacific Ocean Territories.
>
> Also includes listings for wire and photo services, syndicates, newspaper-distributed magazine sections, mat services, and clipping bureaus.

Feature News Publicity Outlets
Morgan-Rand Publishing Company, 2200 Sansom Street, Philadelphia, PA 19103, 800-441-3839.

> Lists and ranks the top 500 newspaper feature departments with names of beauty, fashion, food, home furnishings and lifestyle editors. Includes direct-line telephone numbers and picture requirements.

Greater Philadelphia Publicity Guide
Balset Company, Box 365, Ambler, PA 19002.

> Listings for daily papers including specialized reporters; community newspapers, foreign language and college press; wire services and news bureaus; radio, TV and cable stations; broadcast interview programs with contact names; and broadcast news and public service staff. Covers the eight-county Metro Philadelphia area and Southern New Jersey.

Hispanic Media and Markets
Standard Rate & Data Service, 3004 Glenview Road, Wilmette, IL 60091, 708-256-8333, 800-323-4588.

> Profiles of over 800 Hispanic newspapers, consumer and business publications, and broadcast stations. Although this publication is heavily oriented to advertisers, publicists will also find it useful. Updated quarterly.

Hudson's Newsletter Directory
H&M Publishers, 4 W. Market St., P.O. Box 311, Rhinebeck, NY 12572, 914-876-2081.

> Lists more than 4,000 major subscription newsletters worldwide and gives details on acceptance of press releases and key contact names. Cross-indexed by subject.

International Publicity Checker
Bacon's Information, Inc., 332 S. Michigan Avenue, Chicago, IL 60604, 312-922-2400, 800-621-0561.

> Lists more than 12,000 magazines by category and over 1,000 daily and weekly newspapers for 16 Western European countries. Includes editorial contacts and translation requirements.

Investment Newsletter Contacts
BPI Communications, Inc., 1515 Broadway, 37th Floor, New York, NY 10036, 212-536-5266, 800-876-8506.

> The names and addresses of more than 900 publications in North America, including Canada and Mexico, with information on editorial content and coverage. Free monthly updates.

Media Alerts
Bacon's Information, Inc., 332 S. Michigan Avenue, Chicago, IL 60604, 312-922-2400, 800-621-0561.

> Lists *editorial calendars*, lead times and profiles for 1,200 magazines and 100 major daily newspapers. Updated with a bi-monthly newsletter.

MediaMap
130 The Great Road, Bedford, MA 01730, 617-275-4999.

> This unusually thorough media directory covers the computer industry with detailed data on specialized publications. In addition to an over-

view of each publication, there is information on the audience, circulation, editorial profile, editorial preferences, *editorial calendar,* and lead
time. Media contacts are available on-disk in IBM and Macintosh
format. Available by subscription only.

Mediamatic® Calendar of Editorial Information
Media Distribution Services, Inc. (MDS), 307 W. 36th Street, New York, NY
10018, 212-247-4800.

Describes *upcoming editorial plans* of more than 500 trade, technical
and consumer publications. Includes editorial closing dates, contact
names, addresses and telephone numbers. Published three times a year.

Metro California Media
Public Relations Plus, Inc., P.O. Drawer 1197, New Milford, CT 06776,
203-354-9361, 800-999-8448.

Covers the 22 metropolitan areas in California with 94 percent of the
state's population. Listings for daily papers include address, telephone,
circulation, names of specialized editors and reporters, magazines, and
special sections. Information on broadcasters covers addresses and
telephone numbers, names of directors for news, programming, and
public service, spot interview and guest interview shows (with contact
names), and taping times.

Also gives information on cablecasters; ethnic, foreign language
and weekly newspapers and consumer magazines; as well as newspaper,
magazine, and wire service bureaus. Lists 319 contacts at the *Los
Angeles Times* alone.

National Directory of Magazines
Oxbridge Communications, Inc., 150 Fifth Avenue, Suite 636, New York, NY
10011, 212-741-0231.

Lists and describes all magazines published in the United States and
Canada.

National Radio Publicity Outlets
Morgan-Rand Publishing Company, 2200 Sansom Street, Philadelphia, PA
19103, 800-441-3839.

Listings for over 8,000 radio stations and programs for the U.S. and
Canada include direct-line telephone numbers for producers, talent
bookers and editors, and details on news, talk, and public affairs shows.

News Bureau Contacts

BPI Communications, Inc., 1515 Broadway, 37th Floor, New York, NY 10036, 212-536-5266, 800-876-8506.

> Contact names at more than 1,600 regional, state and local bureaus of daily newspapers, wire services, major magazines and broadcast networks. Includes free monthly updates.

New York Publicity Outlets

Public Relations Plus, Inc., P.O. Drawer 1197, New Milford, CT 06776, 203-354-9361, 800-999-8448.

> Lists media contacts within a fifty mile radius of Columbus Circle, New York City. Includes specialized editors and reporters at dailies, public service and program directors, and guest interview programs with contact names. Also gives contacts for Metro New York's Black press, feature syndicates, networks, magazines, and wire service bureaus. Names New York correspondents for out-of-town newspapers, as well as for radio and TV news bureaus. Includes listings for 2,795 media outlets.

New York Radio-TV Contact Service

Media News Keys, 40-29 27th St., Long Island City, NY 11101, 718-937-3990.

> A directory of more than 100 radio and television programs in the New York Metro area open to personality and product news, and guest interviews. In handy 3 × 5 index card format, updated monthly. Includes contact names and publicity requirements.

Oxbridge Directory of Newsletters

Oxbridge Communications, Inc., 150 Fifth Avenue, Suite 636, New York, NY 10011, 212-741-0231.

> Includes complete editorial information for 19,500 U.S. and Canadian newsletters in 168 subject categories.

Power Media Selects

Broadcast Interview Source, 2233 Wisconsin Avenue, Suite 406, Washington, DC 20007-4104, 202-333-4904.

> A directory of more than 2,000 of the most influential media contacts in the U.S. Includes decisionmakers at the wire services, syndicates, top 50 daily newspapers, major television and radio talk shows, and the most influential business, financial and consumer magazines. Includes

syndicated columnists. Available in bound form and on labels, Rolodex® cards and computer diskettes.

Public Relations Manager™

Cetex Corporation, 37 Thunderhead Road, Medford, NJ 08055, 609-953-1406.

This media directory software comes with up to 80,000 media contacts already entered for you, including newspapers, radio, TV, cable, magazines, trade journals, newsletters and internal corporate publications. Can be customized to meet your specific media contact needs.

Radio Contacts

BPI Communications, Inc., 1515 Broadway, 37th Floor, New York, NY 10036, 212-536-5266, 800-876-8506.

Lists addresses, telephone numbers, descriptions of local programs, preferred guests and types of material wanted from publicists. Includes number and length of news programs, direct-line telephone numbers to newsrooms, contact names for talk shows and names of public service directors. More than 4,100 local listings in 2 volumes. Includes free monthly updates.

Radio/TV Directory

Bacon's Information, Inc., 332 S. Michigan Avenue, Chicago, IL 60604, 312-922-2400, 800-621-0561.

Information on *every* radio and television station in the U.S., including formats, contact names for more than 2,000 shows, programming, target audiences and network affiliations. Includes contact information for 30 cable networks, college radio stations, and Public Broadcasting stations, too. Updated quarterly.

Special Issues

Standard Rate & Data Service, 3004 Glenview Road, Wilmette, IL 60091, 708-256-8333, 800-323-4588.

Detailed *editorial calendars* of 3,800 business publications, 1,150 newspapers, 2,000 consumer magazines and farm publications. Listings for each publication include names of specialized editors, types of editorial material accepted, regular and special sections and features, editorial emphasis for the next 12 months, and circulation. Updated five times a year.

Standard Periodical Directory
Oxbridge Communications, Inc., 150 Fifth Avenue, Suite 636, New York, NY 10011, 212-741-0231.

Listings arranged by subject for more than 75,000 U.S. and Canadian newspapers, magazines, and journals.

State Capitals Directory
H&M Publishers, 44 W. Market St., P.O. Box 311, Rhinebeck, NY 12572, 914-876-2081.

State capitals are the newsmaking centers for news of statewide importance. Lists addresses, telephone numbers and contact names for news bureaus, wire services, radio and television stations in state capitals.

Syndicated Columnists
BPI Communications, Inc., 1515 Broadway, 37th Floor, New York, NY 10036, 212-536-5266, 800-876-8506.

This book gives actual office addresses and telephone numbers of columnists. This is a more valuable resource than others that list only the syndicate's address, since many columnists don't work at or receive mail at syndicate headquarters. Describes more than 1,700 syndicated columns. Includes free monthly updates.

Talk Show Selects
Broadcast Interview Source, 2233 Wisconsin Avenue, Suite 406, Washington, DC 20007-4104, 202-333-4904.

Identifies more than 600 of the most influential radio and television talk show hosts, producers and talent bookers in the U.S. Contact information includes name, title, show name, station, address, telephone and fax number. Includes only regularly scheduled shows that welcome outside sources. Available in bound form and on Rolodex® cards, mailing labels and floppy disks.

Television Contacts
BPI Communications, Inc., 1515 Broadway, 37th Floor, New York, NY 10036, 212-536-5266, 800-876-8506.

Lists names, addresses, and telephone numbers of specialized reporters; names of program, news, and public service directors; general format of interview programs; names of contacts for each show; all special and local programs; audience size; and the names of syndicated network shows with the type of publicity material they want. Includes free monthly updates.

TV News

BPI Communications, Inc., 1515 Broadway, 37th Floor, New York, NY 10036, 212-536-5266, 800-876-8506.

A directory of TV news programs, including listings for specialized reporters, day and night assignment editors, direct telephone lines for key staff, special editorial requirements, satellite media tour requirements, and special interests. Find out which news programs use tapes, slides, scripts, and even book reviews. Includes information on network news programs. Free monthly updates.

TV & Cable Publicity Outlets

Morgan-Rand Publishing Company, 2200 Sansom Street, Philadelphia, PA 19103, 800-441-3839.

Listings for over 5,000 TV and cable programs for the U.S. and Canada include direct-line telephone numbers for producers, talent bookers and editors, and details on news, talk, and public affairs shows.

Washington News Media Contacts Directory

H&M Publishers, 44 W. Market St., P.O. Box 311, Rhinebeck, NY 12572, 914-876-2081.

Listings include Washington, DC newspapers, news bureaus, news services and syndicates, radio and TV stations, and specialized newsletters.

Writer's Market

Writer's Digest Books, 1507 Dana Avenue, Cincinnati, OH 45207, 800-289-0963.

A directory of magazines interested in articles written by freelance writers. Gives information about length, as well as editorial requirements, interests, and needs. Helpful for publicists who want to approach magazine editors with story ideas.

Index

TITLES OF INTEREST IN
PRINT AND BROADCAST MEDIA

ESSENTIALS OF MEDIA PLANNING, Third Edition, by Arnold M. Barban, Steven M. Cristol, and Frank J. Kopec

STRATEGIC MEDIA PLANNING, by Kent M. Lancaster and Helen E. Katz

MEDIA MATH, Second Edition, by Robert W. Hall

INTRODUCTION TO ADVERTISING MEDIA: RESEARCH, PLANNING, AND BUYING, by Jim Surmanek

MEDIA PLANNING, by Jim Surmanek

ADVERTISING MEDIA PLANNING, Fourth Edition, by Jack Sissors and Lincoln Bumba

THE FUTURE OF TELEVISION, by Marc Doyle

HOW TO PRODUCE EFFECTIVE TV COMMERCIALS, Second Edition, by Hooper White

HOW TO CREATE EFFECTIVE TV COMMERCIALS, Second Edition, by Huntley Baldwin

THE RADIO AND TELEVISION COMMERCIAL, Second Edition, by Albert C. Book, Norman D. Cary, and Stanley Tannenbaum

DICTIONARY OF BROADCAST COMMUNICATIONS, Third Edition, by Lincoln Diamant

CHILDREN'S TELEVISION, by Cy Schneider

FUNDAMENTALS OF COPY & LAYOUT, Second Edition, by Albert C. Book and C. Dennis Schick

HOW TO CREATE AND DELIVER WINNING ADVERTISING PRESENTATIONS, by Sandra Moriarty and Tom Duncan

HOW TO WRITE A SUCCESFUL ADVERTISING PLAN, by James W. Taylor

ADVERTISING COPYWRITING, Sixth Edition, by Philip Ward Burton

THE ART OF WRITING ADVERTISING, by Denis Higgins

STRATEGIC ADVERTISING CAMPAIGNS, Third Edition, by Don E. Schultz

WRITING FOR THE MEDIA, by Sandra Pesmen

THE ADVERTISING PORTFOLIO, by Ann Marie Barry

PUBLIC RELATIONS IN THE MARKETING MIX, by Jordan Goldman

HANDBOOK FOR BUSINESS WRITING, by L. Sue Baugh, Maridell Fryar, and David A. Thomas

HANDBOOK FOR PUBLIC RELATIONS WRITING, Second Edition, by Thomas Bivins

HANDBOOK FOR MEMO WRITING, by L. Sue Baugh

HANDBOOK FOR PROOFREADING, by Laura Anderson

UPI STYLEBOOK, by United Press International

FUNDAMENTALS OF SUCCESSFUL NEWSLETTERS, by Thomas Bivins

BUSINESS MAGAZINE PUBLISHING, by Sal Marino

THE PUBLICITY HANDBOOK, by David R. Yale

NTC'S MASS MEDIA DICTIONARY, by R. Terry Ellmore

NTC'S DICTIONARY OF ADVERTISING, Second Edition, by Jack Wiechmann

DICTIONARY OF BROADCAST COMMUNICATIONS, Third Edition, by Lincoln Diamant

PROFESSIONAL ADVERTISING PHOTOGRAPHY, by Dave Saunders

ADVERTISING MEDIA SOURCEBOOK, Third Edition, by Arnold M. Barban, Donald W. Jugenheimer, and Peter B. Tur

HOW TO PRODUCE CREATIVE ADVERTISING, by Ann Keding & Thomas Bivins

HOW TO PRODUCE CREATIVE PUBLICATIONS, by Thomas Bivins and William E. Ryan

For further information or a current catalog, write:
NTC Business Books
a division of *NTC Publishing Group*
4255 West Touhy Avenue
Lincolnwood, Illinois 60646-1975 U.S.A.
800-323-4900 (in Illinois, 708-679-5500)